3D PRINTING AND INTELLECTUAL PROPERTY

IP laws were drafted for tangible objects, but 3D printing technology, which digitizes objects and offers manufacturing capacity to anyone, is disrupting these laws and their underlying policies. In this timely work, Lucas Osborn focuses on the novel issues raised for IP law by 3D printing for the major IP systems around the world. He specifically addresses how patent and design law must wrestle with protecting digital versions of inventions and policing individualized manufacturing, how trademark law must confront the dissociation of design from manufacturing, and how patent and copyright law must be reconciled when digital versions of primarily utilitarian objects are concerned. With an even hand and keen insight, Osborn offers an innovation-centered analysis of and balanced response to the disruption caused by 3D printing that should be read by nonexperts and experts alike.

Lucas S. Osborn is Professor of Law at Campbell University Norman A. Wiggins School of Law. He has spoken about the implications of 3D printing on IP at numerous academic conferences and has published seven articles in leading journals on the topic. Since 2014, he has served as an elected member of the Confidentiality Commission for the Organisation for the Prohibition of Chemical Weapons based in The Hague.

"With great clarity, Lucas Osborn skillfully delineates a normative intellectual property discourse operating in a broad social policy context. He proposes a sound, holistic approach to innovation policymaking in response to the complexities introduced by 3D printing technologies."

Phoebe Li, Senior Lecturer in Law, University of
Sussex Law School

"Lucas Osborn is a leading scholar on the implications of 3D printing for intellectual property theory and practice. No other scholar has addressed as wide a range of issues across the many areas of IP, and this book synthesizes years of his careful and thorough work. It's a must-read for anyone working on issues relating to this cutting-edge technology."

Mark P. McKenna, John P. Murphy Foundation
Professor of Law, Notre Dame Law School

"Lucas Osborn provides a nuanced conceptual framework to begin any analysis of the interaction between 3D printing and intellectual property law. He also articulates the most precise description I have read of how copyright law interacts with 3D files for useful objects. Highly recommended for anyone searching for a sophisticated accounting of where 3D printing could actually disrupt intellectual property law."

Michael Weinberg, Executive Director, Engelberg
Center on Innovation Law & Policy, New York
University School of Law

"Does the uptake of 3D printing challenge prevailing concepts of patentable subject matter and current patentability requirements? Does 3D printing fundamentally alter the scope of rights and the concepts of direct/indirect infringement? Approaching these themes with legal rigor and bold originality, Lucas Osborn provides an exciting journey with well-founded answers and invites readers to look beyond the traditional limits of patent law."

Geertrui Van Overwalle, Professor, University of Leuven, Belgium

"Lucas Osborn brings important intellectual leadership to the law of 3D printing in this ambitious and groundbreaking study. His comprehensive yet straightforward discussion makes a topic saturated with cutting-edge technology and legal nuance remarkably accessible. An engaging read for lawyers, innovators, and technophiles alike."

Daniel Brean, Law Professor, The University of Akron
School of Law, and IP Attorney, The Webb Law Firm

3D Printing and Intellectual Property

LUCAS S. OSBORN

Campbell University School of Law

CAMBRIDGE
UNIVERSITY PRESS

University Printing House, Cambridge CB2 8BS, United Kingdom

One Liberty Plaza, 20th Floor, New York, NY 10006, USA

477 Williamstown Road, Port Melbourne, VIC 3207, Australia

314–321, 3rd Floor, Plot 3, Splendor Forum, Jasola District Centre, New Delhi – 110025, India

79 Anson Road, #06–04/06, Singapore 079906

Cambridge University Press is part of the University of Cambridge.

It furthers the University's mission by disseminating knowledge in the pursuit of education, learning, and research at the highest international levels of excellence.

www.cambridge.org
Information on this title: www.cambridge.org/9781107150775
DOI: 10.1017/9781316584507

© Lucas S. Osborn 2019

First published 2019

Printed in the United Kingdom by TJ International Ltd, Padstow Cornwall

A catalogue record for this publication is available from the British Library.

Library of Congress Cataloging-in-Publication Data
NAMES: Osborn, Lucas S., author.
TITLE: 3D printing and intellectual property : disruption, doctrine and policy / Lucas S. Osborn, Campbell University School of Law.
OTHER TITLES: Three-dimensional printing and intellectual property
DESCRIPTION: Cambridge, United Kingdom ; New York, NY, USA : Cambridge University Press, 2019. | Includes bibliographical references and index.
IDENTIFIERS: LCCN 2019005969 | ISBN 9781107150775 (alk. paper)
SUBJECTS: LCSH: Intellectual property – United States. | Three-dimensional printing – Law and legislation – United States.
CLASSIFICATION: LCC KF2985.T57 083 2019 | DDC 346.7304/8–dc23
LC record available at https://lccn.loc.gov/2019005969

ISBN 978-1-107-15077-5 Hardback
ISBN 978-1-316-60534-9 Paperback

Contents

Acknowledgments

I thank those who read drafts of chapters and provided helpful feedback, including Sarah Burstein, Kevin Collins, Tim Holbrook, Nari Lee, Jake Linford, Ned Snow, and Michael Weinberg and those who worked with me and provided detailed input on earlier articles involving 3D printing and IP, including Dan Brean, Tim Holbrook (again), Mark McKenna, Joshua Pearce, Michael Weinberg (again), and Peter Yu. I also thank the many participants at various academic workshops and conferences too numerous to mention, both in the United States and abroad, where I presented research related to this book. I have been tremendously assisted by hard-working and talented research assistants Melanie Huffines, Jessica Inscore, David Joyner, and Kayla Russell and also by talented volunteer proofreaders Allison Crowder (also known as my big sister) and Barbara Osborn (also known as "mom").

I owe deep gratitude to Dean Rich Leonard and Campbell University for their tremendous support. For their encouragement and cheerleading, I am overwhelmingly thankful to my wife, Dana, and my children, Lucy, Harper, and Jonah (who too often had to hear, "Daddy can't play right now"). This book was written during difficult times. While writing this book, I lost my best friend, Brian Robertson, who was also my wife's brother, to cancer. This book is dedicated to him.

I hope that whatever is good in this book brings God glory.

Abbreviations

CAD	Computer Aided Design
CJEU	Court of Justice of the European Union
CRM	Computer Readable Medium
DMCA	Digital Millennium Copyright Act
DMF	Digital Manufacturing File
DRM	Digital Rights Management
EPC	European Patent Convention
EPO	European Patent Office
EU	European Union
EUIPO	European Union Intellectual Property Office
FOSH	Free and Open Source Hardware
IP	Intellectual Property
JPO	Japanese Patent Office
PGS	Pictorial, Graphic, and Sculptural
TPM	Technological Protection Measures
USPTO	U.S. Patent & Trademark Office

Introduction

They are lined up by the hundreds in the factory, working with steadfastness and precision. They do not take breaks, and yet they don't get tired or make mistakes. They don't complain about working conditions or bargain for higher pay. They don't require much supervision – in fact, there is only one supervisor for the whole factory.

Of course, these workers are not humans. They are 3D printers.

3D printers build objects layer by layer, in contrast to traditional manufacturing processes like molding, casting, or sculpting. Simply put, 3D printers use bits to print atoms; the bits are the digital files that describe the object, and the atoms are the tangible objects made from the digital files. Much like a 2D paper printer deposits a layer of liquid ink, 3D printers create thin, sliced layers of an object. But instead of stopping at one layer, the 3D printer stacks layer upon layer until a 3D object is built, somewhat like how a brick wall is made. 3D printing is known by industrial users as additive manufacturing and rapid prototyping, among other terms, but the term 3D printing has captured the public's imagination and is here to stay.

3D printing technology is revolutionizing design, manufacturing, and innovation processes and is opening doors to new manufacturing possibilities. It was the second fastest growing technology between 2013 and 2017 as measured by published patent application growth rate, faster than machine learning (artificial intelligence), autonomous vehicles, and aerial drones.[1] By just about any metric, the industry has been growing at a dizzying pace. Revenues for the industry as a whole topped $7.3 billion (US billion) in 2017, and

---

[1] Michael Petch, *Interview: New Study of 3D Printing Patents Reveals Second Fastest Growing Technology of 2017*, 3D PRINTING INDUSTRY (Jan. 10, 2018, 5:14 PM), https://3dprintingindus try.com/news/interview-new-study-shows-3d-printing-second-fastest-growing-technology-2017-1 27179/. Only e-cigarettes experienced a faster growth rate.

enjoyed annual growth of 21 percent in 2017, 17.4 percent in 2016, and 25.9 percent in 2015.[2]

Scientific publications relating to the technology have increased at about 40 percent annually from 2002 to 2016.[3] In 1996, around 60 patents related to 3D printing were issued, but by 2016 that number was over 600.[4] And the rate of growth is increasing. The number of patents in the area almost doubled between 2014 and 2016.

Several factors are contributing to increased growth. First, researchers, entrepreneurs, and investors have responded to the technology's growth and market opportunities.[5] At the industrial level, the latest 3D printers serve as cost-effective final product manufacturers for a variety of goods. At the consumer level, sales of desktop 3D printers are accelerating, and their capabilities are rising.[6]

Second, a number of the pioneering patents covering some basics of 3D printing technology have expired or will soon expire.[7] As this book will discuss, patents can be great rewards for invention, but they can also block subsequent development. As key patents expire, the world is free to make, use, and sell the technology, which helps not only to drive down costs, but also to catalyze technological improvements. In the words of one industry expert, when a key patent on a plastic extruding 3D printer expired in 2009, "everything exploded."[8]

---

[2]   TJ McCue, *Wohlers Report 2018: 3D Printer Industry Tops $7 Billion*, FORBES (June 4, 2018, 4:03 AM), www.forbes.com/sites/tjmccue/2018/06/04/wohlers-report-2018-3d-printer-industry-rises-21-percent-to-over-7-billion/#27f2e4002d1a.

[3]   Felix W. Baumann & Dieter Roller, *Additive Manufacturing, Cloud-Based 3D Printing and Associated Services – Overview*, 1 J. MATERIALS PROCESSING & MFG SCI. 1, 11 (2017).

[4]   John Hornick, *3D Printing Patent Landscape*, 3D PRINT.COM (Jul. 17, 2017), https://3dprint.com/181207/3d-printing-patent-landscape/.

[5]   *See, e.g.*, Jing Li et al., *The Current Landscape for Additive Manufacturing Research*, 2016 ICL AMN REPORT 1, 13–36 (2016), https://spiral.imperial.ac.uk/bitstream/10044/1/39726/2/The%20current%20landscape%20for%20additive%20manufacturing%20research_AMN.pdf; Charlie Taylor, *Spending on 3D Printing Set to Explode over Next Five Years*, THE IRISH TIMES (Aug. 9, 2018, 5:00 AM), www.irishtimes.com/business/technology/spending-on-3d-printing-set-to-explode-over-next-five-years-1.3589789.

[6]   *See* Samuel Adams, *Half Million 3D Printers Sold in 2017 – On Track for 100M Sold in 2030*, 3D PRINTING INDUSTRY (Apr. 6, 2018, 11:46 AM), https://3dprintingindustry.com/news/half-million-3d-printers-sold-2017-track-100m-sold-2030-131642/(reporting 52% year-on-year growth in desktop 3D printer sales).

[7]   John Hornick & Dan Roland, *Many 3D Printing Patents Are Expiring Soon: Here's a Round Up & Overview of Them*, 3D PRINTING INDUSTRY (Dec. 29, 2013, 12:04 AM), https://3dprintingindustry.com/news/many-3d-printing-patents-expiring-soon-heres-round-overview-21708/.

[8]   Christopher Mims, *3D Printing Will Explode in 2014, Thanks to the Expiration of Key Patents*, QUARTZ (July 21, 2013), http://qz.com/106483/3d-printing-will-explode-in-2014-thanks-to-the-expiration-of-key-patents.

It is no coincidence that around 2009 desktop printers costing less than a thousand dollars became available.[9]

A third reason for growth is that many important aspects of the technology are being developed in an open source model, which allows collaborative learning and development. The best-known example of open source in 3D printing is the University of Bath's RepRap project, which sought to develop a basic, open source 3D printer that could print parts to make a copy of itself.[10] The RepRap development community is made of hundreds of developers all over the world sharing designs.

Fourth, the technology has several complementary parts, each of which is being deliberately developed. Improvements in 3D printer hardware, 3D printing software, and 3D printable materials all feed into a frenetic cycle of innovation. The results are stunning.

3D printers can manufacture objects in a variety of materials, including myriad plastics, metals, foods, and human tissues. They can print everything from microscopic objects to buildings, prototypes to finished goods, simple blocks to machines with moving parts. They can print statues, jet engine parts, shoes, and functional human organs.

Even beyond what can be printed, the technology's most fundamental impact is the bidirectional path it creates between physical objects and their digital counterparts. This phenomenon, which I call "physitization," challenges assumptions about tangibility and about laws constructed with physical objects in mind. It is no overstatement to say that just about every challenging intellectual property (IP) issue surrounding 3D printing technology is connected to the physitization phenomenon. Because of physitization, manufacturing is democratized, commoditized, and largely anonymized. Much of the economic value associated with goods shifts from their physical embodiment to their digital embodiment. This book explores the implications of these changes.

NOVEL LEGAL QUESTIONS

Though the technology dates back to the 1980s, it erupted into the public sphere beginning around 2012, spurred by technological advances, reduced costs, media attention, and investment opportunity.[11] Joining the media

---

[9]   Terry Wohlers & Tim Gornet, *History of Additive Manufacturing*, WOHLERS REPORT 2014 1, 15 (2014), http://wohlersassociates.com/history2014.pdf.

[10]   Rhys Jones et al., *RepRap – The Replicating Rapid Prototyper*, 29 ROBOTICA 177, 177 (2011).

[11]   *See, e.g.,* HOD LIPSON & MELBA KURMAN, FABRICATED: THE NEW WORLD OF 3D PRINTING (2013); *Special Report: A Third Industrial Revolution*, THE ECONOMIST (Apr. 21, 2012), www.economist.com/node/21552901.

attention, recent academic interest in 3D printing has been intense. Several works have explored legal ramifications of the technology,[12] but each suffers from limitations. Some are excellent but relatively narrow in focus, others misunderstand key aspects of the technology, and still others misunderstand where the new questions arise. Moreover, no work has covered IP law and policy in depth and holistically. This book accomplishes that task.

I will focus on the aspects of IP law that 3D printing technology stresses. And the technology will stress the law, just like past innovations did. The advent of airplanes wiped away centuries of law positing that ownership of a plot of land extended vertically to the heavens. Software continues to confound aspects of patent and copyright law.

With 3D printing, the challenges can be doctrinal, such as whether 3D printable files constitute patentable subject matter. They can also be normative, like whether 3D printing technology lowers the costs of innovation so much that patent rights should be weakened or abolished, or whether instead patent rights should be strengthened in the face of digital appropriations of patented goods. Should copyright law, which is geared toward expressive and aesthetic works, protect 3D printing files that will manufacture purely utilitarian articles?

This book avoids discussing the routine applications of law to the technology. For example, it goes without saying that new and nonobvious 3D printers can be patented. It also avoids legal issues that may be difficult – such as whether a particular 3D shape can be protected by trademark law or whether a particular object is creative enough to garner copyright protection – but that are no more difficult merely because they involve 3D printing technology. Instead, the book seeks to analyze technological nuances that raise novel challenges for IP law. It unpacks those areas doctrinally and theoretically and offers ideas for a way forward through each conundrum.

---

[12] Some of the most relevant early publications exploring 3D printing and IP include Simon Bradshaw et al., *The Intellectual Property Implications of Low-Cost 3D Printing.* 7 SCRIPTED 5, 29 (2010); Deven R. Desai & Gerard N. Magliocca, *Patents, Meet Napster: 3D Printing and the Digitization of Things,* 102 GEO. L.J. 1691 (2014); Timothy R. Holbrook & Lucas S. Osborn, *Digital Patent Infringement in an Era of 3D Printing,* 48 U.C. DAVIS L. REV. 1319, 1353–56 (2015); Michael Weinberg, *It Will Be Awesome If They Don't Screw It Up,* PUBLIC KNOWLEDGE 12 (2010), www.publicknowledge.org/files/docs/3DPrintingPaper PublicKnowledge.pdf. In addition, legal scholarship has also looked at areas outside of IP law. *See, e.g.,* Nora Freeman Engstrom, *3-D Printing and Product Liability: Identifying the Obstacles,* 162 U. PA. L. REV. ONLINE 35 (2013) (discussing the possible impact of 3D printing on the future of products liability law); Lucas S. Osborn, *Regulating Three-Dimensional Printing: The Converging Worlds of Bits and Atoms,* 51 SAN DIEGO L. REV. 553 (2014).

Indeed, digitization has impacted several industries before. Most notably, people previously bought music in some physical form: first as sheet music, then as records and tapes. Beginning in earnest in the 1990s, music was digitized, a phenomenon that struck fear in the hearts of the music industry's stakeholders. Individuals could copy MP3 files costlessly, and, with the roll-out of the internet, "share" those files with the world for copying. Why buy music when you can download it for free? A similar question will now arise with respect to numerous digitized objects and machines.

If music, movies, photographs, and books have already survived digital disruption, one might ask whether anything needs to be said about 3D printing. Is it just more of the same? This book will show why 3D printing raises many issues beyond those already settled by previous rounds of digitization.

Most fundamentally, the digitization of music, movies, photographs, and books all implicated primarily one branch of IP law: copyright. 3D printing brings digital disruption to patent law, trademark law, and design law in addition to copyright law. Whereas copyright law is generally well prepared for 3D printing's challenges – with an important exception – other branches of IP are not. Even copyright law will face a unique challenge: how to treat digital versions of physical objects when the physical object is not protected by copyright law. Design law has a similar question to answer.

Patent law, including utilitarian and design patents, faces several difficult questions. Which kinds, if any, of 3D printable files are eligible for patenting? Does the making, using, and selling of those files constitute direct patent infringement? Trademark law also must contend with disruptions. Trademarks have traditionally indicated the source of manufactured goods. But 3D printing technology commoditizes manufacturing and separates design from manufacturing. It also bifurcates questions of source: those related to source of the physical object and those related to source of the file.

This book analyzes these and other questions doctrinally but recognizes that doctrine alone cannot supply the answers. They are inescapably matters of policy, and this book analyzes them as such.

OVERVIEW

I write for a wide audience. This book aims to be helpful not only to lawyers, lawmakers, and judges, but also policymakers, technologists, and artists. It considers IP laws in numerous jurisdictions, with a strong focus on the United States and the EU/Europe, but also including other large jurisdictions like Australia, Canada, and Japan.

Chapters 1 and 2 introduce key aspects of 3D printing technology. Chapter 1 describes the technology's capabilities and its limitations. It also explains the important concept of physitization, which is the term I use to describe the bidirectional path that 3D printing creates between physical and digital versions of objects.

Chapter 2 tackles a key technological concept – the various file formats used in the design and manufacturing process. Collectively, I refer to these files as digital manufacturing files (DMFs). 3D printing technology shifts economic value from tangible objects to DMFs. Understanding how IP law will apply to 3D printing requires an understanding of these file formats because the law will treat each format differently. The chapter also describes the various kinds of 3D printers on the market and important complementary technologies, like 3D scanners. Finally, it describes the many participants in the IP ecosystem.

Chapter 3 provides a short overview of IP law for those not familiar with it. It introduces the major concepts of patent law, copyright law, trademark law, and design patent law, focusing on internationally agreed upon frameworks and treaties such as the Berne Convention, the Paris Convention, and TRIPS. It also walks readers through fundamental concepts like territoriality, validity, direct and indirect infringement, and remedies.

Chapters 4, 5, and 6 concern patent law. Chapter 4 analyzes the doctrine of patentable subject matter in American, European, and Japanese patent jurisprudence. It applies that jurisprudence to 3D printable files to demonstrate why only one of the three DMF formats is likely to constitute patentable subject matter. Chapter 4 also analyzes jurisdictions' differential treatment of patent claims directed to electronic signals, which is important because most 3D printable files are sold as internet signal transmissions.

Chapter 5 turns from patentable subject matter to patent infringement. It introduces a fundamental tension between patent holders and good-faith users of the technology. 3D printing will expose unsuspecting individuals and 3D print shops to patent infringement liability when they print patented objects. To spare unintentionally infringing individuals and 3D print shops the ruinous costs of litigation, I explore options for exemptions and safe harbors that simultaneously consider the rights of patentees.

In addition, Chapter 5 demonstrates how the patent protection gap described in Chapter 4 carries over into the infringement analysis. DMFs will not infringe traditional patent claims directed to tangible objects, and claims directed to digital files suffer from severe limitations. Attempting to alleviate some of the protection gaps for patent holders while balancing the needs of users, I consider a novel theory of "digital patent infringement," whereby commercializing a DMF would constitute infringement but merely creating and manipulating the file would not.

Chapter 6 explores the doctrines of indirect patent infringement in the United States, Europe, and Japan, focusing primarily on novel statutory interpretation issues brought about by 3D printing technology. Indirect infringement generally requires knowledge of the patent or some sort of intent to infringe. Because 3D printing technology will empower many legally unsophisticated actors to assist – even if unwittingly – others to infringe, virtually every jurisdiction will need to clarify how to measure knowledge or intent when numerous individuals or small businesses are involved. In Europe, courts will also need to decide the fundamental issue of whether the knowledge requirement implies a culpable mental state. After discussing additional statutory interpretation issues, the chapter concludes by recommending that courts and lawmakers resolve interpretive issues in a manner that captures at least the most egregious actors, namely, those who repeatedly and knowingly facilitate infringement by distributing DMFs. How much further the law should go depends on the overall effect of 3D printing technology on innovation incentives, a topic more fully considered in Chapter 10.

Chapters 7, 8, and 9 cover trademark law, copyright law, and design law, respectively. One might fairly ask why patent law deserved three chapters while each of these areas of IP law only receives one chapter. In part I believe that patent law is less doctrinally and theoretically equipped to contend with 3D printing technology than these other areas of law. In addition, Chapters 5 and 6 introduce the concepts of direct and indirect infringement and describe some basics of litigation realities. For the benefit of nonlawyer readers, I spend a bit more time on these topics when I first introduce them because they have relevance for other areas of IP as well.

Chapter 7 begins by considering how 3D printing technology will disrupt trademark law's core function of indicating the source or origin of manufactured goods. The technology dissociates product design from product manufacturing. Design is embodied in a 3D printable file, while manufacturing is commoditized and democratized. These changes result in a world where source indication works very differently for digital versions of tangible objects. They also fundamentally upset the doctrine of post-sale confusion.

Chapter 8 focuses on a specific issue created by 3D printing technology: whether DMFs of purely (or primarily) utilitarian objects should receive copyright protection. Tangible objects dominated by utilitarian concerns do not receive copyright protection. Neither should the corresponding DMF, I argue. This novel argument has attracted criticism, but I defend it as a matter of doctrine and policy. Doctrinally, most jurisdictions around the world extend copyright protection only to works containing creativity, and I argue that DMFs of utilitarian objects contain no copyrightable creativity. As a matter of policy, allowing copyright protection for DMFs of useful articles would cause copyright law, which is geared toward aesthetic works, to trespass on patent law, which is geared toward utilitarian works.

Chapter 9 considers the role of design rights for DMFs. In it, I argue that DMFs should only receive design protection if the object they will print would receive such protection. Current practice in many jurisdictions is to the contrary. It protects any qualifying images if they appear on a computer screen. I argue that this approach impermissibly protects mere artistic images, which should be protected, if at all, by copyright law. I offer a framework for a teleological approach to design right in digital images and focus the approach on DMFs specifically. In addition, I describe how, unlike the situation in the United States, the EU Design Directive includes many important safeguards for free speech, experimentation, and private use.

Chapter 10 takes a broader look at IP protection as an incentive to innovate. Patent protection gaps brought about by 3D printing technology must be viewed in conjunction with how the technology lowers the costs of innovation and imitation for 3D printable goods. Moreover, although patents serve as a primary incentive to innovate, they are not the only incentive. The chapter looks at other IP rights, contracts, and extralegal appropriability mechanisms, as well as nonmonetary incentives to innovate, to determine how the IP regime should respond to 3D printing technology. I describe the need for a better empirical understanding of 3D printing technology's effects on innovation incentives and make recommendations for what to do as we await that evidence.

***

Technological change can be disruptive, even uncomfortable, but that alone is no reason to resist it. In the face of 3D printing technology, the desires of IP owners will skew toward stronger protections, and the desires of the technology's users will skew in the opposite direction. Bowing to neither but balancing both, I offer an expert appraisal of the changes and challenges wrought by 3D printing technology. I recommend numerous avenues for balancing the rights of IP owners and technology users while leaving ample space for the technology itself to achieve its full potential.

1

3D Printing Technology's Capabilities and Effects

Chapter Outline:

At their most basic level, 3D printers construct physical objects based on input from a digital file. But 3D printing technology's effects on the law cannot be addressed without a deeper understanding of certain aspects of the technology. This chapter and the next extend this basic understanding with explanations and examples of the technology's current abilities and limitations, its promise, and its details most relevant to IP law.

Though the technology has garnered tremendous attention in the last few years, the technology was born decades ago. Most credit Charles Hull with inventing 3D printing in 1983 even though he was not the first to research or experiment with precursors to 3D printing technology.[1] Early 3D printers were unable to print many products suitable for final uses, and instead focused on printing prototypes. That is why one of the 3D printing's sobriquets is "rapid prototyping" – it allows an innovator to bypass the time-consuming and costly machining of parts used to build prototypes.[2] 3D printing continues to be an excellent strategy for rapid and iterative prototyping, but the industry has experienced tremendous research, development, and growth, opening the door to final product production and mass production. The fruits of this growth almost strain the imagination.

---

[1]   *See* Terry Wohlers & Tim Gornet, *History of Additive Manufacturing*, WOHLERS REPORT 2014 1, 29 (2014), http://wohlersassociates.com/history2014.pdf.

[2]   *See, e.g.*, Juho Vesanto, *Saving Resources by Prototyping with 3D Printing – A Lamplight Case Study*, 3D PRINTING INDUSTRY (Sept. 30, 2013, 12:03 AM), https://3dprintingindustry.com/n ews/saving-resources-prototyping-3d-printing-lamplight-case-study-17629/.

A. TECHNOLOGICAL CAPABILITIES

3D printing is prized for many reasons, not least because it can manufacture geometrically complex objects as easily as it can make simple ones. This allows users to print objects in a single pass, whereas traditional manufacturing methods would have required the manufacture and assembly of multiple components. For instance, GE, which is a leader in adopting 3D printing technology, developed a theory for a fuel injection nozzle having a complex tip geometry that reduced fuel consumption. The problem was that they couldn't make the complex part using traditional methods. According to Mohammad Ehteshami, a lead GE engineer who worked on the project, the complex welding and brazing needed to assemble the twenty subcomponents prevented manufacture: "We tried to cast it eight times, and we failed every time."[3]

That was when GE turned to 3D printing to try to mass-produce the complex part. A 3D printer was able quickly to print the fuel injection nozzle in nickel alloy, and the result exceeded the team's hopes. The printed nozzle combined all twenty parts into a single unit, weighed 25 percent less than an ordinary nozzle, and was more than five times as durable. The result was an epiphany for Ehteshami. In his words, "I was excited but also disturbed. I knew that we found a solution, but I also saw that this technology could eliminate what we've done for years and years and put a lot of pressure on our financial model."[4]

Many 3D printable objects, from simple phone cases to complex medical implants, have no moving parts. But even objects with moving parts can be printed in a single pass. Objects with ball bearings[5] and multiple rotating gears[6] have been printed in this way. NASA has produced an advanced fabric a little like chain mail consisting of multiple interlocking silver squares, all printed in one pass.[7] Single-pass print jobs eliminate the need to assemble parts, saving time and obviating the need for assembly expertise.

While printing finished machines in one pass is a good goal, sometimes it is not possible or cost-effective with current technology. In these cases, 3D printing may bring value as part of hybrid manufacturing wherein some parts are 3D

---

[3] Tomas Kellner, *An Epiphany of Disruption: GE Additive Chief Explains How 3D Printing Will Upend Manufacturing*, GE REPORTS (Nov. 13, 2017), www.ge.com/reports/epiphany-disruption-ge-additive-chief-explains-3d-printing-will-upend-manufacturing/.

[4] *Id.*

[5] Yeong-Jae Lee, *Friction Performance of 3D Printed Ball Bearing: Feasibility Study*, 10 RESULTS IN PHYSICS 721 (2018), www.sciencedirect.com/science/article/pii/S2211379717325196.

[6] *3D Printing Moving Parts Fully Assembled – 28-Geared Cube*, INSTRUCTABLES, www.instructables.com/id/3D-printing-moving-parts-28-Geared-Cube/.

[7] *'Space Fabric' Links Fashion and Engineering*, NASA JET PROPULSION LABORATORY (Apr. 18, 2017), www.jpl.nasa.gov/news/news.php?feature=6816.

printed and others are made using traditional processes. For instance, in a turboprop's engine, GE reduced 855 parts down to twelve 3D printed parts, which were combined with other parts made by traditional manufacturing.[8] Other examples include cars[9] and planes[10] made of many 3D printed components. The reductions in cost, time, and supply-chain logistics can be substantial.

The range of 3D printable products stretches from the tiny to the huge. On the tiny side, researchers at TU Wein University printed an intricate castle that measured 230 x 250 x 360 microns.[11] Miniature plastic castles may be fun, but the technology has been extended to metals, as shown by Cal Tech scientists who printed a latticed cube measuring just six microns across.[12] Micro and nanoprinting hold promise for electronic circuits and microrobots, among other applications.

On the huge side, companies now offer 3D printed buildings.[13] These systems lay down the concrete–like contours of a building, with humans installing any windows, plumbing, and wiring. 3D printed structures generate less waste than traditional construction and can enjoy much greater geometric complexity with ease. Most importantly, they can be inexpensive, leading to potential applications in low-income housing.

And in between tiny and huge are a litany of impressive objects, including bicycle frames, entire bicycles,[14] food,[15] and shoes.[16] Some objects, most

---

[8]   *Additive Manufacturing: Aviation and Aerospace Industry*, GE ADDITIVE, www.ge.com/addi tive/additive-manufacturing/industries/aviation-aerospace.

[9]   Vanessa Bates Ramirez, *This 3D Printed Electric Car Will Enter Production This Year*, SINGULARITYHUB (Apr. 1, 2018), https://singularityhub.com/2018/04/01/this-3d-printed-electric-car-will-enter-production-this-year/#sm.00000hqxzl2g7ffus8k27zgbqye19.

[10] Clay Dillow, *UK Engineers Print and Fly the World's First Working 3-D Printed Aircraft*, POPULAR SCI. (July 28, 2011), www.popsci.com/technology/article/2011-07/uk-engineers-print-and-fly-worlds-first-working-3-d-printed-aircraft.

[11] Beau Jackson, *3D Printing with Pencil-Point Precision at TU Wien Produces Miniature Castle*, 3D PRINTING INDUSTRY (Jan. 3, 2017, 11:59 AM), https://3dprintingindustry.com/news/3d-printing-pencil-point-precision-tu-wien-produces-miniature-castle-101927/.

[12] Andrey Vyatskikh et al., *Additive Manufacturing of 3D Nano-Architected Metals*, 9 NATURE COMMUNICATIONS 593 (2018), www.nature.com/articles/s41467-018-03071-9.

[13] APIS COR, http://apis-cor.com/en/; 3D NATIVES, www.3dnatives.com/en/3d-printed-house-companies-120220184.

[14] Richard Lai, *EADS's Airbike Is a 3D-Printed Nylon Bicycle, Actually Looks Rather Decent*, ENGADGET (Mar. 9, 2011, 2:50 PM), www.engadget.com/2011/03/09/eadss-airbike-is-a-3d-printed-nylon-bicycle-actually-looks-rat.

[15] Bianca Bosker, *3D Printers Could Actually Make Donuts Healthy*, HUFFINGTON POST (Apr. 24, 2013, 3:13 PM), www.huffingtonpost.com/2013/04/24/3d-printed-food_n_3148598.html.

[16] Brian Heater, *Adidas Joins Carbon's Board as Its 3D Printed Shoes Finally Drop*, TECHCRUNCH (Jan. 2018), https://techcrunch.com/2018/01/18/adidas-joins-carbons-board-as-its-3d-printed-shoes-finally-drop/; Michael Fitzgerald, *With 3-D Printing, the Shoe Really Fits*,

prominently guns, cause public concern. Others offer amusement, like 3D printed "selfie" statues. Though there are numerous areas from which to choose, the following subparts highlight a few additional applications for 3D printing final objects.

Medical Products

The medical community was an early adopter of 3D printing technology. Established products like customized hearing aid shells, dental products, and prosthetics have been 3D printed for years.[17] 3D printing's low cost and geometrical freedom is a boon to these products, which must be adapted to each user's body. It is particularly helpful to reduce costs of prostheses for children who quickly outgrow the devices.[18]

The technology is also useful for surgical planning and implants. A dramatic illustration comes from Belgium, where surgeons implanted the world's first titanium 3D printed mandible for an eighty-three-year-old woman.[19] The uses go from head to foot,[20] and everywhere in between.

Drug manufacturing, too, may be revolutionized. The U.S. Food and Drug Administration approved the first 3D printed drug, Spritam, which treats epilepsy.[21] Of course, to manufacture drugs you need the proper starting materials, which can sometimes be difficult for specific compounds. But 3D printing is also being used to create small reactors that can make a variety of drugs starting with basic ingredients.[22]

MIT SLOAN MGMT. REV. (May 15, 2013), http://sloanreview.mit.edu/article/with-3-d-print ing-the-shoe-really-fits.

[17] E.g., Helena Dodziuk, *Applications of 3D Printing in Healthcare*, 13 POLISH J. THORACIC AND CARDIOVASCULAR SURGERY 283 (2016), www.ncbi.nlm.nih.gov/pmc/articles/PM C5071603/.

[18] Mick Ebeling, *How a 3-D Printed Arm Gave Hope to Boy Maimed in Bomb Blast*, VITAL SIGNS (Mar. 19, 2014, 7:09 AM), www.cnn.com/2014/03/19/opinion/3d-print-arm-daniel/index .html.

[19] Monica Dybuncio, *Woman Gets World's First 3D Printed Jaw Transplant*, CBS NEWS (Feb. 6, 2012, 3:03 PM), www.cbsnews.com/news/woman-gets-worlds-first-3d-printed-jaw-trans plant/.

[20] T. J. Dekker, *Use of Patient-Specific 3D-Printed Titanium Implants for Complex Foot and Ankle Limb Salvage, Deformity Correction, and Arthrodesis Procedures*, 39 FOOT ANKLE INT'L 916 (2018).

[21] Jennifer Kite-Powell, *FDA Approved 3D Printed Drug Available in the US*, FORBES (Mar. 22, 2016, 4:38 PM), www.forbes.com/sites/jenniferhicks/2016/03/22/fda-approved-3d-printed-drug-available-in-the-us.

[22] Robert Service, *You Could Soon Be Manufacturing Your Own Drugs – Thanks to 3D Printing*, SCIENCE (Jan. 18, 2018, 2:50 PM), www.sciencemag.org/news/2018/01/you-could-soon-be-manufacturing-your-own-drugs-thanks-3d-printing.

On the cutting edge of medicine sits bioprinting, which has the goal of printing complete organs.[23] As early as 2004, scientists were able to bioprint a bladder and implant it in a patient.[24] But as they move away from thin tissues, difficulties such as obtaining the correct vasculature increase. Nevertheless, researchers have applied 3D printing to the production of liver tissue, blood vessels, and cartilage.[25] These materials are not yet at the stage to be implantable organs, but the race is certainly on to achieve that goal. In the meantime, the printed tissues are very valuable for experimentation and drug testing.[26]

Aesthetic Creations

Most of the technological capabilities discussed thus far involved utilitarian objects, but 3D printing promises to benefit aesthetic creations as well. The jewelry industry is discovering the advantages and appeal of bespoke and on-demand jewelry created with 3D printing.[27] Printers can either create wax molds for casting or print jewelry directly. Materials range from inexpensive plastics and metals to precious metals. Jewelry designs are available for download on numerous sites and can be printed at home or using one of the many available 3D print services. One jeweler reported spending $25,000 to have Shapeways print her pieces, an amount of money that would have netted far fewer pieces using traditional manufacturing methods.[28]

Sculptors too are adopting the technology to increase their creative freedom because it allows complex shapes that would be difficult or impossible to create using traditional methods. One sculptor described his frustrations before 3D printing was available, stating, "I wanted to develop the drawings

---

[23] For a discussion of patent-related issues implicated by bioprinting, see Phoebe H. Li, *3D Bioprinting Technologies: Patents, Innovation and Access*, 6 L. Innovation Tech. 282 (2014).

[24] Brian Lord, *Bladder Grown From 3D Bioprinted Tissue Continues to Function After 14 Years*, 3D Printing Industry (Sep. 12, 2018, 1:41 PM), https://3dprintingindustry.com/news/blad der-grown-from-3d-bioprinted-tissue-continues-to-function-after-14-years-139631

[25] *See, e.g.*, S. V. Murphy & A. Atala, *3D Bioprinting of Tissues and Organs*, 32 Nature Biotechnology 773 (2014); Rui Yao, *Three-Dimensional Printing: Review of Application in Medicine and Hepatic Surgery*, 13 Cancer Biology & Medicine 443 (2016), www .ncbi.nlm.nih.gov/pmc/articles/PMC5250601.

[26] *Bioprinters: Printing a Bit of Me*, The Economist (Mar. 8, 2014), www.economist.com/ne ws/technology-quarterly/21598322-bioprinting-building-living-tissue-3d-printer-becoming-new-business.

[27] *E.g.*, Clare O'Connor, *How a Jewelry Company Is Making $250,000 Pieces Using 3D Printing and Google Earth*, Forbes (Feb. 28, 2014, 3:49 PM), www.forbes.com/sites/clareoconnor/20 14/02/28/how-a-jewelry-company-is-making-250000-pieces-using-3d-printing-and-google-earth.

[28] *Id.*

I was doing three-dimensionally and there was absolutely no way to do it."[29] Sculptures range from the microscopic[30] to the huge,[31] and all sizes in between. And the sculptures aren't limited to high-end pieces; there are thousands of inexpensive digital files of sculptures for sale online.

In a somewhat troubling example of technological power, artist Dewey-Hagborg relied on 3D printing to complete her Stranger Visions project.[32] The project took DNA samples from things like hair and gum in public spaces and extracted information about the owner's physical traits such as ethnicity, eye color, and the like. Armed with that information, she used a custom-designed computer program to generate a three-dimensional resemblance of the owner's face, which she then 3D printed.

Beyond fine art, photographs and selfies can now enjoy a third dimension with 3D scans. 3D scanners are discussed in more detail in Chapter 2, but in essence they allow users to obtain a digital file of the physical object in near exact dimensional accuracy. President Obama became the first president to have a 3D scanned and printed portrait made.[33] But you don't have to be a president to enjoy printing yourself, many companies are sprouting up to offer this service at affordable prices. One unfortunate side effect is that engaged couples, perhaps already too self-absorbed, can add to their nuptial narcissism with self-replicas atop their own wedding cakes.

Personal digital scans can be creatively altered and combined with other figures. For example, designing and printing a centaur version of yourself would not be difficult. More ominously from an intellectual property perspective, neither would printing your head on the body of a copyrighted and trademarked action figure.[34]

---

[29] *How 3D Printing Is Changing the Arts and Crafts World*, NDTV GADGETS (May 16, 2013), http://gadgets.ndtv.com/laptops/news/how-3d-printing-is-changing-the-arts-and-crafts-world-3 67601 (quoting Joshua Harker).

[30] Sarah Anderson Goehrke, *3D Prints Smaller Than an Ant's Forehead Are Printed and Then Inevitably Lost*, 3DPRINT.COM (Nov. 14, 2014), https://3dprint.com/24892/nanosculpture-jonty-hurwitz/ (depicting intricate sculptures of humans that can fit on a human hair).

[31] Alec, *Gigantic 2.3 Meters Tall 3D Printed Iron Knot Sculpture by Rinus Roelofs Revealed at RapidPro 2016*, 3DERS.ORG (Mar. 2, 2016), www.3ders.org/articles/20160302-gigantic-3d-printed-iron-knot-sculpture-by-rinus-roelofs-revealed-at-rapidpro-2016.html.

[32] Amanda Kooser, *Artist 3D-Prints Portraits from DNA Left in Public Places*, CNET (May 8, 2013, 8:31 AM), http://news.cnet.com/8301-17938_105-57583442-1/artist-3d-prints-portraits-from-dna-left-in-public-places.

[33] Günter Waibel, *Smithsonian Creates the First-Ever 3D Presidential Portrait*, SMITHSONIAN INSTITUTION (Dec. 2, 2014, 1:00 PM), https://dpo.si.edu/blog/smithsonian-creates-first-ever-3 d-presidential-portrait.

[34] Mark Fleming, *3D Printing Can Turn You into a Superhero*, 3DPRINTER.NET (May 10, 2012), www.3dprinter.net/3d-printing-can-turn-you-into-a-superhero.

A final example of the benefits of 3D printing technology comes from artifacts and museums. Museums can replicate priceless works in case a disaster ruins the original,[35] a concern made all the more urgent in 2015–16 when the world watched in horror as ISIS extremists destroyed thousands of years of history in Syria.[36] 3D scanning and printing methods are superior to previous reproduction methods, which involved risky physical contact – sometimes even using messy plaster. 3D scans do not require contact and allow high-fidelity reconstructions.[37]

The Smithsonian began to three-dimensionally digitize its collection of 137 million objects in 2009.[38] Motivations extend beyond preservation. Replicas allow intimate expert study and the dissemination of multiple replicas for better public access.[39] Indeed, anyone with the digital file can print a version at home or through a 3D printing service.

Hybrid Creations

Product designers are also finding new inspiration from the flexibility 3D printing brings. The technology allows designers to merge aesthetic and utilitarian goals in ways not previously practical. Freed from geometric constraints imposed by traditional manufacturing techniques, designers have poured creativity into everyday objects like lamps, tables, and chairs.

In addition to printing models during the design process, designers have printed final products such as a coffee table based on biomimicry of tree growth,[40] chairs inspired by botany,[41] and lamps of all shapes and

---

[35] See, e.g., Jane J. Lee, 5 Ways Smithsonian Uses 3-D Scanning to Open Up History, NAT'L GEOGRAPHIC (Sept. 5, 2013), http://news.nationalgeographic.com/news/2013/09/130904-3d-printing-smithsonian-whale-skeleton-technology-science.

[36] Dan Bilefsky, *ISIS Destroys Part of Roman Theater in Palmyra, Syria*, N.Y. TIMES (Jan. 20, 2017), www.nytimes.com/2017/01/20/world/middleeast/palmyra-syria-isis-amphitheater.html. Thanktully, many of the artifacts destroyed in the Mosul museum were plaster replicas fortuitously made when the originals were moved to Baghdad in preparation for a major renovation. Ben Wedeman, *ISIS Devastated Mosul Museum, or Did It?*, CNN (Mar. 13, 2017, 4:00 AM), www.cnn.com/2017/03/12/middleeast/mosul-museum-isis/index.html.

[37] Lee, *supra* note 35.

[38] *Id.*

[39] *Id.*

[40] HOD LIPSON & MELBA KURMAN, FABRICATED: THE NEW WORLD OF 3D PRINTING 177 (2013).

[41] Natashah Hitti, *Nagami's First Collection Features 3D-Printed Chairs by Zaha Hadid Architects*, DEZEEN (Mar. 26, 2018), www.dezeen.com/2018/03/26/nagamis-first-furniture-collection-features-3d-printed-chairs-by-zaha-hadid-architects/.

sizes.[42] And it is not only custom furniture being created – IKEA has sold several 3D printed pieces and is working on more.[43] Additional examples abound of 3D printable functional designs, from clothes and cars to simple objects like protective phone cases.[44]

To look more closely at one functional-aesthetic hybrid, consider prosthetics and assistive exoskeletons. This industry was an early adopter of 3D printing, in part because of the reduction in costs of generating tailor-fit devices. The accessibility of the technology to relatively unskilled workers has given rise to a worldwide, open source network of people who seek to provide 3D printed prosthetics to everyone in need, regardless of income.[45] The technology is accessible enough that teenagers are using it to make prosthetics for others.[46]

It is not just the functional side of prosthetics that is influenced by 3D printing. Creators can use it to introduce artistic and expressive personalizations to any prosthetic. From video game and sports-based themes[47] to intricate, beautiful, and personal fairings (covers), 3D printing allows patients to help design what will be a part of themselves in a more intimate, emotionally satisfying way.[48]

---

[42]   Jessica Van Zeijderveld, *20 Incredible 3D Printed Lamps to Brighten Up Home Decor*, SCULPTEO (Jan. 31, 2018), www.sculpteo.com/blog/2018/01/31/20-incredible-3d-printed-lamps-to-brighten-up-home-decor.

[43]   Alexandrea P., *IKEA Customizes Gaming Chairs Using 3D Printing*, 3D NATIVES (June 14, 2018), www.3dnatives.com/en/ikea-3d-printed-chair150620184/.

[44]   *See* Laird Borrelli-Persson, *Iris van Herpen*, VOGUE (Jan. 1, 2013), www.vogue.com/fashion-shows/spring-2013-couture/iris-van-herpen (describing flexible 3D printed clothing); Amandine Richardot, *3D Printed Car: The Future of the Automotive Industry*, SCULPTEO (Dec. 27, 2017), www.sculpteo.com/blog/2017/12/27/3d-printed-car-the-future-of-the-automotive-industry (describing a car with many 3D printed interior and exterior components).

[45]   *3D-Printable Prosthetic Devices*, NAT'L INSTITUTES OF HEALTH, https://3dprint.nih.gov/collections/prosthetics.

[46]   *See, e.g.*, John Ramos, *Bay Area Teen Designs, Builds Prosthetic Hand for Romanian Man*, CBS SF (Apr. 20, 2018, 6:56 PM), https://sanfrancisco.cbslocal.com/2018/04/20/teenager-3d-prints-hand-for-man-romania/. At the same time, concerns arise about the safety of devices made by nonprofessionals. *See* ANGELA DALY, SOCIO-LEGAL ASPECTS OF THE 3D PRINTING REVOLUTION 71–80 (2016).

[47]   *Products: Deus Ex Covers*, OPEN BIONICS, https://shop.openbionics.com/products/deus-ex-covers; LIMBITLESS SOLUTIONS, https://limbitless-solutions.org/about/.

[48]   *Bespoke Prosthetic Fairings: The Art of Personalized Medicine with Industrial 3D Printing*, 3D SYSTEMS, www.3dsystems.com/learning-center/case-studies/bespoke-prosthetic-fairings-art-personalized-medicine.

B. PHYSITIZATION AND ITS EFFECTS

3D printing technology's current abilities capture the imagination, and the technology will continue to improve. Having given an overview of 3D printing technology's capabilities, I now introduce some of the technology's impacts. Increasingly, 3D printing will affect not only manufacturing and design, but also health, the environment, entrepreneurship, and global trade.[49]

Physitization

Two of the most important aspects of 3D printing from an IP standpoint are that numerous physical objects will have a digital counterpart, and that moving back and forth between the digital and physical realms will become easy. More succinctly, a key aspect of 3D printing technology is physitization.

The term *physitization* is meant to express the bidirectionality of 3D printing technology. Someone can create ("draw") a digital version of an object and translate that file into a tangible object. And one can go in the opposite direction. Starting with a tangible object, someone can use a 3D scanner to automatically create a digital version of the object. As 3D printing matures, traveling between the digital and physical worlds will become increasingly effortless.

In that world, digital objects will have almost as much value as tangible objects, and in some ways will embody more value. With the ubiquity of computers and the Internet, digital objects can be stored, shared, transferred, and modified with ease. And with access to the right 3D printer, owning the digital file is in many ways as good as owning the tangible object. In one important way, it is better: one can print as many copies of the tangible objects as desired.

Physitization will have a cascade of effects on product design and creation. The following subsections catalog the impacts most relevant to IP law.[50]

---

[49]   See, e.g., *Special Report: Manufacturing and Innovation: A Third Industrial Revolution*, THE ECONOMIST (Apr. 19, 2012), www.economist.com/node/21552901.

[50]   The literature discusses a range of other impacts that are less directly relevant to IP, but are no less important to society. See, e.g., NEIL GERSHENFELD, FAB: THE COMING REVOLUTION ON YOUR DESKTOP (2005); Matt Ratto & Robert Ree, *Materializing Information: 3D Printing and Social Change*, 17 FIRST MONDAY 1 (2012), http://firstmonday.org/ojs/index.php/fm/article/view/3968/3273.

Effect #1: Democratization

Digital tools like CAD drawing programs bring individuals into more meaningful contact with the design of tangible objects. Although individuals have been free to design by hand or digitally before 3D printing technology, few did so because they had no easy way to bring those creations into the physical realm. Now, however, individuals will be far more motivated to design because they can easily turn those designs into tangible creations.

More fundamentally, manufacturing is democratized, commoditized, and largely anonymized.[51] 3D printing technology captures the imagination not only because of what things are printed, but also because of *where* things are printed. 3D printers are making their way into homes, much like computers and 2D printers did in the 1980s. Similar to early desktop computers, affordable 3D printers are currently somewhat limited in their abilities. But they will continue to improve. And as they do, homes become manufacturing hubs for 3D printable goods. In addition, individuals have access to more sophisticated printers through print-on-demand services that are accessible locally and on the Internet.

The democratization of design and manufacturing portends global changes. To the extent manufacturing is localized and commoditized, supply chains decrease and global trading patterns are disrupted. The environmental impacts will be important as the need to ship components and finished goods long distances decreases or vanishes.[52] This shift in manufacturing can also have substantial humanitarian impacts by providing developing countries with access to manufacturing capabilities.[53] The impacts extend also to developed countries where businesses and households can save money by self-printing needed items.[54]

---

[51] See, e.g., R. E. Devor et al., *Transforming the Landscape of Manufacturing: Distributed Manufacturing Based on Desktop Manufacturing (DM)2*, 134 J. Manufacturing Sci. & Engineering 041004-1 (2012).

[52] These gains would need to be offset by the environmental impacts of distributing the raw printing materials and of performing the actual printing. Abundant research into the environmental impacts of 3D printing exists. See, e.g., M. A. Kreiger et al., *Life Cycle Analysis of Distributed Recycling of Post-Consumer High Density Polyethylene for 3-D Printing Filament*, 70 J. Cleaner Production 90 (2014).

[53] See, e.g., J. M. Pearce et al., *3-D Printing of Open Source Appropriate Technologies for Self-Directed Sustainable Development*, 3 J. Sustainable Dev. 17 (2010).

[54] B. T. Wittbrodt et al., *Life-Cycle Economic Analysis of Distributed Manufacturing with Open-Source 3-D Printers*, 23 Mechatronics 713 (2013) (finding that an average household could achieve between 40 and 200 percent ROI for a 3D printer); Joshua M. Pearce, *Building Research Equipment with Free, Open-Source Hardware*, 337 Science 1303 (2012); Nicole Gallup et al., *Economic Potential for Distributed Manufacturing of Adaptive Aids for Arthritis Patients in the U.S.*, 89 Geriatrics 1 (Dec. 6, 2018).

In addition, design will increasingly reside in the digital space and will be fundamentally dissociated from manufacturing, which is commoditized. As a result, much of the value of goods can no longer be captured by mass-manufacturing. In the past, IP owners could rely on tangible distributed goods to embody the value of underlying IP. By controlling the manufacture of tangible goods, IP owners in turn recouped the value of their IP. But when anyone can manufacture objects based on a digital file, the value of IP undergirding the goods is shifted upstream to the digital files. Whoever controls the digital files obtains the value of the IP.

When individuals hold the power of design and manufacturing, they will also shift how they view brands. Individual empowerment will figuratively lift the veil that currently separates consumers from branded goods. To the extent that individuals comprehend their ability to create goods, brands will be demystified. Companies will be less able to dictate brands to customers, and customers will demand participation with product design and manufacturing.

Not all aspects of decentralized manufacturing are widely celebrated. Localized manufacturing, especially in the home, brings relative anonymity. Though it is not impossible to learn who is printing what, it is difficult technologically and overwhelming in scale. Under this reality, many worry about public safety since guns can be 3D printed. Critics have likewise sounded the alarm about the public health impact of 3D printable illegal drugs.[55] And of course, the need for this book arises in part because of the fear many IP owners express about the impacts of 3D printing on IP infringement.[56]

Effect #2: Customization – Complexity Is Free

With 3D printing, complexity is free. This catchphrase conveys the fact that it is generally no more difficult for a 3D printer to print a mundane cube than to print an intricate, multifaceted object.[57] This technological aspect brings utilitarian and aesthetic advantages.

---

[55] Mike Power, Drugs 2.0: The Web Revolution That's Changing How the World Gets High (2013).

[56] *See, e.g.*, U.S. Intellectual Property Enforcement Coordinator, 2013 Joint Strategic Plan On Intellectual Property Enforcement 6 (2013)("[J]ust as 3D printing offers the opportunity to make meaningful contributions to our society, there also exists the opportunity for individuals who look to exploit others' hard work to abuse this technology by trading in counterfeit and pirated goods, of which we must be cognizant and diligent in our efforts to prevent.").

[57] It should be noted that printing certain shapes, like large overhanging parts, may require printing temporary supports with certain printers to prevent the overhang from falling while the printed material cools and strengthens.

On the utilitarian side, free complexity allows engineers to create more aerodynamic and hydrodynamic parts.[58] Moreover, previously separate sub-parts can be combined into a single unitary 3D printed part, improving manufacturing time, supply chain logistics, and product durability. Finally, free complexity allows engineers to print customized object infills as opposed to simply making the object solid. Like the internal lattice structure of bones, objects can be infilled only to the extent and manner needed for the physical demands of the part. This results in porous objects that use less material and weigh less (hence the name "lightweighting") while maintaining strength. Through this technology, researchers have printed a graphene structure twenty times lighter than steel but ten times more powerful.[59] Car and airline manufacturers eagerly use lightweighting to reduce the weight and hence fuel consumption of their vehicles.[60]

On the aesthetic side, ornate flourishes or uncommon shapes do not incur increased cost of manufacturing. In addition, bespoke consumer goods are more readily attainable. Sellers can easily offer a range of different designs because they need not sink money into mass-manufacturing. Goods are printed on demand. Individuals can easily personalize digital versions of goods; it is no costlier to print a monogrammed version than a plain one. In fact, as demand for individualized goods increases, if companies do not offer buyers personalized options, consumers may obtain digital versions and self-customize them.

Effect #3: Innovation

3D printing catalyzes innovative and creative works by lowering the costs of their creation and dissemination. In terms of utilitarian inventions, the technology can affect every stage of the innovation cycle. As detailed in Chapter 10, 3D printing can lower the costs and improve the speed of basic research, design, prototyping, iterative improvements, and product launch/commercialization. The lowered costs allow inventions to be created and commercialized with less or no outside investment, freeing innovators to create rather than raise funds (or give up).

---

[58]   Sarah Saunders, *Shark Skin, 3D Printing, and Aerodynamics*, 3DPRINT.COM (Feb. 15, 2018), https://3dprint.com/203849/3d-print-shark-skin-aerodynamics/.

[59]   Zhao Qin et al., The Mechanics and Design of a Lightweight Three-Dimensional Graphene Assembly, 3 SCI. ADVANCES E1601536-1 (2017).

[60]   *See, e.g., Advanced Software Design Technology Leads GM into Next Generation of Vehicle Lightweighting*, GM (May 3, 2018), https://media.gm.com/media/us/en/gm/news.detail.html/content/Pages/news/us/en/2018/may/0503-lightweighting.html (describing a seat bracket 40 percent lighter and 20 percent stronger than the original part).

Innovation (in its broader sense) can come on the cultural and artistic side too. 3D printing allows artists and cultural commentators to better express themselves in another medium. The open culture of many 3D printing enthusiasts fosters various design competitions. One contest offered prizes for the best functional remixes of design files from furniture designer Tom Dixon's latest creations.[61] Another contest invited participants to remix a 3D file of a T-Rex skull.[62] The creative contestants thought up remixes like a T-Rex showerhead, T-Rex high heels, and a T-Rex bike seat.

Beyond lighthearted remix competitions, 3D printing technology has helped produce more pointed social commentary. If a picture is worth a thousand words, perhaps a three-dimensional object is worth a million. Artist Nickolay Lamm was thinking along these lines when he used the technology together with the Centers for Disease Control's measurements of the average nineteen-year-old woman to transform the iconic Barbie doll into one having average measurements.[63] The 3D printed doll represented his commentary that "average is beautiful."[64]

Effect #4: Imitation

Just as 3D printing technology fosters innovation, it also fosters imitation. Indeed, imitation and reverse engineering often lead to innovation, as when the imitator adds an improvement. Imitation can be good or bad, depending on the context and one's perspective.[65] On the one hand, imitation is the basis of a capitalist society – good ideas and technology spread to make everyone better off. On the other hand, imitation can dampen the fire of innovation if the imitation runs the first innovator out of business.

There are several ways imitation can happen. First, if an imitator has access to a digital file that will print an object, copying the file is instantaneous and costless. Second, if the imitator does not have access to a digital version of the object, 3D scanners can be used to make a digital copy of the physical object.

---

[61] Carrie Wyman, *Disrupt Tom Dixon – A New Design Competition*, STRATASYS (Apr. 16, 2013), http://blog.stratasys.com/2013/04/16/tom-dixon-design-competition-3d-printing.

[62] Eddie Krassenstein, *3D Designers Submit Some Incredible T-Rex Remix Designs for MakerBot Competition*, 3DPrint.com (May 21, 2014), https://3dprint.com/4131/3d-t-rex-remix/.

[63] Scott Stump, *'Normal' Barbie Uses Real Women's Measurements*, TODAY (July 3, 2013, 4:56 PM), www.today.com/news/normal-barbie-uses-real-womens-measurements-6C10533511.

[64] *Id.*

[65] *See* Pamela Samuelson & Suzanne Scotchmer, *The Law and Economics of Reverse Engineering*, 111 YALE. L. J. 1575 (2002).

Finally, imitation can happen through carefully studying a product and creating the digital file from scratch with a computer drafting program.

In any of these scenarios, once the copy is obtained, it can be printed numerous times and shared around the world though the Internet. It is no wonder, therefore, that IP owners fear the digital proliferation of their files.[66] But imitators may do more than merely copy the object. They may manipulate the digital file to introduce improvements in the design and functionality of the object. Or they may simply study the product to understand how it works and decide to build something different. How people use the imitative powers of 3D printing technology may vary, but the key point for now is that the technology lowers the costs and increases the speed of imitation.

C. TECHNOLOGICAL LIMITATIONS

Having spent the bulk of this chapter considering the capabilities and potential of the technology, it is important also to consider its current limitations. While the technology will continue to improve, it is impossible to accurately predict how quickly and how much. Improvements will come in the areas of software, hardware, and materials, among others, and each will have its own trajectories and challenges.

It is equally important to emphasize that even with current technological limitations, the IP problems and challenges discussed in this book are currently salient – they are not reserved for the future. The existing technology has already digitized and 3D printed objects directly implicating patent, copyright, trademark, and design law. What will change as the technology progresses is the frequency and magnitude of those intersections.

Limitations in Industrial Use

The technology's general limitations can be measured against the holy grail goal of being able to cost effectively mass-produce completed machines that are ready to use right out of the printer. But focusing on that objective only is

---

[66] *Gartner Says Uses of 3D Printing Will Ignite Major Debate on Ethics and Regulation,* GARTNER (Jan. 29, 2014), www.gartner.com/en/newsroom/press-releases/2014-01-29-gartner-says-uses-of-3d-printing-will-ignite-major-debate-on-ethics-and-regulation ("Gartner predicts that by 2018, 3D printing will result in the loss of at least $100 billion per year in IP globally."). Gartner's 2014 prediction was wildly off base, and very few significant losses in IP have been attributable to 3D printing to date. Significant losses will eventually happen, but probably not for several years to come.

unwise, because 3D printed components represent a huge potential market. Furthermore, components can also be protected by IP.

Whether complete machines or components thereof, 3D printed objects may require post-printing treatments like removing supports, curing (baking in an oven), and smoothing (to smooth the edge interfaces of each printed layer). Post-printing treatments are relatively inexpensive and are not generally considered a big impediment for specialized products, but they can be more substantial in the context of mass production.

A more serious limitation both for mass production and specialized applications is the difficulty of printing in multiple materials at the same time.[67] Even if an object is made of all metal or all plastic, incorporating different kinds of metals or different kinds of plastic in a single object poses challenges in terms of software, hardware, and material cooperation. More difficulties arise when products have a mixture of metal and plastic components. For example, the high temperatures used in many metal processes would melt some plastics.

The difficulty with simultaneously printing multiple materials also explains why current technology is not widely used to print electrical components or electromechanical objects. Circuits and electromechanical devices can be printed,[68] and the technology continues to advance, but the goal of printing a smart phone in one pass is a long way off. On the other hand, 3D printing holds promise for creating a new branch of printed circuitry that transcends the limitations of 2D printed circuit boards and allows circuitry to fit in smaller volumes and reduce electronic interference within the circuitry.[69] The U.S. Army recently invested in this technology.[70]

---

[67] For recent advances in the area, see Kavin Kowsari et al., *High-Efficiency High-Resolution Multimaterial Fabrication for Digital Light Processing-Based Three-Dimensional Printing*, 5 3D PRINTING & ADDITIVE MANUFACTURING 185 (2018), and sources cited therein.

[68] *See, e.g.*, Yong He et al., *Three-Dimensional Coprinting of Liquid Metals for Directly Fabricating Stretchable Electronics*, 5 3D PRINTING & ADDITIVE MANUFACTURING 195 (2018); Anan Tanwilaisiri et al., *Design and Fabrication of Modular Supercapacitors Using 3D Printing*, 16 J. ENERGY STORAGE 1 (2018).

[69] *See, e.g.*, Amit Joe Lopes et al., *Integrating Stereolithography and Direct Print Technologies for 3D Structural Electronics Fabrication*, 18 RAPID PROTOTYPING J. 129, 129–33 (2012); Kenneth H. Church et al., *Printed Circuit Structures, the Evolution of Printed Circuit Boards*, UTMI-NERS.UTEP.EDU (2013), *available at* http://utminers.utep.edu/pdeffenbaugh/printed_circuit_structures_ipc.pdf; Multilayer Three-Dimensional Circuit Structure and Manufacturing Method Thereof, U.S. Patent No. 7,987,589 (filed Dec. 11, 2008).

[70] Tia Vialva, *nScrypt Enhances U.S Army's Additive Manufacturing Capabilities with Factory in a Tool Platform*, 3D PRINTING INDUSTRY (Dec. 12, 2018, 11:56 AM), https://3dprintingindustry .com/news/nscrypt-enhances-u-s-armys-additive-manufacturing-capabilities-with-factory-in-a-tool-platform-145382/.

Other general limitations include lack of speed, the limited number of printable materials, limits on the size of printable objects, and costs.[71] If 3D printing is to be used in more mass-manufacturing operations, its speed will need to improve. Recent breakthroughs have increased some metal printing speeds tenfold and some polymer printing speeds a hundredfold,[72] and there is optimism that printing speeds will continue to increase. And despite the large variety of printable materials currently available, the range of materials currently used in traditional manufacturing is remarkable. Adding to the arsenal of printable materials will broaden the appeal of 3D printing for more finished products.

Finally, costs are a concern. Some industrial printers cost hundreds of thousands of dollars, meaning that the savings from using the technology needs to be of a similar magnitude to justify the investment. Lowering the technology's costs will obviously broaden its appeal. Similarly, the costs of some printable materials will need to be reduced to make the technology competitive for certain mass production operations.

Limitations in Personal Use

3D printing is already being used by individuals in their homes, but desktop printers are even more limited than their industrial counterparts. To be affordable to many individuals, 3D printers would need to cost less than a thousand dollars, and the only printers currently in that price range are simple plastic extruding devices. Thus, the user is generally limited to printing plastic parts.[73] In addition, the cheaper the device, the more prone it tends to be toward error and the more rudimentary are its products.[74]

At the same time, individuals have access to much more sophisticated 3D printers via many 3D printing services, what I will call 3D print shops. These shops can be local spaces like UPS stores that individuals physically visit. But many 3D print shops like Shapeways, Ponoko, and i.Materialise accept digital uploads of 3D printable files, which are then printed and mailed to the customer.

---

[71] *See, e.g.,* Li, *supra* note 23, at 1.

[72] *See* John R. Tumbleston et al., *Continuous Liquid Interface Production of 3D Objects,* SCIENCEXPRESS, Mar. 16, 2015.

[73] *But see infra* Chapter 2 note 39(describing experimental desktop printers using a variety of materials).

[74] *See* Chandrakana Nandi et al., *Programming Language Tools and Techniques for 3D Printing,* 2ND SUMMIT ON ADVANCES IN PROGRAMMING LANGUAGES 8 (2017), https://homes .cs.washington.edu/~ztatlock/pubs/incarnate-nandi-snapl17.pdf.

Another substantial limitation to individual use is the complexity of the technology. 3D printing is not currently easy for nonexperts. Creating the digital files requires a certain amount of training, and understanding the 3D printers and how best to print the files also requires some expertise. Although many people can and have taught themselves the skills, and free tools are widely available to help interested people learn, the process still takes time and effort.

Another futuristic vision of 3D printing technology is a "factory in every home" that can print just about anything the owner wants. This vision, frankly, is a long way off and in some ways will likely never be achieved. Even if 3D printing technology became exceedingly inexpensive and easy to use, the likelihood of a homeowner keeping a stock of the multitude of print materials needed to print "almost anything" is close to nil.

Even with these limitations, it should be reiterated that desktop 3D printers are currently able to print a huge variety of objects. These objects may be covered by patents, copyright, trademarks, and design law. As with industrial uses, the question is not whether individuals can use 3D printing to infringe IP, but how often and to what extent such infringement will occur.

For an example of an individual use that almost certainly infringed a patent, consider a college student who used 3D printing to make his own set of dental aligners (similar to the branded Invisalign invisible braces).[75] He created a digital model of his current teeth from a mold, then created a series of digital molds that slowly repositioned his teeth to be straight. He then 3D printed the series of molds and wore them until his teeth were straightened. His total cost was about $60, compared to the thousands of dollars charged by dentists. In addition to safety concerns, his activity almost certainly infringed Invisalign's patents.[76]

Examples implicating copyright and trademark rights are legion. One only needs to search a 3D printing file repository like MyMiniFactory, Thingiverse, or Turbosquid for well-known trademarks or fictional characters.

At this point, the basic IP implications of the technology should be clear. But before those implications can be properly analyzed, a deeper understanding of the technology is needed. For this reason, the next chapter discusses key aspects of the technology, most notably the different file types used in 3D printing.

---

[75] Hope King, *College Student 3D Prints His Own Braces*, CNN (Mar. 16, 2016, 4:38 PM), http://money.cnn.com/2016/03/16/technology/homemade-invisalign.

[76] *See, e.g.*, U.S. Pat. No. 6,406,292 (filed May 13, 1999).

2

How 3D Printing Works and Why it Matters

Chapter Outline:

It may seem strange that a book about IP law goes two chapters without really discussing the law. But the law does not exist in a vacuum. The law only finds its purpose in its interactions with the real world, or what lawyers call the law applied to the facts. In this case, the relevant facts relate to 3D printing technology.

Technology is an amoral tool. People can use it for good or for ill, and people did just that in the earlier – and ongoing – copyright battles over digital music and movies. There is no reason to expect anything different with 3D printing. In the movie and music area, industries collectively resisted the technological change, suing everyone from software developers to the end listener. In those battles, intellectual property law played an important role. Most of the music and movies were protected by copyright, making infringers out of those who downloaded files without paying for them. But the "infringer" moniker didn't deter many people, at least not at first. Instead, a blend of technology and law worked together to solve the issue of digital copying. The law played a role by providing avenues for copyright holders to pursue those who infringed – both individual downloaders when necessary and centralized hubs of infringement like Napster.

But technology played a very important role too. From digital rights management, to IP address detection, to the development of sleek, authorized sellers of music (iTunes and Spotify), technology helped maintain a system where IP rights continued to incentivize creation without (arguably) imposing unnecessary collateral costs. Importantly, copyright law allowed MP3 and internet technologies that "created" the problems to continue to develop. Lawmakers understood that although the internet and MP3 technologies facilitated prodigious amounts of copyright infringement, they also brought tremendous benefits.

In this sense, lawmakers viewed the technologies themselves as neutral; what mattered was how people employed them.[1] And lawmakers wisely have allowed such neutral technologies to proliferate generally unhindered (with some exceptions) even as they tweak IP law to balance competing interests. A page of history is worth a volume of logic, and on either front it is expected that the law will follow the same course and allow 3D printing technology to develop largely unhindered by the IP infringement it may facilitate.[2]

It is important, therefore, to understand the technology well. Moreover, details of the technology can matter greatly to IP law, making a technological foundation all the more important. This chapter first considers the important issue of the various 3D printing file formats, or stages, which is critical to subsequent analysis. The second subsection provides details on the different types of 3D printers. The final subsection describes important complementary technologies, including 3D scanners, CNC machines, and technological protection measures.

A. FILE FORMATS IN 3D PRINTING

Before a 3D printer can manufacture anything, it needs a digital file to provide instructions for how to build the object. Chapter 1 described how these files can serve as the new locus of economic value for 3D printable goods. In fact, different file formats are used at different stages of digital design and manufacturing.

Unfortunately, just about every academic discussion of 3D printing and IP law fails to distinguish among the various file formats used in 3D printing. Most of the writing refers to 3D printable files generically as CAD files, but this is inexact and misleading. This imprecise usage brings to mind the warning echoed by Judge Easterbrook about the risks of multidisciplinary dilettantism.[3] The CAD file format is only the first of three formats important to 3D printing. As this book will make clear throughout, the law will treat different file formats differently. To heed Judge Easterbrook's warning, this

---

[1]   This view preceded digital technology. For instance, courts refused to hold makers of VCRs liable for indirect copyright infringement for merely selling their technology. *See* Sony Corp. of Am. v. Universal City Studios, Inc., 464 U.S. 417 (1984).

[2]   If there is a legal worry that might restrain the technology, it is the ability to 3D print guns.

[3]   Frank H. Easterbrook, *Cyberspace and the Law of the Horse*, 1996 U. CHI. LEGAL F. 207, 207 (1996).

subsection carefully analyzes the file formats used in the various stages of 3D design and printing.

The process of creating the digital file used by 3D printers is usually a three-step process:

1. create a design file,
2. convert the design file into a surface-mesh file, and
3. convert the surface-mesh file into a machine-instruction file.

Each of these file types differs in very important ways from the others, both in terms of its function and economic importance. These differences may have profound effects on how IP law categorizes and treats them. In fact, one of the tensions that will reappear throughout this book is how these file types are both different and yet similar. They are different in their function but are similar in that translation between the file types can be relatively easy and will become easier as the technology matures.

Design Files

Design files predate 3D printing. Engineers often refer to them as CAD files (computer aided design files). The most basic form is an electronic version of a traditional blueprint. A user can create a design file from scratch using a CAD program such as AutoCAD, TurboCAD, SolidWorks, or any number of commercial or open source programs. There are many design file extensions, including DWG and DXF.

CAD programs allow users to draw essentially freehand if they desire, but typically drafters use prefigured shapes (cylinders, screws, etc.) that can be manipulated by shrinking, growing, stretching, and the like. Lines or shapes can also be drawn that are exact lengths or that snap precisely to other existing shapes.

A simple CAD 2D program mimics the process of hand-drawn blueprints. A basic 2D CAD drawing might generate a top, side, and elevation view of an object, together with labels of parts and a parts list. The drawing might also include manufacturing notes such as design tolerances. More advanced 3D CAD programs are now commonplace. A basic 3D CAD program would allow representation of the object in three dimensions as a wireframe model or as a compilation of solid surfaces.

More advanced 3D CAD programs allow much more extensive manipulation of shapes and the ability to specify relationships between objects (concentricity, tangency, etc.). The virtual representation of the final product permits users to validate the form, fit, and function of a product before building it. CAD programs can be enhanced by the inclusion of other engineering tools, such as materials properties, stress analysis, and motion modeling.

An important point is that design files, especially those made with a view toward 3D printing, will often contain much more than mere geometric information about the object depicted. It may contain parts names and numbers, author comments, material information, histories of changes to the drawing, and rules or guidelines input by the draftsperson.

In addition to creating design files from scratch, users can create files in two other ways. First, a user can take an existing design file and modify it into a different shape. Alternatively, a user can rely on a 3D scanner (discussed in more detail in subsection C) to scan an existing physical object. Software is available that translates the scan into a surface-mesh file. Additional software, such as Geomagic Design, can translate the surface-mesh file into a design file for further manipulation or processing.

Design files are the file type most useful for the initial creation and subsequent editing of objects to be 3D printed. CAD programs offer a great deal of precision, power, and flexibility for designing objects of complex geometry. For this reason, although design files cannot speak directly to 3D printers, they are important in 3D design and manufacturing processes. They are also the easiest to edit and change.

Usually, objects are viewed and manipulated using a visual representation of the design file in a CAD program. But like any computer file, a design file can be viewed in a code format, which is basically a text file with numerous lines of code. A very adept user can even edit this code directly to change the drawing.

Surface-Mesh Files (STL)

Software converts design files into surface-mesh files. A surface-mesh file represents the surfaces of an object through tessellations, which are geometric shapes such as triangles, squares, etc. Surface-mesh files are the coin of the realm in the 3D printing ecosystem. They are not directly 3D printable, but they are the type most often shared, sold, and downloaded.[4] Because of this, they are the most economically significant of the file formats and embody much of the economic value of the underlying object.

---

[4] Chandrakana Nandi et al., *Programming Language Tools and Techniques for 3D Printing*, 2ND SUMMIT ON ADVANCES IN PROGRAMMING LANGUAGES 5 (2017), https://homes .cs.washington.edu/~ztatlock/pubs/incarnate-nandi-snapl17.pdf.

Currently, the most common surface-mesh file format is the STL format, which is a shortening of the word *stereolithography*, one type of printing technique.[5] STL files describe the surface geometry of a three-dimensional object through a series of connected triangles that approximate the shape of the object. It is a bit like the pixels in a 2D picture on a computer screen. Instead of square pixels approximating an image, the STL file approximates an object's surfaces with tiny triangle tiles. As with pixels, the smaller the triangles, the better the resolution and thus the smoother the object appears. At the same time, a higher resolution means the file itself takes up more computer memory. The surface-mesh file's resolution will eventually correlate to the resolution of the printed object.

Importantly, the conversion to an STL file strips away a great deal of information from the design file. Color and texture are removed, as are design notes, materials, tolerances, and build histories. All that is left is the triangulated surface geometry.

While STL is the most common surface-mesh file specification, others have been developed to try to enhance functionality. OBJ, AMF, and 3MF files also use surface-meshes, but they can include texture and color information. Some can also use curved triangles in addition to straight triangles, which allows smoother images and fewer facets. Despite their advantages, these other formats have not truly supplanted STL files, which are typically much easier to work with.

It is very important for a surface-mesh file to be "water tight," meaning that there are no gaps or holes where a surface should be. The smallest gap can cause a print job to fail. For this reason, it is sometimes necessary for a human with the proper skills and know-how to check the surface-mesh file and manually repair any gaps. As software improves, the need for human intervention should decrease, but it is currently a limitation in the technology in terms of unskilled users.

As with design files, users can change the shape and dimensions of objects in surface-mesh files, but editing surface-mesh files is much clumsier and more limited.[6] It is possible, though, to add and subtract components or otherwise manipulate the digital object without needing to translate the file back to the design format.

---

[5]   3D printing pioneer Chuck Hull coined the term to describe his 3D printing technique. *Our Story*, 3D SYSTEMS, www.3dsystems.com/30-years-innovation (last visited Dec. 5, 2018). Industry participants also understand *STL* to be an acronym for "Standard Tessellation Language." HOD LIPSON & MELBA KURMAN, FABRICATED: THE NEW WORLD OF 3D PRINTING 101 (2013).

[6]   *See* Nandi et al., *supra* note 4, at 5.

Like design files, surface-mesh files can be represented as textual code. For example, an excerpt of a file might read as follows:

```
facet normal 0.0000e+00 0.000000e+00–1.0000e+00
        outer loop
        vertex 5.0000e+01–5.0000e+01 0.00000e+00
        vertex -5.0000e+01 5.0000e+01 0.00000e+00
        vertex 5.0000e+01 5.0000e+01 0.00000e+00
        endloop
    endfacet
```

Skilled users can edit the code directly to make changes to the digital object. In addition, users can insert comments into the text of the file. Comments are non-executable portions of code. They don't cause the computer to do anything, but rather are typically present to communicate aspects of the project to other users who are viewing the code.

As important as surface-mesh files are, they are not directly 3D printable. They must be translated into a third file format for printing.

Machine-Instruction Files (Gcode)

Software must convert surface-mesh files into machine-instruction files, the most popular of which are GCODE files.[7] So called slicer software creates machine-instruction files by slicing the digital object from the surface-mesh file into hundreds or thousands of discrete layers, which correspond to the layers that will be printed. The file contains specific instructions for the 3D printer to follow when manufacturing the product. For example, if a simple plastic extruding 3D printer is involved, the file would instruct the extruder nozzle to move to a certain X-Y coordinate and begin extruding molten plastic, and to continue doing so until a second coordinate is reached. Once the first layer is deposited, the file instructs the printer nozzle to move up to the second layer's level, and so on.

Machine-instruction files are filled with information specific to a particular 3D printer and its settings. If someone tried to use a machine-instruction file generated for one 3D printer on a different type of 3D printer, it would not work properly. For this reason, people do not typically trade, sell, or download files in this format. Instead, they obtain the surface-mesh version and use slicer

---

[7] GCODE predates 3D printing. It was originally created for controlling machine tools like CNC milling machines. Its name comes from the fact that many of the control commands begin with the letter G. *See, e.g.,* JOAN HORVATH, MASTERING 3D PRINTING 66 (2014).

software to create a machine-instruction file specific to their 3D printer. The flexibility of surface-mesh files across all types of 3D printers explains why they are more economically valuable than machine-instruction files in the 3D printing ecosystem.

It is sometimes possible to slice directly from a design file instead of a surface-mesh file,[8] but no technique for doing so has proven to be robust and reliable. Instead, the progression is currently almost always "design" file to "surface-mesh" file to "machine-instruction" file.

Like surface-mesh files, machine-instruction files generated automatically by software sometimes need skilled human tailoring, particularly for more complex objects. One common problem is that an overhanging area of the printed object will need supports printed under it to sustain it while the "ink" cools and hardens.[9] The operating temperature might also be wrong, resulting in a mushy print. Even with the same surface-mesh file input, different slicer software may generate slightly different GCODE commands. Some slicer software may be better at handling curved surfaces or automatically generating supports, for example. Of course, as software continues to improve, human intervention will be required less often. GCODE can be represented as text, an excerpt of which follows:

> G1 Z15.0 F9000 ;this command moves the platform down 15mm
> G1 F200 E3 ;this command extrudes 3mm of printer feedstock
> M107
> G0 F9000 X58.549 Y59.387 Z0.300
> G1 F1800 X59.715 Y58.239 E0.03847

Note that the text following each semicolon on a given line constitutes a comment that has no effect on the file's functionality. The comments are directed to human readers of the text and explain why a particular portion of code is organized a certain way or what it does.

---

[8]   *See* Zhiwen Zhao & Zhiwen Luc, *Adaptive Direct Slicing of the Solid Model for Rapid Prototyping*, 38 INT'L J. OF PRODUCTION RES. 89 (2000); Ron Jamieson & Herbert Hacker, *Direct Slicing of CAD Models for Rapid Prototyping*, 1 RAPID PROTOTYPING J. 4 (1995).

[9]   *See, e.g.,* Dibya Chakravorty, *2018 3D printer G-Code Commands—Tutorial & Manual*, ALL3DP (July 7, 2018), https://all3dp.com/g-code-tutorial-3d-printer-gcode-commands/ ("[A] utomatically generated code is often not ideal. You will often find that there are problematic areas that do not have enough support, leading to a failed print. In this case, you need to modify the code to ensure successful printing.").

Digital Manufacturing Files (DMFs)

Throughout this book I apply the generic label "digital manufacturing file" (DMF) to any file involved in the 3D printing design and manufacturing process. Most relevant are files that can, with minimum human intervention, provide manufacturing instructions to a 3D printer.

B. 3D PRINTERS

When most laypeople think of 3D printers, they probably think of the inexpensive plastic extruding machines used by hobbyists. These printers have a nozzle a bit like a glue gun that melts and extrudes a plastic feed stock and builds objects up layer-by-layer. After a first layer is printed, the print head moves up (or the base moves down) and a second layer is placed on top of the first layer, with the layers fusing together. The thicker the layers, the lower the resolution of the print job. The process continues until the object is complete.

Machines

Common home-based printers using plastic are a type of deposition printer.[10] Deposition printers deposit materials layer-by-layer until a three-dimensional object is built. The "ink" is the deposited material, which can be plastic, paste, food, and even human cells.

Deposition printers using plastic are referred to as fused filament fabrication, also called fused deposition modeling.[11] They use a variety of thermoplastic polymers, including polycarbonate, polylactic acid (PLA), acrylonitrile butadiene styrene (ABS), high density polyethylene, recycled plastics, and even some polymer-based composites.[12] Many fused filament fabricators have a relatively poor resolution (meaning each layer is thick and thus surfaces are not smooth), but offer the advantage of low prices and fast print speeds.[13] Their fast speed and low price contribute to their wide use in homes and schools.

More advanced deposition printers use a process of continuous metallic welding.[14] The process is very similar to fused filament fabrication, but instead

---

[10] Much of the information on types of 3D printers is based in part on Lucas S. Osborn, Joshua M. Pearce & Amberlee Haselhuhn, *A Case for Weakening Patent Rights*, 89 ST. JOHN'S L. REV. 1185 (2015).

[11] D. T. Pham & R. S. Gault, *A Comparison of Rapid Prototyping Technologies*, 38 INT'L J. OF MACHINE TOOLS & MANUFACTURE 1257, 1269 (1998).

[12] *Id.* at 1270.

[13] *Id.*

[14] Yu Ming Zhang et al., *Automated System for Welding-Based Rapid Prototyping*, 12 MECHATRONICS 37, 38 (2002).

of extruding plastic through a hot nozzle, an electric arc melts a metal filament, such as aluminum.[15] Most welding printers must use shield gases like argon to prevent undesired oxide layer formation. Many weld-based 3D printers are relatively inexpensive for metallic printing and produce quality parts.[16]

In addition to deposition printers, binding printers use lights, lasers, or adhesive to bind together layers of material, such as a liquid polymer or a powdered bed of metal, cement, sawdust, or plastic.[17] The process binds the top layer in the container and then successively melts layers. In such processes, the final objects arise from the bed of material.

In a separate set of processes, lasers can be used to melt, sinter, or clad metals, ceramics, or polymers.[18] Sintering processes often leave undesired small pores throughout the object. To remove the pores the printed object is put under heat or pressure to homogenize the material and remove any porosity.[19] Cladding processes can add a coating to an existing object, repair parts, or build a part from scratch.[20] Laser-based processes often allow for very high resolution and complex shapes.[21] The downsides can include slower build times and increased costs.[22]

Another binding method is actually the first commercialized 3D printing method. Stereolithography (SLA) uses ultraviolet light to cure (harden) successive layers of a liquid photopolymer.[23] Watching the process can be somewhat surreal because the part slowly rises from a vat of liquid goo. Like some laser-based processes, SLA processes can be slow and expensive, but provide high resolution and allow for great shape complexity.[24]

New methods of SLA, especially the Continuous Liquid Interface Production (CLIP), have dramatically improved build times from hours to minutes.[25] CLIP can print in various materials, including silicone

---

[15] *Id.* at 37–38.

[16] Edson Costa Santos et al., *Rapid Manufacturing of Metal Components by Laser Forming*, 46 Int'l J. Machine Tools & Manufacture 1459, 1460 (2006).

[17] Lipson & Kurman, *supra* note 5, at 68, 73, 75.

[18] Santos, *supra* note 16, at 1459.

[19] *Id.* at 1463.

[20] M. W. Khaing et al., *Direct Metal Laser Sintering for Rapid Tooling: Processing and Characterisation of EOS Parts*, 113 J. of Materials Processing Tech. 269, 269 (2001).

[21] *Id.* at 270.

[22] *See* Santos, *supra* note 16, at 1462.

[23] Pham & Gault, *supra* note 11, at 1259. Perhaps the best-known use of SLA is in making the Invisalign clear dental braces.

[24] *Id.* at 1263–64.

[25] John R. Tumbleston et al., *Continuous Liquid Interface Production of 3D Objects*, Sciencexpress, Mar. 16, 2015.

and rigid, flexible, or elastomeric polyurethane. The technology is still young, but the company behind the technology has contracted with Adidas to 3D print customized midsoles for the Adidas Futurecraft 4D shoe[26] and is partnering with companies to produce medical devices.[27]

A final printer type is material jetting, which deposits droplets of photosensitive material that solidify under ultraviolet light.[28] Material jetting is adept at providing multiple materials and colors. But the parts made tend to be brittle and therefore not well suited for mechanical parts.

Research and development continue to pour into 3D printing technology, leading to a constant stream of technological advances in printing materials and methods. Many advances are incremental, while others like CLIP are more dramatic. But the cumulative effect is the steady expansion of capabilities. Ongoing developments include improving the software controlling 3D printers, continuing to increase the variety of printable materials, and enhancing the ability to print in multiple materials simultaneously, including to print electronics.[29]

Materials Used in 3D Printing

Most home-based 3D printers on the market are simple deposition printers that extrude one of two basic plastics, PLA or ABS.[30] But 3D printers can print in an astonishing array of materials. The plastic options are too numerous to list but include materials for use in end products in high-stress and -temperature

---

[26] Barry Hochfelder, *Carbon Copy? Adidas' 3D-Printed Sneaker Hints at New Supply Chain Models*, SUPPLYCHAINDIVE (Sept. 13, 2018), www.supplychaindive.com/news/adidas-3D-printed-shoe-design-to-market-cycle/532284/.

[27] Chris Newmarker, *Resolution Medical Inks 3D Printing Partnership with Carbon*, MEDICALDESIGN & OUTSOURCING (Sept. 14, 2018), https://www.medicaldesignandoutsourcing.com/resolution-medical-3d-printing-partnership-carbon/.

[28] Kaufui V. Wong & Aldo Hernandez, *A Review of Additive Manufacturing*, 2012 ISRN MECHANICAL ENGINEERING 1, 5 (2012).

[29] *See, e.g.*, Pitchaya Sitthi-Amorn et al., *MultiFab: A Machine Vision Assisted Platform for Multi-Material 3D Printing*, 34 ASS'N FOR COMPUTING MACHINERY TRANSACTIONS ON GRAPHICS 129-1 (2015); Mohammad Vaezi et al., *Multiple Material Additive Manufacturing*, 8 VIRTUAL & PHYSICAL PROTOTYPING 19 (2013); J. Hoerber et al., *Approaches for Additive Manufacturing of 3D Electronic Applications*, 17 PROCEDIA CIRP 806 (2014); Sen Wai Kwok et al., *Electrically Conductive Filament for 3D-Printed Circuits and Sensors*, 9 APPLIED MATERIALS TODAY 167 (2017).

[30] Low cost 3D printers are not limited to plastic. Gerald C. Anzalone et al., *A Low-Cost Open-Source Metal 3-D Printer*, 1 IEEE ACCESS 803 (2013) (describing an open source metal 3D printer).

environments.[31] Hybrid mixtures of plastics and other materials allow for a large array of materials, including ceramic, wood, and concrete. Flexible and elastomeric materials open possibilities for medical devices, shoes, and even the fashion industry.

Beyond plastics, metal is the next most common printing material. Printing in metal is especially important as 3D printing technology continues its expansion from making prototypes to manufacturing finished parts. Metal printing is presently the fastest growing area, and the number of metal 3D printing systems purchased in 2017 increased about 80 percent from the previous year.[32] Many of these were for industrial users, but about 20 percent of the growth was from desktop metal 3D printers (defined as costing less than $5,000).

Printing has also extended to graphene, a material prized for its strength and light weight. Recent methods to print with graphene allow complex shapes and enhanced durability.[33] The material allows the manufacture of objects that are ten times stronger than steel versions but 95 percent lighter.[34]

Other specialized printable materials include skin[35] and other human tissues in bioinks,[36] food,[37] and nanomaterials.[38] While some of these materials require specialized machines, several can be printed with open source RepRap printers. RepRaps have been used to print with steel, elastomers,

---

[31] *See, e.g.,* Alexandrea P., *3D Printer Materials Guide: 3D Printing Plastics,* 3Dnatives (Feb. 23, 2018), www.3dnatives.com/en/plastics-used-3d-printing110420174/.

[32] Michael Petch, *Interview: Terry Wohlers on the 2018 Wohlers Report,* 3D Printing Industry (Apr. 4, 2018, 9:39 PM), https://3dprintingindustry.com/news/2018-wohlers-report-interview-terry-wohlers-3d-printing-131524/.

[33] Ryan M. Hensleigh et al., *Additive Manufacturing of Complex Micro-Architected Graphene Aerogels,* 5 Material Horizons 1035 (Aug. 13, 2018), https://pubs.rsc.org/en/content/article landing/2018/mh/c8mh00668g#!divAbstract.

[34] David L. Chandler, *Researchers Design One of the Strongest, Lightest Materials Known,* MIT News (Jan. 6, 2017), http://news.mit.edu/2017/3-d-graphene-strongest-lightest-materials-0106.

[35] Peng He et al., *Bioprinting of Skin Constructs for Wound Healing,* Burns & Trauma, Jan. 2013, at 1.

[36] David Grossman, *New 3D Printer Can Make Complex Body Tissues,* PopularMechanics (May 14, 2018), www.popularmechanics.com/technology/a20686462/new-3d-printer-can-make-complex-body-tissues/; A. Ovsianikov et al., *Laser Printing of Cells Into 3D Scaffolds,* 2 Biofabrication (2010).

[37] *3D Food Printing,* 3Dprinting.com, https://3dprinting.com/food/ (last visited Dec. 7, 2018).

[38] *See, e.g.,* Thomas A. Campbell & Olga S. Ivanova, *3D Printing of Multifunctional Nanocomposites,* 8 Nanotoday 119 (2013); Harpreet Singh et al., *Synthesis of Flexible Magnetic Nanowires of Permanently Linked Core-Shell Magnetic Beads Tethered to a Glass Surface Patterned by Microcontact Printing,* 5 Nano Letters 2149 (2005).

PEEK (polyetheretherketone), brick composite, wood composite, and carbon fiber composites, among other materials.[39]

C. COMPLEMENTARY TECHNOLOGIES

The 3D printing ecosystem includes several technologies not strictly necessary to 3D printing. These technologies work harmoniously with 3D printing to increase design and manufacturing capabilities and to control and monitor DMFs.

3D Scanners

3D scanners are an important complementary technology to 3D printers. 3D scanners allow the user quickly to turn a physical object into a digital one and can be used as a step toward reverse engineering an object.[40] Laser scanners, computed tomography (CT) scanners, and white light scanners each use electromagnetic radiation to collect data about an object. Each has its advantages and disadvantages. For instance, CT scanners are able to see inside of parts and have excellent accuracy but tend to be more expensive. Even digital cameras and smartphones can be turned into 3D scanners with the proper software. Beneficially, none of these scanner types need to physically touch an object.

Contact-based scanners (also called digitizing scanners) use one or more probes to touch the object at various points to obtain data. They are often the most accurate, but sometimes are not a good choice because they must physically contact the object.

The data obtained by scanners is point cloud data, which is essentially a bunch of spatially related dots. Software helps convert this cloud data into some more usable form, typically a surface-mesh file format like STL. But despite the sophisticated software, an experienced user often must manually clean up the surface-mesh file for a high quality output – things like sharp corners. Nevertheless, the process can be much faster than creating the file from scratch. If more comprehensive manipulation of the digital file is desired, additional software can convert the surface-mesh file into a design file, though the resulting file may need manual processing.

---

[39] *RepRap Materials*, APPROPEDIA, www.appropedia.org/RepRap_materials (last visited Dec. 7, 2018).

[40] *See generally Almost Everything You Always Wanted to Know About 3D Scanning*, DIRECT DIMENSIONS, www.dirdim.com/lm_everything.htm (last visited Dec. 7, 2018).

Other Digital Manufacturing Technology

Although this book focuses on 3D printing technology, digital manufacturing includes other technologies such as computer numerical controlled (CNC) machines, laser cutting, and molecular manufacturing. Like 3D printers, CNC machines use digital files as inputs, but instead of additively building up an object's layers, they cut, drill, or otherwise remove material from an existing object until obtaining the desired shape.[41] Laser cutting, another subtractive technology, uses lasers to cut materials and can be thought of as a subset of CNC manufacturing.

At the cutting edge of digital manufacturing technology is molecular manufacturing, which, as its name suggests, builds molecules from atoms or molecules.[42] Much of molecular manufacturing is at the conceptual stage, and it is typically considered a branch of nanotechnology rather than 3D printing. But one of its goals is to manufacture molecules, cells, and systems from digital files, similar in principle to the digital inputs to 3D printers.[43]

Each of these technologies relies on digital files as inputs and thus raises many similar issues to 3D printing technology. In fact, CNC technology was developed before 3D printing.[44] Because these technologies use digital file inputs and can help manufacture objects protected by IP, this book's analysis applies to them as well.

Technological Protection Measures

A final group of technologies important to the intersection of 3D printing and IP is the universe of technological protection measures (TPM). The authenticity and traceability of 3D printed parts and the corresponding digital files

---

[41] *See* Adrian McEwen & Hakim Cassimally, Designing the Internet of Things 154–68 (Wiley 2014).

[42] *See* J. P. Renault et al., *Fabricating Arrays of Single Protein Molecules on Glass Using Microcontact Printing*, 107 J. Physical Chemistry B 703, 703–04 (2003) (describing a microcontact printing method for printing proteins and protein arrays); Press Release, Nat'l Sci. Found., *Drag-and-Drop DNA* (Dec. 4, 2012), *available at* www.nsf.gov/news/news_summ.jsp?cntn_id=125990 (describing technology that allows one to "'print,' molecule by molecule, exactly the [desired] compound" and "to rapidly, and precisely, specify the placement of every atom in a compound").

[43] *See* Robert F. Service, *The Synthesis Machine*, 347 Science 1190 (2015); Kyle Maxey, *3D Printing Martian DNA?*, Engineering (Oct. 9, 2013), www.engineering.com/3DPrinting/3DPrintingArticles/ArticleID/6443/3D-Printing-Martian-DNA.aspx (discussing the potential to 3D print synthetic DNA).

[44] Norman Sanders, *A Possible First Use of CAM/CAD*, 387 IFIP Advances in Info. & Comm. Tech. 43, http://dl.ifip.org/db/series/ifip/ifip387/Sanders12.pdf.

will often be of central importance in 3D printing manufacturing. TPMs assist in these objectives. In addition, just as many creators will want to use IP law to prevent copying of their DMFs, they will also rely on TPMs to achieve the same goal. TPMs exist to prevent or dissuade copying or other unwanted behavior and have been used for years on all sorts of digital files. They can include digital rights management (DRM), file comparison methods, and file tracking methods. Though it will not be necessary to understand these technologies in detail, it is helpful to have a basic understanding of them.

DRM controls the access, use, and distribution of files through encryption or other blocking devices.[45] Simple DRM can require a password or product key before granting access to the file. Other DRM encrypts the digital content and allows only authorized users to decrypt it. Some creators will doubtless rely on DRM to attempt to protect their creations,[46] and companies have even patented DRM strategies for use with 3D printing.[47]

TPMs can work cooperatively with IP laws. For instance, because proving copying can be essential in a copyright infringement case, file comparison methods use software to compare the content of two files to see if one is a copy of the other. In addition, file tracking methods trace the digital history of files, including copying and usage information. Digital watermarks, which are covert digital stamps embedded in a file, play an important role in these systems.[48]

More broadly, TPM can include content delivery strategies. Just as Netflix streams movies to users over the Internet, companies can stream printing data to the buyer's 3D printer for a single print.[49] The buyer does not retain a copy of the file, thus preventing the unauthorized redistribution of the file.

---

[45] *See, e.g.,* Julie E. Cohen, *DRM and Privacy*, 18 BERKELEY TECH. L.J. 575, 580–88 (2003) (describing various types of DRM).

[46] *See, e.g.,* Jong-Uk Hou et al., *3D Print-Scan Resilient Watermarking Using a Histogram-Based Circular Shift Coding Structure*, PROC. OF THE 3RD ACM WORKSHOP ON INFO. HIDING & MULTIMEDIA SECURITY 115 (2015); *More on 3D Printing and DRM*, MICHAELWEINBERG. ORG (Jan. 14, 2013), http://michaelweinberg.org/post/107999782805/more-on-3d-printing-and-drm.

[47] *See, e.g.,* U.S. Patent No. 10,061,906 (Issued Aug. 28, 2018); U.S. Patent No. 8,286,236 (Issued Oct. 9, 2012).

[48] Andre, *MarkAny Develops DRM and Piracy Protection for 3D Print Files*, 3DERS.ORG (Mar. 31, 2016), www.3ders.org/articles/20160331-markany-develops-drm-and-piracy-protection-for-3 d-print-files.html (describing TPM such as "Feature Extraction, which is capable of extracting information from a particular design and examining it against other similar designs to better prevent piracy; Digital Forensics, a feature which essentially watermarks digital designs and can track ownership information if a leak does occur").

[49] F. W. Baumann et al., *Model-Data Streaming for Additive Manufacturing Securing Intellectual Property*, 1 SMART SUSTAINABLE MANUFACTURING SYST. 142 (2017);

TPMs can also be used in the physically printed product to ensure authenticity. For example, objects can be printed with some visually perceptible microdistortions.[50] Another version of this technology uses under-the-surface taggant layers that are detectable using portable chemical analyzers such as spectrometers.[51]

TPMs, however, are not foolproof. Hackers can circumvent them,[52] though doing so will sometimes violate the law if the TPM protects a copyrighted work. All it takes is one person somewhere in the world to circumvent the TPM, and the resulting file can be instantly shared across the globe. Moreover, TPMs result in collateral damage. A TPM that limits illegal copying might also inhibit research or follow-on innovation that does not violate any IP law.

D. THE 3D PRINTING ECOSYSTEM

It is worthwhile briefly to highlight the constituent parts of the 3D printing ecosystem, each of which has been mentioned already in this chapter or in Chapter 1. Key physical components include 3D printing hardware, 3D printable materials, and 3D printing software. In addition, the people involved in the ecosystem include the developers and purveyors of the hardware, materials, and software, and of course the creators of 3D printable digital files. Buyers and end users of all the above are a part of the ecosystem, and buyers/users may be interested in the digital files or only the printed objects.

Also included should be purveyors of services, including print services (print shops), design services, file hosting and selling services (such as Thingiverse, MyMiniFactory, or TurboSquid), and services that can take designs and translate them into printable files. Another important set of participants are those involved with making and using 3D scanners.

Keeping this ecosystem in mind allows the reader to appreciate the range of uses for the technology, from the individual who designs and prints a file in the home to the industry participant utilizing professional designers and high-end

---

Tom Simonite, *Copy Protection for 3-D Printing Aims to Prevent a Piracy Plague*, MIT TECH. REV. (Aug. 27, 2013).

[50] *See, e.g.,* Frederik Mayer et al., *3D Fluorescence-Based Security Features by 3D Laser Lithography*, 2 ADVANCED MATERIALS TECHS. 1700212-1 (2017).

[51] Sharon Flank et al., *Anticounterfeiting Options for Three-Dimensional Printing*, 2 3D PRINTING ADDITIVE MANUFACTURING 180 (2015).

[52] Michael Weinberg, *DRM on 3D Printers Is a Big Deal. Nathan Myhrvold's Patent Is Not.*, PUBLIC KNOWLEDGE (Oct. 22, 2012), www.publicknowledge.org/news-blog/blogs/drm-3d-printers-big-deal-nathan-myhrvolds-pat.

printers.[53] It also allows the reader to appreciate the variety of avenues for additional innovation. Most importantly for this book, understanding the ecosystem sheds light on the many opportunities for IP issues to arise.

[53] *See, e.g.,* Felix W. Baumann & Dieter Roller, *Additive Manufacturing, Cloud-Based 3D Printing and Associated Services,* 1 J. MANUFACTURING MATERIALS PROCESSING 1 (2017).

3

Primer on Intellectual Property Law

Chapter Outline:

At times enthusiasts will yield to the temptation to proclaim that the law is completely unprepared for a new technology and that whole new laws must be created to cope with it. In part, it was this temptation that Judge Frank Easterbrook had in mind when he pejoratively equated mid-1990s discussions of the law of cyberspace (the Internet) with the law of the horse.[1] One of his points was that activities involving horses don't need their own separate laws; the law of contracts, torts, etc., will do just fine.

So, is 3D printing like a horse? In Easterbrook's meaning, mostly yes. But then again, so is anything, including the Internet, software, and every other momentous technological change. Easterbrook's narrow point was simply that we don't need an entirely new law for things like 3D printing. Instead of arguing for a new set of laws, this book focuses on the aspects of IP law that 3D printing technology stresses.

This chapter provides a basic overview of IP laws with an emphasis on areas most relevant to 3D printing technology. It is by no means a comprehensive treatise. Later chapters dive deeper into the most relevant legal rules and policy. Readers familiar with IP law are likely to desire to skip this chapter.

This chapter will cover the laws related to patents, copyrights, trademarks, and design rights (also referred to as design patents or industrial design). Before discussing these areas individually, some basics common to all IP are introduced.

---

[1] Frank H. Easterbrook, *Cyberspace and the Law of the Horse*, 1996 U. CHI. LEGAL F. 207 (1996).

Territorial Nature of IP Rights

IP rights are generally territorial in nature, meaning that an IP right only grants power over acts done in the granting jurisdiction. For example, making a patented machine in the United States is only an act of infringement if there is a U.S. patent. To obtain IP protection in multiple countries, one must obtain rights in each country. In some cases, groups of countries can work together to provide a single avenue for applicants either to obtain or to enforce IP rights across the group of counties. For example, the European Union is close to finalizing a unitary patent system whereby a patentee may sue in a single court to capture infringement across all participating countries, but at the time of this writing, the system has not been finalized.[2]

Validity

A given IP right only exists if certain legal (and sometimes procedural) requirements are met. If all the requirements are met, the right is said to be valid. Some IP rights only come into existence after an office examines an application for validity. Other rights are not examined unless and until they are asserted in court. Importantly, even if an office has granted an IP right after an examination process, a court can reanalyze the alleged right during a proceeding for infringement. If the court determines a requirement is not met, it can invalidate the IP right.

Many countries also include administrative (non-court) venues that can adjudicate IP validity challenges. These venues are generally faster and cheaper than courts.

Direct and Indirect Infringement

Possessing an IP right allows the owner to stop someone from continuing to infringe that right, or at least to obtain monetary damages for the ongoing infringement. In addition, the owner can collect damages for past infringement. The law defines various acts that constitute "direct" infringement, and these acts may be different for different IP rights. As an example, making

---

[2]   Kieren McCarthy, *Europe's Unified Patent Court Fate in the Balance Amid German Probing*, THE REGISTER (Feb. 22, 2018), https://www.theregister.co.uk/2018/02/22/european_patent_court_under_doubt_as_german_court_agrees_to_take_on_case/. European countries cooperate on various aspects of obtaining and enforcing IP rights. Other regions have also created cooperative organizations, such as the African Regional Intellectual Property Organization. Beyond these cooperatives, there are international treaties open to all countries that set standards for procedural or substantive law.

a device that is covered by a patent will constitute direct patent infringement if done without the patentee's permission.

Sometimes there are numerous infringers spread out across a territory, each of whom only engages in a single or few acts of infringement. In those cases, enforcing an IP right would involve suing each person individually in a series of separate lawsuits. That would be expensive and time consuming for the rightsholder. Even worse, the individuals may be unable to pay any judgment, defeating one of the main purposes of the lawsuit (the other main purpose is to stop the infringement).

Rightsholders would therefore strongly prefer to sue a centralized actor who is responsible for multiple infringements, such as the one who made a batch of goods or sold the goods to the individuals. Although the individuals may be infringing by using the goods, the rightsholder can choose to sue the centralized actor and recoup damages for each infringing act of making or selling, efficiently collecting the damages for all the sales in a single lawsuit for direct infringement. There is no requirement to sue the individuals. (One can sue both the seller and the buyer, but cannot "double recover.") In addition, the lawsuit will likely result in a court order for the infringer to stop infringing.

Often a centralized actor does not itself engage in infringing acts, but only helps others to do so. For example, the actor may not make the complete device, but instead only supply components or services used by others to make the infringing object. In these cases, rightsholders may be able to sue on a theory of indirect infringement. Indirect infringement is analogous to aiding and abetting a crime. It is more difficult to prove than direct infringement because the law typically requires the rightsholder to prove that the indirect infringer knew of the IP right and, in some sense, understood that there was infringement. In other words, innocent indirect infringement, even on a massive scale, is not actionable in most cases.

Despite these limitations, indirect infringement theories can be extremely important to protecting IP rights. Suing the many spread-out direct infringers would be less efficient than suing the centralized facilitator. In addition, the indirect infringer usually has more resources to pay any damages ordered by a court.

Remedies

Assuming infringement exists, the next issue is the rightsholder's remedy. Remedies fall into two primary categories: monetary and injunctive. Monetary remedies can include compensation for past infringement (to approximate actual damages) as well as future infringement. Injunctive relief typically takes the form of a court order to cease the infringement. IP owners can obtain both types – money for past infringement and an injunction to prevent future infringement. Importantly, the amount of recovery is correlated to the amount of infringement. Engaging in a single act of infringement will give rise to smaller damages than engaging in one million of the same acts. Sometimes, particularly where infringement is willful, courts can enhance the damages by doubling or even tripling the recovery.

The costs of being found guilty of infringement go beyond the court ordered compensatory damages. The legal fees incurred during an IP dispute can be considerable. Many countries force the losing party to pay their own legal fees as well as the other party's. The default system in the United States is that each party pays its own legal fees, which can lead to wealthier parties bullying smaller parties with the threat of litigation costs even if the suit will ultimately fail. But in some IP cases, particularly where the infringement is willful or a claim is egregious, a court may order the losing party to pay the prevailing party's legal fees.

A. PATENT LAW

Patents cover utilitarian inventions like better mousetraps or methods of production. Patent law is justified across the world on utilitarian grounds. It seeks to incentivize the invention and commercialization of utilitarian creations like machines and methods of manufacturing.[3] Patent law's incentive is fueled by a powerful right: it provides exclusivity to the inventor, regardless of whether the second comer copies or independently invents.

Patent law attempts to overcome the problem of upfront innovation costs. The inventor (and investors) bear the time, effort, and costs involved in inventing and commercializing a new machine. If a competitor could copy the creation without incurring all those costs, it could profitably sell the copycat product at a price cheaper than that of the original creator. The patent right allows the original inventor time to sell without that competition, which generally means selling at a higher price to recoup the upfront costs.

Most of the world has the same basic requirements for patents based on the TRIPS Agreement.[4] Patents generally last twenty years from their filing date.[5]

---

[3] Patents also incentivize the inventor to disclose the invention rather than attempting to keep it as a trade secret. *See, e.g.*, Jeanne C. Fromer, *Patent Disclosure*, 94 IOWA L. REV. 539 (2009).

[4] Agreement on Trade-Related Aspects of Intellectual Property Rights, art. 23, Apr. 15, 1994, 1869 U.N.T.S. 299 [hereinafter TRIPS Agreement].

[5] *Id.* art. 33.

A patent is only granted if the invention meets three technological-related requirements.[6] First, it must be useful (also phrased as capable of industrial application), a requirement that divides patent law from copyright law, which involves creative works. Second, the invention must be novel or new, meaning (roughly) that it had not been previously known. Third, it must be nonobvious, meaning it involves some nontrivial inventive step above what is already in existence.

Obtaining a Patent

To obtain a patent, an inventor must file an application with a country's patent office. The office will examine applications to see if they meet the relevant legal and procedural requirements. Applications (or issued patents) are eventually published for the world to see,[7] which in essence forces a bargain. The patentee gets the exclusive rights to the invention, but in exchange, the application must "disclose the invention in a manner sufficiently clear and complete for the invention to be carried out by a person skilled in the art."[8] As a result, the patentee gets exclusivity for twenty years, but the public gets to learn how the invention works.

If an application fails to meet any of the requirements, the examiner will reject the application, notify the applicant, and explain the reasons for the rejection. The applicant can respond to the rejection by amending the application to fix the issue (if possible) or by arguing that the examiner's reasons for rejection are incorrect. This back-and-forth can continue for several iterations. Eventually, if the applicant makes changes and/or arguments that convince the examiner, the patent application will issue as a patent. If not, the application is abandoned.

Obtaining a patent is not cheap. There are various fees, including a filing fee, examination fee, and an issuance fee. In the United States, for example, these fees are each several hundred dollars. In addition, the cost to hire an attorney to help draft and "prosecute" (the term of art for navigating the patent examination process) the patent application runs several thousands of dollars.

---

[6] *Id.* art. 27(1) (requiring that any patented inventions are "new, involve an inventive step and are capable of industrial application").

[7] There are exceptions, including in the United States, when an applicant requests nonpublication of the application and the application never issues as a patent.

[8] TRIPS Agreement art. 29(1); *see* 35 U.S.C. § 112(a). In patent law, the word "art" means (approximately) "technology."

Patent Claims

Patent claims appear at the end of a patent as numbered sentences. They define the boundaries of the right to exclude others from practicing (i.e., making, using, etc.) what is claimed.

Patent claims are full of technical subtleties. So much can be packed into a single claim that one is tempted to analogize them to short poems rich with hidden meaning, except that patent claims are, in their lack of literary beauty, so far from poetry that the analogy invites strong protest. Suffice it to say that every word in a patent claim is (or should be) present for a reason, and just about every word is meaningful in determining whether the person accused of infringement is guilty.

To give readers an idea of a traditional patent claim, a portion (but due to length, only a portion) of a claim to a fuel injector from U.S. Patent Number 4,317,542 is presented here:

> A fuel injector comprising: a housing, a fuel feed port arranged on one end of said housing; a fuel injection port arranged on the other end of said housing; a fuel passage formed in said housing and interconnecting said fuel feed port to said fuel injection port; a valve seat formed on an inner wall of said fuel passage; a needle movable in said housing and having a tip which cooperates with said valve port dividing said fuel passage into a first passage section located between said fuel feed port and said valve port and a second passage section located between said fuel injection port and said valve port . . .

A patent claim can be thought of as a checklist. If the accused device includes everything in the checklist, it infringes. If, instead, it omits something in the claim, it generally avoids infringement. For example, if a claim specifies an injector made of steel, then an injector made of aluminum would not literally infringe the claim. In short, a patent generally only protects what is claimed, and courts generally read the claims very mechanically.

One caveat is that most claims are drafted to be "open-ended," meaning that it will not matter if the infringer *adds* additional bells and whistles to the infringing device. As long as everything listed in the patent claim is present in the accused device, it infringes no matter how many extra improvements it has. A classic example is an open-ended claim to a stool with three legs. The claim might recite a "horizontal surface" for sitting attached to "three legs extending approximately perpendicularly downward." A chair, even though it has a fourth leg and a back-supporting portion, would infringe the claim because the chair includes the horizontal support and three legs.

Patentable Subject Matter

Every nation's patent laws exclude certain things from patentability. In the United States, the Supreme Court created the basic rule that laws of nature (e=mc^2), natural phenomena (the workings of the digestive system), and abstract ideas (diversification of risk) are not patentable.[9] Many countries legislatively exclude certain subject matter, such as article 52 of the European Patent Convention's exclusion of discoveries, scientific theories, mathematical methods, computers programs, and presentations of information, among other things.[10]

It should be obvious that exclusions of this sort do not extend to practical applications of the excluded categories. Thus, a 3D printer that works in part because of gravity and the laws of thermodynamics is not excluded. Many claims will easily pass the subject matter threshold, including claims to a physical machine, a method of making the new machine, a new material used in printing, and a new process for printing.[11] Moreover, a physical machine constitutes patentable subject matter regardless of whether it is 3D printed or made through more traditional processes.

The difficulty often comes from things close to the unpatentable end of the spectrum that nevertheless may be said to be practical applications. Because the law in this area is key to 3D printing technology, it is explored in depth in Chapter 4.

Patent Infringement

The main point of owning a patent is to exclude others from trespassing on your invention. Around the world, patents generally allow their owners to exclude others from "making, using, offering for sale, selling, or importing" the claimed invention.[12]

Any one of these acts constitutes direct infringement. Direct infringement is generally a strict liability regime: Regardless of the actor's intent or knowledge of the patent, performing any prohibited act is infringement. If you sell the claimed invention without permission, you infringe even if you did not know of the patent and you independently developed the same invention. And even

---

[9] *See, e.g.,* Alice Corp. Pty. Ltd. v. CLS Bank Int'l, 134 S.Ct. 2347, 2354 (2014).

[10] Convention on the Grant of European Patents (European Patent Convention), Oct. 5, 1973, 1065 U.N.T.S. 199 (entered into force Oct. 7, 1977) [hereinafter EPC]. These things are only excluded if they are claimed "as such." *Id.*

[11] *See, e.g.,* 35 U.S.C. § 101 (listing as patentable subject matter categories "process, machine, manufacture, [and] composition of matter").

[12] TRIPS Agreement art. 28; *see* 35 U.S.C. § 271(a).

if you merely offer to sell the invention, but never consummate the sale, you can be liable for infringement.

There is an important exception in countries that excuse the private, non-commercial making and using of an invention. But in other countries, like the United States, privately making or using the invention constitutes infringement even if it is not sold. As Chapter 5 demonstrates, the private, noncommercial use exception will garner a great deal of attention in a 3D printing world where huge numbers of individuals can privately print the same object for personal use.

One of patent infringement doctrine's fundamental tenets is that one only infringes what is claimed in the patent. It doesn't matter what the inventor thinks the invention is, or what is described in the patent's other text – the patent claims govern whether someone infringes or not. Infringement is determined by studying the claim line-by-line to see if the device accused of infringement includes each thing required by the claim. This provides some measure of certainty to competitors, who can study the claims and determine whether they infringe. It also incentivizes competitors to "design around" the patent – that is, to develop a competing product that works differently from the patented technology.

If a court determines infringement has occurred, it will grant remedies as discussed above.

B. COPYRIGHT LAW

In the United States, copyright law is justified as an incentive for creative works, as opposed to the utilitarian works of patent law's province. Creative works include things like sculptures, paintings, novels, and movies. In contrast to patent law's exclusive rights against even independent inventors, a copyright protects against *copying* another's creative expression. In other words, independent creation is a defense.

Like patent law, copyright law seeks to overcome the problem of upfront creation costs. The time, effort, and cost involved in writing a novel or making a movie need to be recouped if an author is to make money from the creation. Copying a book or movie is much cheaper than creating one from scratch, so a copycat could undersell the original creator. Indeed, because digital copying is so easy, copiers are often willing to give the copies away for free. As the saying goes, it is difficult to compete against free.

In other parts of the world, particularly continental Europe, the incentive rationale for copyright law is complemented or even eclipsed by a focus on a natural rights theory or personhood theory. Under a natural rights theory, the copyright is a right the author deserves for the creative efforts. Indeed, many European countries do no use the term "copyright," but rather "author's right." Another popular theoretical justification for copyright stems from a personhood theory, which posits that works represent an extension of their creator and thus are entitled to protection.

Obtaining Copyright Protection

Obtaining protection for copyrights is much easier than it is for patents. Copyright protection attaches automatically when the work is created in some tangible form, and the protection immediately extends to all signatories to the Berne Convention.[13] Nevertheless, enforcement of those rights typically must be done on a country-by-country basis. Jurisdictions may offer registration, but it is not required for basic protection. Some countries, like the United States, tie certain important benefits to obtaining a registration, such as the ability to recover statutory damages.

Copyrightable Subject Matter

Most legislation does not claim to provide exhaustive lists of works covered by copyright, but works commonly protected include literary works, movies, musical compositions, paintings, drawings, sculptures, and photographs.[14] Fundamentally, copyright protects creativity, and thus it does not protect basic ideas like "a love story."

In addition, to divide copyright protection from patent protection, copyright protection does not extend to procedures or methods of operation.[15] It will extend, however, to creative explications of the excluded categories. This is known as the idea-expression dichotomy.

Copyright law generally protects works if they (1) are original to the author, meaning not copied, and (2) contain some basic level of creativity.[16] Some countries have granted copyrights (or similar rights) in works that may lack creativity but nevertheless involve significant effort on the part of the

---

[13]   *See* Berne Convention for the Protection of Literary and Artistic Works, art. 5(2), Sept. 9, 1886, 25 U.S.T. 1341, 828 U.N.T.S. 221(as last revised July 24, 1971) [hereinafter, Berne Convention].

[14]   *See, e.g.*, 17 U.S.C. § 102(a); Berne Convention art. 2(1).

[15]   *See, e.g.*, 17 U.S.C. § 102(b); TRIPS Agreement art. 9(2).

[16]   Feist Publ'ns, Inc., v. Rural Tel. Serv. Co., 499 U.S. 340, 345 (1991) ("[T]he requisite level of creativity is extremely low; even a slight amount will suffice. The vast majority of works make the grade quite easily, as they possess some creative spark, 'no matter how crude, humble or obvious' it might be.").

creator.[17] For instance, UK courts have traditionally defined originality to include any work that is a result of the author's own skill, labor, judgment, and effort.[18] Recent EU decisions have required some level of creativity,[19] so it will be interesting to see how UK law develops if and when Brexit is finalized. As demonstrated in Chapter 8, the creativity requirement will play an important role for certain 3D printable files.

Copyright Infringement & Moral Rights

As one might expect based on its name, a copyright protects against copying. Copying includes not only making a full and exact copy, but also making a work that is substantially similar. This can include (1) copying sizable portions of a work, and (2) nonliteral copying that nevertheless co-opts the author's original expression. Thus, it is infringement to copy half of a book or to rewrite a novel by simply substituting synonyms throughout. Some jurisdictions conceptualize nonliteral copies as derivative works. Common examples of derivative works include adaptations (turning a book into a movie) and translations into a different language. The right to prevent or authorize copying is not the only right encompassed by a copyright. Added to that are the rights to prevent or authorize the public performance, recordation, and broadcasting of certain works.

The above rights can be thought of as economic rights because they assist the owner in recouping the time and money needed to create the work. Alongside economic rights are moral rights, which allow creators to protect and preserve their links to their works. The two most widely recognized moral rights are the right to attribution (also known as the right of paternity, which is the right to be identified as the creator of a work) and the right to integrity (to oppose changes to a work that could harm the creator's reputation).[20] They

---

[17] For a general review of the creativity requirement in Europe, see generally ELEONORA ROSATI, ORIGINALITY IN EU COPYRIGHT: FULL HARMONIZATION THROUGH CASE LAW (2013); *see also* Daniel J. Gervais, *Feist Goes Global: A Comparative Analysis of the Notion of Originality in Copyright Law*, 49 J. COPYRIGHT SOC'Y U.S.A. 949 (2002). European protection for databases represents an example of protection where creativity may be lacking. *See* European Parliament & Council Directive 96/9 on the Legal Protection of Databases, 1996 O.J. (L 77) 20 (EC).

[18] *See, e.g.*, Indep. Television Publ'ns. Ltd. v. Time Out Ltd. [1984] FSR 64.

[19] *See, e.g.*, Case C-5/08, Infopaq Int'l. v. Danske Dagblades Forening, 2009 E.C.D.R 16; Case C-604/10, Football Dataco Ltd v. Yahoo! UK Ltd, 1 C.M.L.R. 29 (2013); Andreas Rahmatian, *Originality in UK Copyright Law: The Old "Skill and Labour" Doctrine Under Pressure*, 44 INT'L REV. INTELL. PROP. & COMPETITION L. 4 (2013).

[20] *See* Berne Convention art. 6*bis*.

can also include the right to decide when to publish and the right to withdraw a work from public dissemination.

There is much to be said about moral rights and digital works, but because the issues do not uniquely affect 3D printing technology, they will be touched on only briefly herein. For example, moral rights must be balanced against the freedom downstream creators need to make new works.[21] This is especially true where works have a utilitarian aspect to them, such as software. French law, which has among the strongest moral rights provisions, prohibits authors from opposing modifications of software by assignees where such modifications do not prejudice the author's honor or reputation.[22]

Moral rights can exist in perpetuity and be inalienable.[23] Economic rights, in contrast, are time limited, though they last for a long time. The Berne Convention provides for a minimum copyright term of the life of the author plus fifty years. The United States and Europe have extended that an additional twenty years.[24] Where the work is authored by a business (which may never die), a specific time limit is given. In the United States, that time is 95 years from the date of publication or 120 years from the date of creation, whichever expires first.[25]

Fair Use (Fair Dealing)

Even though copyrights encompass partial and nonliteral copying, there are times when the law excuses copying because it is a fair use (also called fair dealing) of the work. Quintessential examples of fair use are quoting portions of a work for news reporting or criticism and reproducing a work for educational purposes. Fair use inquiries are generally complex and involve a case-by-case balancing of interests. For example, the U.S. statute requires courts to consider at least the following factors:

> (1) the purpose and character of the use, including whether such use is of a commercial nature or is for nonprofit educational purposes; (2) the nature of the copyrighted work; (3) the amount and substantiality of the portion used in relation to the copyrighted work as a whole; and (4) the effect of the use upon the potential market for or value of the copyrighted work.[26]

---

[21] *See, e.g.,* Adolf Dietz, *The Moral Right of the Author: Moral Rights and the Civil Law Countries,* 19 COLUM.-VLA J.L. & ARTS 199, 220–25 (1995).

[22] CODE DE LA PROPRIÉTÉ INTELLECTUELLE art. L121-7.

[23] *See, e.g., id.* at L121-1 ("It shall be perpetual, inalienable, and imprescriptible.").

[24] 17 U.S.C. § 302(a).

[25] *Id.* § 302(c).

[26] *Id.* § 107.

U.S. law is considered one of the most solicitous toward fair uses; European law is less so. It provides lists of specific exceptions to infringement rather than a holistic factor-balancing approach.[27] The result is more certainty but less flexibility.

Copyright Remedies

Like with other areas of IP, copyrights provide monetary and equitable remedies. In many jurisdictions, monetary relief is in the form of actual damages.[28] In some jurisdictions,[29] most prominently the United States, a copyright owner may choose to collect statutory damages, which typically range from $750 to $30,000 per infringement.[30] In the United States, the availability of statutory damages (and attorney's fees) and the ability to sue in federal court (as opposed to state court) are conditional on obtaining a copyright registration before the infringement occurs (or within three months of publication of the work).[31]

C. TRADEMARK LAW

Trademarks are in some ways a crude fit under the IP umbrella. Rather than incentivizing the creation of new works or inventions, they serve as indicators of the source of goods or services to distinguish them from those provided by others.[32] Stated another way, trademarks reduce consumer search costs because consumers can choose to rely on the trademark when selecting among a sea of competing goods whose quality cannot be fully ascertained at the point of sale. Loosely speaking, trademarks correlate with brand names. They have twin purposes of preventing fraud against consumers and allowing producers to capitalize on the reputation of their goods.

[27] *See* European Parliament & Council Directive 2001/29 on the Harmonisation of Certain Aspects of Copyright and Related Rights in the Information Society, 2001 O.J. (L 167) 10 (EC) art. 5 [hereinafter Copyright Directive].

[28] 17 U.S.C. § 504. In the United States, actual damages and infringer's profits are apportioned based on the damages attributable to copying. *Id.* § 504(b); Sheldon v. Metro-Goldwyn Pictures Corp., 309 U.S. 390 (1940).

[29] *See* Pamela Samuelson et al., *Statutory Damages: A Rarity in Copyright Laws Internationally, But for How Long?*, 60 J. COPYRIGHT SOC'Y U.S.A.529, 534–36 (2013) (describing the countries that provide statutory copyright damages, which include Canada, Israel, and the Republic of Korea).

[30] 17 U.S.C. § 504(c).

[31] *Id.* §§ 411–12.

[32] *See* TRIPS Agreement art. 15(1). The mark must indicate that a source exists, but the consumer need not know the source's specific identity.

Trademark law is not as harmonized globally as patent law, though the Paris Convention for the Protection of Industrial Property[33] and the TRIPS Agreement harmonize some aspects, and additional treaties primarily make applying for protection in multiple countries more convenient. In most countries, a trademark registration lasts ten years and can be renewed indefinitely.[34]

Obtaining Trademark Protection

In some countries, including the United States, the United Kingdom, and Canada, trademark rights are obtained by using the mark in commerce on the relevant goods or services. For example, if you adopt a brand name ZUZU for blue jeans and make bona fide sales of blue jeans in interstate commerce bearing that logo, you immediately gain trademark rights. But because the right is use based, you only obtain rights in the geographic location(s) where you use the mark.

That being said, there are advantages for going an extra step and registering your trademark rights. For example, in the United States, registration immediately expands your zone of use to the entire country (subject to anyone else who may have been using the same mark on the same goods before you filed for your registration).[35] Registration also allows you to sue in federal court,[36] to gain access to stronger remedies, and to have your registration considered "incontestable" after five years of registration and use.[37]

In other countries, like those in Europe, rights are governed not by use, but by registration (though even most of these countries eventually require use; you can't simply reserve marks indefinitely). Whether in a use-based or registration-based country, applications for registration must be filed with the relevant office, whereupon an examiner will examine the application to make sure it meets all legal requirements. In addition, even in registration-based systems, if a registration owner fails to use the mark it can be subject to cancellation.

---

[33] Paris Convention for the Protection of Industrial Property, Mar. 20, 1883 (as revised at Stockholm, July 14, 1967), 21 U.S.T. 1583, 828 U.N.T.S. 305.

[34] *See, e.g.,* 15 U.S.C. § 1058.

[35] *Id.* § 1072.

[36] *Id.* § 1121.

[37] *Id.* § 1065.

Trademark Subject Matter

To serve as a trademark, a mark must be distinctive, meaning it can identify the source of a particular good or service. This rule forecloses the use of generic terms for goods as trademarks, like MILK for milk or APPLE for apples. Descriptive terms, which describe qualities or features of a good or service, are permissible as long as they serve as a source indicator. Thus, YUMMY could become a trademark for delicious ice cream if through advertising and use the public began to associate the term with an ice cream producer.

A key feature of trademarks is that the right is tied to the specific goods or services for which they are used. Thus, you can use a word like APPLE as a trademark for goods other than apples, like computers. Because trademarks are specific to certain goods, two different companies can own trademarks for the same word on two different types of goods (e.g., Delta airlines and Delta faucets).

Trademark Infringement

Trademark registrations (and common law rights where applicable) give the owner the right to prevent others from using "in the course of trade identical or similar signs for goods or services which are identical or similar to those in respect of which the trademark is registered where such use would result in a likelihood of confusion."[38] Confusion can be as to origin of the goods or to the sponsorship or approval of such goods. For identical marks used on identical goods, confusion is generally presumed.[39]

Where the marks and/or the goods are different, courts weigh a number of factors to ascertain whether consumers are likely to be confused: (1) the strength of the mark; (2) the proximity of the goods; (3) the similarity of the marks; (4) evidence of actual confusion; (5) the similarity of marketing channels used; (6) the degree of caution exercised by the typical purchaser; and, (7) the defendant's intent.[40]

Many countries provide extra protections to well-known (famous) marks, such as marks that are household names. Chapter 7 discusses these rights.

---

[38] TRIPS Agreement art. 16(1).
[39] *Id.*
[40] *See, e.g.*, Polaroid Corp. v. Polarad Elecs. Corp., 287 F.2d 492 (2d Cir. 1961).

D. INDUSTRIAL DESIGN/DESIGN PATENT LAW

In a loose sense, design rights sit at the intersection between patent and copyright[41] and offer protection to "articles of manufacture" embodying ornamental design features.[42] Given their similarity to other areas of IP, I will cover the basics of protection more briefly in this section. I will use the term "design rights" to refer to all forms of design protection, including design patents as found in the United States and registered and unregistered designs as found in Europe.

Design Patents in the United States

The United States, Canada, and Australia are some of the few countries to have a design protection system that requires examination as opposed to pure registration. The U.S. design patent scheme relies heavily on the statutes governing utility patents.[43] Much of the law of design patents, therefore, superficially appears similar to utility patents. Thus, applications are examined by the U.S. Patent & Trademark Office (USPTO) for certain requirements, including novelty and nonobviousness (though the tests for these requirements are different for design patents).[44] As with utility patents, an application may be rejected by a USPTO examiner for failing to meet the various requirements, and applicants have opportunities to make some changes and to submit counterarguments to the examiner's positions.

Some of the main differences between utility patents and design patents are that design patents

- have a different term length (fifteen years from the date of grant),[45]
- primarily use drawings instead of words for claims,
- require ornamentality (in addition to novelty and nonobviousness),

---

[41]   *See In re* Mogen David Wine Corp., 328 F.2d 925, 928–29 (C.C.P.A. 1964) (referring to design patents as "a hybrid which combines in itself features of both a patent and a copyright"). In truth, this oversimplification is subject to many caveats.

[42]   *See* 35 U.S.C. § 171(a).

[43]   *Id.* § 171(b) ("The provisions of this title relating to patents for inventions shall apply to patents for designs, except as otherwise provided.").

[44]   Novelty is determined by "whether the [patented and prior art reference's] designs would be viewed as substantially similar in the eyes of the ordinary observer armed with the knowledge of the prior art." Int'l Seaway Trading Corp. v. Walgreens Corp., 589 F.3d 1233, 1243 (Fed. Cir. 2009). Obviousness is determined by "whether the claimed design would have been obvious to a designer of ordinary skill who designs articles of the type involved." Durling v. Spectrum Furniture Co., 101 F.3d 100, 103 (Fed. Cir. 1996).

[45]   35 U.S.C. § 173.

- are infringed if the two designs would look substantially similar in the eye of an ordinary observer,[46] and
- include an additional remedy for infringement.[47]

Like copyrights, design patents cover nonfunctional aspects of an article of manufacture. But the standard of nonfunctionality (or ornamentality) is more permissive with design patents than copyrights. Whereas copyrightable subject matter must be separable from utilitarian aspects, a design patent is nonfunctional if its design is not "dictated by function."[48] A design for an article is dictated by function if no "alternative designs for the article of manufacture are available,"[49] which in practice means that most designs are not considered functional. Under current doctrine, a work can simultaneously enjoy design patent and copyright protection (and trade dress protection).[50]

Acts of infringement are the same as those for utility patents, such as making, using, selling, offering to sell, and importing the article of manufacture that includes the design.[51]

Design Rights in Most of the Rest of the World

Much of the rest of the world uses some form of an industrial design registration (as opposed to examination) system. Like in the United States, the protections are for designs used for not-purely utilitarian aspects of articles of manufacture for a limited term. Unlike the United States, most other jurisdictions do not have a formal nonobviousness requirement, though they have somewhat analogous requirements that take account of small changes from the prior art.

Europe has industrial design protection through each country's domestic law and in the European Union through the Design Regulation.[52] EU designs must be novel[53] and have "individual character," meaning that "the overall

---

[46]   Egyptian Goddess Inc. v. Swisa, Inc., 543 F.3d 665, 677 (Fed. Cir. 2008) (en banc).

[47]   35 U.S.C. § 289.

[48]   Best Lock Corp. v. Ilco Unican Corp., 94 F.3d 1563, 1566 (Fed. Cir. 1996) ("However, if the design claimed in a design patent is dictated solely by the function of the article of manufacture, the patent is invalid because the design is not ornamental.").

[49]   *Id.*

[50]   *See* Mazer v. Stein, 347 U.S. 201, 217 (1954) ("Neither the Copyright Statute nor any other says that because a thing is patentable it may not be copyrighted."); *In re* Yardley, 493 F.2d 1389 (C. C.P.A. 1974).

[51]   35 U.S.C. § 271. Acts that will trigger an additional remedy are spelled out in § 289.

[52]   Council Regulation 6/2002 on Community Designs, 2002 O.J. (L 3) 1 (EC) [hereinafter Design Regulation].

[53]   *Id.* art. 5.

impression [a design] produces on the informed user differs from the overall impression produced on such a user by any design which has been made available to the public."[54] The nonfunctionality test is worded similarly to that of the United States, and requires in part that the design is "not solely dictated by [the product's] technical function."[55]

EU designs and domestic designs can be unregistered or registered.[56] Unregistered designs come into being when they are "made available to the public" in the European Union.[57] The downside is that unregistered protection lasts only for three years and infringement requires actual copying.[58] Registered designs, in contrast, can subsist for up to twenty-five years and infringement is based on similarity, not copying.[59] The EU law and each member country's domestic law have been largely harmonized for registered designs, but this is not true for unregistered designs.[60]

Unlike U.S. law, the Design Regulation spells out numerous exceptions to infringement. The most relevant to 3D printing include the exceptions for acts done privately and for noncommercial use, acts done for experimental purpose, and "acts of reproduction for the purpose of making citations or of teaching, provided that such acts are compatible with fair trade practice and do not unduly prejudice the normal exploitation of the design, and that mention is made of the source."[61]

E. TRADE SECRET LAW

This book will not cover trade secret law. As the name implies, trade secret law protects nonpublic information from being misappropriated. Although the area of law is of immense importance to innovation, 3D printing technology does not raise any truly novel issues in it. It may be that misappropriation becomes more common (because manufacturing from a DMF is relatively

---

[54] *Id.* art. 6. This requirement is roughly similar to U.S. law's nonobviousness requirement.
[55] *Id.* art. 8. Other countries' basic frameworks are broadly similar. *See, e.g.*, Australian Designs Act 2003, § 15 (requiring, inter alia, newness and distinctiveness). In Australia, functionality is handled by the common law.
[56] Outside of Europe, countries vary on whether they protect unregistered designs. Australia and Canada, for instance, do not.
[57] Design Regulation art. 11.
[58] *Id.* arts. 11, 19.
[59] *Id.* art. 12. Acts of infringement for registered designs cover "making, offering, putting on the market, importing, exporting or using of a product in which the design is incorporated or to which it is applied, or stocking such a product for those purposes." *Id.* art. 19(1).
[60] *See* European Parliament & Council Directive 71/1998 on the Legal Protection of Designs, 1998 O.J. (L 289) 28 (EC).
[61] Design Regulation art. 20(1).

easy), but the law treats misappropriating a DMF no differently than misappropriating a blueprint, whether electronic or paper. In addition, 3D scanners may make reverse engineering[62] certain products easier, but that is a difference in degree, not kind.

---

[62] Reverse engineering, which is permissible under trade secret law, refers to studying a product to figure out how to build it.

4

Can You Patent a 3D Printable File? (and Why it Matters)

Chapter Outline:

Patents can help protect the time and expense of invention and commercializa-tion. But patents only protect what the patent claims. This chapter first explains the basic function of a patent's claims for those not familiar with patent law. Second, it turns to the rules in the U.S., European, and Japanese patent systems regarding what sort of inventions patent law will protect. As shown, these rules have profound ramifications for the different DMF formats described in Chapter 2 (design, surface-mesh, and machine-instruction formats).

A word of caution for readers not thoroughly familiar with patent law: Aspects of this chapter are highly technical and interrelate to the subject matter of Chapter 5 regarding patent infringement. Reading this and Chapter 5 together will help you understand the bigger picture.

A. PATENT CLAIMS

Suppose someone invents an ingenious fuel injector and obtains a patent protecting it. (This is not a far-fetched hypothetical, insofar as there are hundreds of patents covering fuel injectors. Moreover, GE and NASA have 3D printed fuel injectors for jet and rocket engines, respectively.) If someone makes a similar injector, will the patent stop the alleged infringer? The answer lies primarily in the patent's claims. Chapter 3 explained the function of patent claims and included an excerpt from one directed to a fuel injector. It is important to recall that the claim language controls the patentee's right to exclude. To infringe a patent, the accused device generally must contain each and every element listed in the claim.

In many aspects, 3D printing doesn't pose any challenges to patent claims. Hundreds of patents have issued in the last few years with claims directed to new and nonobvious 3D printing hardware, 3D printing materials, and methods of printing. The number of such patents issued in the United States in 2016 was about double the number from 2014, and the trend looks likely to continue climbing.[1] These sorts of claims are no different than claims to other machines and processes that patent offices around the world have issued for over a hundred years. Further, if a patent claim covers a specific fuel injector, third parties who make the same injector will infringe whether they use a 3D printer or traditional manufacturing techniques.

Yet the centrality of patent claims has important implications for 3D printing technology. Patent holders will want to control not only the manufacture of the invented device, which can be difficult to detect, but also the creation and dissemination of DMFs of it. But, of course, a problem looms: if the patent claim is worded to describe a physical device, it will not cover a DMF of it. In other words, a digital version of an object will generally not infringe a patent claim directed to the physical object. (Chapter 5 explores the doctrine of patent infringement more generally and discusses possible exceptions to this statement.)

The most straightforward solution to this problem would be to draft a patent claim covering the DMF version of the fuel injector. For example, to claim a DMF version of the fuel injector from patent number 4,317,542 reproduced in Chapter 3, one might attempt to claim, "A digital manufacturing file containing data to additively manufacture a fuel injector comprising [all the limitations of claim 1 of U.S. Patent Number 4,317,452]."

Formidable, perhaps insurmountable, obstacles stand in the way of this solution. These obstacles all center around the doctrine of patentable subject matter.

B. PATENTABLE SUBJECT MATTER AND TANGIBILITY

Recall from Chapter 3 that patent systems across the world insist on certain substantive requirements before granting a patent, including usefulness, novelty, nonobviousness, and some form of disclosure in the patent document. None of these requirements will require much attention in this book, and I will mostly assume their presence because they do not present novel questions for 3D printing technology. But the reader must keep this assumption in

---

[1] John Hornick, *3D Printing Patent Landscape*, 3DPRINT.COM (Jul. 17, 2017), https://3dprint.com/181207/3d-printing-patent-landscape/.

mind. Thus, for example, if a machine is not new or is obvious, a DMF that will manufacture the same machine will not – and should not – enjoy patent protection. To do otherwise would protect old technology with a patent system meant only for new inventions.

This chapter focuses on patentable subject matter: whether DMFs are the kinds of things patent systems will protect. Each country's patent system excludes things from patentable subject matter, such as abstract ideas, but generally allows patents for practical applications of the excluded categories. At the margins, however, it becomes exceedingly difficult to draw a clear line between what is patent eligible and what is not.

The European Patent Convention (EPC)[2] explicitly excludes certain subject matter, such as computer programs, but then cryptically limits the exclusions only "to such subject-matter or activities as such."[3] The meaning of "as such" has a decidedly protean character in the hands of national courts and patent offices. The U.S. Supreme Court's most recent line-drawing exercise, which dramatically narrowed the eligibility for certain type of inventions, sets forth a two-step test: first, a court must determine whether the patent claim is directed to a patent-ineligible category; if so, the court must next determine whether any element, or combination of elements, in the claim is sufficient to transform the nature of the claim into a patent-eligible application.[4] Exacerbating the opacity of the inquiry, the Court has made clear that the determinations are to be made on a case-by-case basis, thus reducing predictability.

Scholars and lawyers generally agree that these rules do not provide clear guidance in close cases. One industry in particular has haunted patent (and copyright) systems the world over because its outputs often involve close cases: software.[5] Even the terms *software* and *program* are inexact. Among other

---

[2]   Convention on the Grant of European Patents (European Patent Convention), Oct. 5, 1973, 1065 U.N.T.S. 199 (entered into force Oct. 7, 1977) [hereinafter EPC]. The EPC is a multilateral treaty whose signatories are different than the members of the European Union. The term European patent is used to refer to patents granted under the European Patent Convention, but an EPC patent is not a unitary right. Instead, it is a group of essentially independent, nationally enforceable, nationally revocable patents. The European Union is attempting to finalize a unitary patent system whereby a patentee may sue in a single court to capture infringement across all participating countries, but as of this writing the system has not been finalized.

[3]   *Id.* art. 52(3).

[4]   Alice Corp. Pty. Ltd. v. CLS Bank Int'l 134 S. Ct. 2347, 2355 (2014). The Court refers to the second step as an inquiry into the inventive concept, thus conflating eligible subject matter with novelty and nonobviousness.

[5]   For an extensive history of the patenting of software-related inventions, see Julie E. Cohen & Mark A. Lemley, *Patent Scope and Innovation in the Software Industry*, 89 CALIF. L. REV. 1, 7–11 (2001).

things, they can refer to a set of instructions in the abstract, or to the lines of code as embodied in a tangible storage medium such as a disk or a computer's memory.

Although this author disagrees, some believe that an important threshold issue is whether DMFs are in fact software (which is used interchangeably with the term computer program in patent law). Neither U.S. patent statutes nor the EPC defines the terms software or computer program.[6] The European Patent Office (EPO) has publicly stated that the term software is ambiguous and thus avoided in favor of the term computer-implemented invention.[7] The Japanese Patent Office (JPO), following the Japanese Patent Act,[8] defines the term broadly as "a set of instructions given to a computer which are combined in order to produce a specific result."[9]

Under a narrow definition, *software* relates to application programs, whereas *files* connote collections of data stored as a unit and used by application programs.[10] Under this usage, Microsoft Word is a program and DOC documents are mere files that contain data used by the program. Extending this usage to 3D printing, a slicer program would be software (e.g., Slic3er or NetFabb) that slices a surface-mesh file,[11] which contains mere data. Likewise, a program on a 3D printer reads data from a machine-instruction file.[12] And yet

---

[6] The U.S. copyright statute defines a computer program capaciously as "a set of statements or instructions to be used directly or indirectly in a computer in order to bring about a certain result." 17 U.S.C. § 101.

[7] EPO, PATENTS FOR SOFTWARE? EUROPEAN LAW AND PRACTICE 3 (2013), http://documents .epo.org/projects/babylon/eponet.nsf/0/a0be115260b5ff71c125746d004c51a5/$FILE/patents_ for_software_en.pdf.

[8] Patent Act, Act No. 121 of 1959, art. 2(4) (Japan) (unofficial English translation available at www.wipo.int/edocs/lexdocs/laws/en/jp/jp198en.pdf) [hereinafter, Japanese Patent Act] (defining computer program).

[9] See JPO, EXAMINATION GUIDELINES FOR PATENT AND UTILITY MODEL IN JAPAN at Part III, Ch. 1, § 2.2.1 (defining "program" as "a set of instructions given to a computer which are combined in order to produce a specific result" and defining "equivalent to a program" as "those which are not direct instructions to computers and thus cannot be called programs, but have similar properties to programs in terms of prescribing computer processing. For example, 'data structure' (a logical structure of data that is expressed by correlations between data elements) can be equivalent to a program."), *available at* www.jpo.go.jp/tetuzuki_e/t_tok kyo_e/files_guidelines_e/03_0100_e.pdf.

[10] See File, TECHTERMS.COM, www.techterms.com/definition/file (last visited Sept. 21, 2018).

[11] Recall that a surface-mesh file, such as an STL file, is a 3D model of an object that has been processed from a CAD format and is ready to be translated into a machine-instruction file. A machine-instruction file is typically in GCODE and provides specific instructions to a 3D printer about where to move, operating temperature, etc.

[12] See, e.g., RepRap Firmware, REPRAP, https://reprap.org/wiki/RepRap_Firmware (last visited Sept. 14, 2018) (describing the program that reads GCODE files on a RepRap 3D printer).

the line between files and programs is somewhat arbitrary. The Microsoft Word program exists as a file (e.g., as an EXE file) and is mediated by other software, including the operating system and BIOS (though BIOS is perhaps more specifically labeled firmware).[13]

On the other hand, many DMFs are software under a broad definition like that of the JPO. Some DMFs, particularly machine-instruction files, certainly contain instructions that tell a computer-controlled printer to do certain things, such as "move the printing nozzle to location XYZ." Surface-mesh files also contain a set of instructions to achieve a result on a computer, but in their case the result is typically merely an editable image on a screen. This book will use a broad definition of program and software, which includes surface-mesh and machine-instruction files.

But labeling files as software, while perhaps helpful to clarify analogies to other software patent cases, does not answer the question of whether DMFs constitute patentable subject matter. On this key question, scholars disagree. Some contend DMFs are patentable,[14] and others argue they are merely data and thus not patentable.[15] In fact, they are both correct in a sense. But many scholars have failed to appreciate the important differences between different DMF formats, which were discussed in Chapter 2. It turns out that some formats will almost certainly qualify as patentable subject matter, and others likely will not.

Patent Claims to Files in the Abstract – The American Perspective

Patentees would like the broadest patent claims possible – to capture the most infringement – and thus would prefer to claim software or a DMF file in the abstract, untethered to anything physical. But this goal has been stymied by patent systems around the world.

In the United States, the patent statute requires an invention to fall into one of only four categories: "process, machine, manufacture, or composition of

---

[13] See, e.g., Communicating with Computers, OREGONSTATE.EDU, http://oregonstate.edu/instruct/ch590/lessons/lesson1_files/chap2.html ("An operating system is a system of programs that controls the computer's input and output devices; [and] coordinates the processing of computer tasks . . .").

[14] See, e.g., Daniel Harris Brean, Patenting Physibles: A Fresh Perspective for Claiming 3D-Printable Products, 55 SANTA CLARA L. REV. 837, 845–48 (2015) (properly distinguishing among different 3D printable file formats and arguing that computer-readable medium claims could protect machine-instruction files).

[15] See, e.g., Geertrui Van Overwalle & Reinout Leys, 3D Printing and Patent Law: A Disruptive Technology Disrupting Patent Law?, 48 INT'L REV. OF INTELL. PROP. AND COMPETITION L. 504, 512 (2017).

matter."[16] If a claim falls outside of those categories, it is not patent eligible.[17] This presents a problem for software in the abstract. One of the categories, process, denotes intangible steps that are performed, but that is not what software in the abstract is: software is a set of instructions for what steps to perform, rather than the actual performance of those steps.[18] As far as the other three categories, courts have long held that machines, manufactures, and compositions of matter must be tangible in nature. For instance, the Supreme Court has defined *machine* as "a concrete thing, consisting of parts, or of certain devices and combination of devices."[19] In addition, the Court defined *composition of matter* to mean "all compositions of two or more substances and ... all composite articles, whether they be the results of chemical union, or of mechanical mixture, or whether they be gases, fluids, powders or solids."[20] Software and DMFs as abstract data are not concrete and thus do not fall under these categories.

Abstract software's best (but vanishingly slim) hope to qualify as patentable subject matter lies in the category of *manufactures*. The term manufacture has appeared in the patent statutes since the Patent Act of 1790.[21] The Supreme Court has defined it (strangely in its verb form even though the statute uses it as a noun) as "the production of articles for use from raw or prepared materials by giving to these materials new forms, qualities, properties, or combinations, whether by hand-labor or by machinery."[22] Building off this definition, the question becomes, what is an *article*? Here the courts have again required tangibility. In a widely followed 2007 opinion, *In re Nuijten*, the U.S. Court of Appeals for the Federal Circuit (Federal Circuit), which has exclusive jurisdiction for patent case appeals, rejected the patentability of transient electric or electromagnetic transmissions because the relevant definitions of "articles" of "manufacture" require "tangible articles or commodities."[23] In 2017 the

---

[16]   35 U.S.C. § 101.

[17]   *See, e.g., In re* Nuijten, 500 F.3d 1346, 1353–55 (Fed. Cir. 2007).

[18]   Inventors can protect software-related inventions by drafting claims to a process (also called a method), such as a method of 3D printing a fuel injector using a 3D printer. But for reasons explored in Chapter 5, those method claims are only infringed when someone actual performs the steps (e.g., prints the file).

[19]   Burr v. Duryee, 68 U.S. 531, 570 (1863).

[20]   Diamond v. Chakrabarty, 447 U.S. 303, 308 (1980).

[21]   Patent Act of 1790, § 4, 1 Stat. 109, 111 (1790).

[22]   Diamond v. Chakrabarty, 447 U.S. 303, 308 (1980) (quoting Am. Fruit Growers, Inc. v. Brogdex Co., 283 U.S. 1, 11 (1931)).

[23]   *In re* Nuijten, 500 F.3d 1346, 1356–57 (Fed. Cir. 2007). In a related context the Federal Circuit has also interpreted the term article to require tangibility. ClearCorrect Operating, L.L. C. v. Int'l Trade Comm'n, 810 F.3d 1283, 1286 (Fed. Cir. 2015) (holding that the word "articles" in the Tariff Act of 1930, which provides the International Trade Commission with authority to

court followed *Nuijten* in holding that "carrier waves" did not constitute patentable subject matter.[24]

Besides signs and carrier waves, a related issue is whether data structures are patentable subject matter or, instead, intangible. In 2014, the Federal Circuit held they were not eligible in *Digitech Image Technologies, L.L. C. v. Electronics for Imaging, Inc.*,[25] stating that "[d]ata in its ethereal, non-physical form is simply information that does not fall under any of the categories of eligible subject matter under section 101." Digitech attempted to claim a device profile for describing the properties of a digital image device (e.g., a camera or photoprinter).[26] The claimed device profiles comprised nothing more than data, causing the three-judge panel to reject the claims because they were "not directed to any tangible embodiment of this information (*i.e.*, in physical memory or other medium)" and did not "claim any tangible part of the digital processing system."[27]

Applying *Digitech*'s reasoning to DMFs, one can see that DMFs in the abstract will not constitute patentable subject matter even though they contain data describing tangible objects; the same was true in *Digitech*. The data in *Digitech*'s failed claims represented "device dependent" information, where the device was a physical object like a camera or printer.[28] *Digitech* thus spells doom for any claim to a DMF in the abstract because the data in DMFs comprise intangible information about the shape and properties of the physical object or intangible instructions to a 3D printer.

In an important 2015 article, Professor Brean disagreed, both doctrinally and normatively, with a tangibility requirement for manufactures.[29] Doctrinally, he sided with Judge Linn's dissent in *Nuijten*, questioning among other things the majority's reliance on a definition from an 1895 dictionary, when the word *manufacture* has appeared in the statute since 1790.[30] Regardless of the definition used, the statutory interpretation duel carried out in *Nuijten*'s majority and dissent is at best indeterminate. Congress, of course, had no

remedy only those unfair acts that involve the importation of articles, includes only material things and does not include transmission of digital data).
[24] Mentor Graphics Corp. v. EVE-USA, Inc., 851 F.3d 1275, 1294–95 (Fed. Cir. 2017) (holding that a claim encompassing "carrier waves" was invalid under § 101).
[25] 758 F.3d 1344, 1350 (Fed. Cir. 2014).
[26] *Id.* at 1349.
[27] *Id.*
[28] *Id.* at 1347–48.
[29] Brean, *supra* note 14, at 848–63.
[30] *Id.* at 805. The *Nuijten* majority counterargued that Congress readopted the term manufacture after relevant Supreme Court precedent interpreted it, suggesting an acquiescence in the interpretation. *In re* Nuijten, 500 F.3d 1346, 1356 n.5 (Fed. Cir. 2007).

opinion in 1790 as to whether abstract data capable of being stored on computer files constituted patentable subject matter. And Judge Linn's refrain about the Supreme Court's *Chakrabarty* opinion as signaling a policy of permissiveness toward abstract claims looks laughable after recent Supreme Court cases,[31] as Brean acknowledges.

Brean also attempts to distinguish *Digitech* from 3D printable files. He argues that "the information claimed [in *Digitech*] is unconnected to something physical, [whereas] a CAD file representing a complete three-dimensional object is a far cry from such disembodied data."[32] Though Brean's work is excellent and generally careful, this is an overstatement. The claimed data in Digitech explicitly relates to "data for describing a *device* dependent transformation of color information content of the *image*."[33] The device referred to can include things like a digital camera, printer, or display screen, all of which are clearly tangible (as is an image when printed or displayed).[34] Although Digitech's data is one degree removed from directly describing the tangible device or image, the decision nevertheless presents a significant hurdle for DMFs.

Finally, Brean asserts that "a CAD file is remarkably concrete" compared to the data in *Digitech*.[35] But the data in a DMF is of course intangible, not concrete. Moreover, just as *Digitech*'s data relates to intangible spatial information about an image and its correlation to a device,[36] a fuel injector DMF's data relates to intangible information such as lengths and widths of pieces of a fuel injector (which is a type of spatial information). Thus, one also cannot easily distinguish *Digitech* on this ground.[37]

Even aside from *Digitech* and *Nuijten*, a canvas of patentable subject matter jurisprudence over the last several decades leaves little hope for claims directed to files in the abstract. Indeed, even during its most permissive era of patentable subject matter jurisprudence, roughly the 1990s and early 2000s,

---

[31]   *See* Alice Corp. Pty. Ltd. v. CLS Bank Int'l, 134 S.Ct. 2347 (2014).

[32]   Brean, *supra* note 14, at 851.

[33]   U.S. Patent No. 6,128,415 col. 5 l. 36–37 (filed Sept. 6, 1996) (emphasis added).

[34]   The district court in *Digitech* recognized the connection to a tangible device but disparaged the connection as "only represent[ing] intangible properties of a device." *See* Digitech Image Techs., LLC v. Fujifilm Corp., 2013 WL 3947120 at *4 n.4 (C.D. Cal. 2013). The same could be said of data in a DMF, which only represents intangible properties like lengths and widths of the tangible object.

[35]   Brean, *supra* note 14, at 852.

[36]   And note that the image (i.e., picture) in *Digitech* would be considered a tangible item (a printed photograph) in the pre-digital era.

[37]   It would perhaps be more accurate to say that a DMF's data is more specific (as opposed to concrete) than the data claimed in *Digitech*, which I believe is Professor Brean's position. The consequences of this fact are explored in the discussion of *Alice* and pre-emption.

the Federal Circuit required tangibility. The capacious "useful, concrete, and tangible result" test required tangibility on its face.[38] Likewise, the Freeman-Walter-Abele test of the 1980s required any claimed algorithm to be "applied in [some] manner to physical elements or process steps"[39] and rejected claims to intangible inventions such as data structures.[40]

Going back further, commentators have long understood manufactures to be tangible objects.[41] As Professor Sarah Burstein's research shows, the difference between manufactures and machines was difficult to discern, but often centered on whether they were unitary objects or multicomponent objects, respectively.[42] But there was no belief that manufactures could be intangible. With tangibility required for both categories, distinguishing between manufactures and machines was not urgent: as long as an invention was one or the other, it constituted patentable subject matter.[43] In sum, there is no reason to believe that, doctrinally speaking, the category of manufactures in U.S. law encompasses intangible inventions.

---

[38] *See, e.g.*, State St. Bank & Trust Co. v. Signature Fin. Grp., 149 F.3d 1368, 1373 (Fed. Cir. 1998) ("Today, we hold that the transformation of data, representing discrete dollar amounts, by a machine through a series of mathematical calculations into a final share price, constitutes a practical application of a mathematical algorithm, formula, or calculation, because it produces 'a useful, concrete and tangible result.'"). One can reasonably question whether a share price is in fact tangible, but the claim in *State Street* was to a system, which the court characterized as a machine. *Id.* Regardless, the point is that even during this permissive era, data in the abstract was not patentable, notwithstanding whether the transformation of data by a system or process was.

[39] *In re Pardo*, 684 F.2d 912, 915 (C.C.P.A. 1982) (quoting *In re Walter*, 618 F.2d 758, 767 (C.C.P.A. 1980)). Commentators have criticized *State Street* for failing to follow the then-binding Freeman-Walter-Abele test. *See* John R. Thomas, *The Patenting of the Liberal Professions*, 40 B.C. L. Rev. 1139, 1159 (1999).

[40] *In re Warmerdam*, 33 F.3d 1354, 1361–62 (Fed. Cir. 1994). *Warmerdam* distinguishes *In re Bradley*, 600 F.2d 807 (C.C.P.A. 1979). *In re Bradley*, although involving a claim to data structures, construed the data structures to be tangible hardware "which results from the arrangement of the recited hardware elements in the claimed manner." 600 F.2d 807, 812 (1979), *aff'd by an equally divided court* Diamond v. Bradley, 450 U.S. 381 (1981).

[41] *See, e.g.*, George Ticknor Curtis, A Treatise on the Law of Patents for Useful Inventions in the United States of America § 102 (1849) (defining manufacture as "fabrics or substances made by the art or industry of man, not being machinery"); Albert H. Walker, Text-Book of the Patent Laws of the United States of America § 339 (1885) (referring to machines and manufactures as "classes of tangible things").

[42] Sarah Burstein, *The "Article of Manufacture" in 1887*, 32 Berkeley Tech. L.J. 1, 25–68 (2017); *see also Ex parte* Ackerson, 1869 Dec. Comm'r Pat. 74, 75 (stating that manufacture is "used to distinguish the thing made from the art, i.e., process, of making it, or from the machine that makes it, or from the mere union of the materials which compose it.").

[43] Burstein, *supra* note 42, at 31.

*Patent Claims to Files in the Abstract – The European
and Japanese Perspectives*

Claiming a DMF in the abstract has no better prospects in Europe than in the
United States. One would think the issue is clearly dealt with by EPC Article
52(2)(c), which states that computer programs *as such* are not patentable. But
a review of EPO decisions shows that "software as such" is a malleable term
that has changed meaning over time. The Technical Boards of Appeal of the
EPO (Board)[44] has decided that "programs for computers must be considered
as patentable inventions when they have a technical character."[45] But when
software has technical character is not clear.

Perhaps the closest the Board came to allowing claims for software in the
abstract was *IBM/Computer Program Product*, where the Board considered
several patent claims, including a claim to a "computer program product
directly loadable" onto a computer. The Board stated that "a computer
program claimed *by itself* is not excluded from patentability if the program,
when running on a computer or loaded into a computer, brings about, or is
capable of bringing about, a technical effect which goes beyond the 'normal'
physical interactions between the program (software) and the computer (hardware) on which it is run."[46]

The Board also stated that "it does not make any difference whether
a computer program is claimed *by itself or as a record on a carrier*."[47] This
could suggest that claims to a program by itself will not be interpreted as
requiring a carrier (e.g., a memory device) and would thus protect the software
in the abstract. Alternatively, the Board might have meant that whether or not
a claim explicitly mentions a carrier, it is implicitly treated as a claim to
a program on a carrier. In favor of the latter interpretation, the presence of
the word "product" suggests tangibility. In addition, the Board stated that
programs as such, which are excluded by the EPC, are those that are "abstract
creations,"[48] suggesting that the software product claim was somehow not

[44] The EPO's decisions, especially those from the Board, have more significance than its
U.S. counterpart's decisions, in part because the EPO is currently the only significant
European-wide actor. The EPO can rule on patent applications and oppositions to issued
patents, and those decisions apply across Europe, but litigation is left to national courts unless
and until the unified patent court becomes a reality. Moreover, Board decisions generally
cannot be appealed further. In rare instances, an Enlarged Board can hear a case, but only
under narrow circumstances amounting to irreconcilable conflict among Board decisions.
[45] Computer Program Product/IBM, Case T-1173/97, 14 (Tech. Bd. App., July 1, 1998), reasons
for decision at ¶ 5.3.
[46] *Id.* at ¶ 13 (emphasis added).
[47] *Id.* (emphasis added).
[48] *Id.* at ¶ 5.2.

abstract. But again, whether the nonabstractness was due to storage on a tangible medium or instead because of some further technical effect is not clear from the opinion itself.

Regardless of any potential ambiguity in the decision, subsequent decisions and analysis assume tangibility as a requirement for software product claims. In a subsequent line of cases, the Board allowed claims if they recited any hardware, i.e., any storage medium or computer. These cases have been criticized on other grounds, but what is relevant here is their use of language indicating the importance of tangibility. For example, *Controlling Pension Benefits System/PBS Partnership* stated that even a business method is not excluded from patentability if claimed as a computer system suitably programmed, because the claimed invention "has the character of a concrete apparatus in the sense of a physical entity."[49] Likewise, *Auction Method/ Hitatchi* opined that "activities falling within the notion of a non-invention 'as such' would typically represent purely abstract concepts devoid of any technical implications."[50] Finally, *Microsoft/Clipboard Formats* reiterated that a claim to a program stored on a tangible medium is not excluded as a program "as such" because "[the claim] relates to a computer-readable medium, i.e. a technical product involving a carrier."[51]

Commentators and courts have also interpreted the Board's decisions as only excluding programs in the abstract. For example, the UK Court of Appeal, while voicing its opposition to the Board's narrow interpretation, thought it clear that only "abstract or intangible" claims would be excluded.[52] In addition, the EPO website indicates that a computer program product claim "was introduced in order to provide better legal protection for computer programs distributed on a data carrier and not forming part of a computerised system."[53] Finally, Professors Marsnik and Thomas, in their thorough discussion of European patentable subject matter jurisprudence, focus on the Board's "any hardware" approach to subject matter eligibility,

---

49 Controlling Pension Benefits Systems/PBS Partnership, Case T-0931/95, 12–13 (Tech. Bd. App., Sept. 8, 2000), reasons for decision at ¶ 5. The Board went on to hold the computer claim unpatentable as obvious because the machine simply performed a business method, which is excluded as patentable subject matter, and anything excluded cannot contribute to nonobviousness.
50 Auction Method/Hitatchi, Case T-258/03, 6 (Tech. Bd. App., Apr. 21, 2004), reasons for the decision at ¶ 4.5.
51 Clipboard Formats I/Microsoft, Case T-0424/03, 10–11 (Tech. Bd. App., Feb. 23, 2006), reasons for decision at ¶ 5.3.
52 Aerotel Ltd. v Telco/ In re Macrossan's Application [2006] EWCA (Civ) 1371 at [30]-[31].
53 EPO, *supra* note 7, at 13.

without any discussion of protecting software in the abstract.[54] Thus, as in the United States, in Europe one cannot simply claim software in the abstract.

The JPO also allows patent "product" claims for computer programs, independent of the medium on which the program is stored,[55] but the courts continue to require some level of tangibility.[56] Interestingly, the JPO considers claims directed to data structures to be eligible subject matter in some circumstances,[57] and the JPO's recent guidelines specifically discuss 3D printing data.[58] But a claim to 3D printing data only consisting of the "[m]ere presentation of information (where the feature resides solely in the content of the information, and the main object is to present information)," does not constitute patentable subject matter.[59]

Even though no major patent office allows patent claims to software in the abstract, such claims may not be necessary to adequately protect at least some DMF formats if they can be claimed as an internet signal, as will be discussed immediately below.

Patenting Signals Versus Tangible Storage Media

If an inventor cannot patent software in the abstract, the next best option would be to claim the program as encoded on a signal. These claims are valuable in an era when most software is transferred via internet downloads (i.e., signals), rather than sales of tangible objects like CDs or floppy disks. If a patent claim covers the program encoded on a signal, a third party who sells the program as an internet download directly infringes. Where the infringing seller has sold numerous copies to many different buyers, the patent owner prefers the simplicity and efficiency of suing a single seller as opposed to the multiple buyers.[60]

---

[54] Susan J. Marsnik & Robert E. Thomas, *Drawing a Line in the Patent Subject-Matter Sands: Does Europe Provide a Solution to the Software and Business Method Patent Problem?*, 34 B.C. INT'L. & COMP. L. REV. 227, 287–97 (2011).

[55] Japanese Patent Act art. 2(3).

[56] Nari Lee, *Computer Program Patents and the Law and Policy of Patent Eligible Subject Matter: The Creation of a Private Social Contract?*, 8 ICFAI J. INTELL. PROP. RIGHTS 26 (2009).

[57] *See* JAPANESE PATENT OFFICE, EXAMINATION HANDBOOK FOR PATENT AND UTILITY MODEL IN JAPAN Annex B, Ch. 1, §2.1.2 (2018) [hereinafter JPO HANDBOOK], www.jpo.go.jp/tetuzuki_e/t_tokkyo_e/files_handbook_sinsa_e/app_b1_e.pdf.

[58] *See id.* at Annex B, Ch. 1, at 120–26.

[59] *Id.* at Annex A, CH. 3, at 23; *see also* METI, *The Intellectual Property System for the Fourth Industrial Revolution* 19–20 (2017), *available at* www.jpo.go.jp/tetuzuki_e/t_tokkyo_e/files_handbook_sinsa_e/app_a3_e.pdf.

[60] Stephen G. Kunin & Bradley D. Lytle, *Patent Eligibility of Signal Claims*, 87 J. PAT. & TRADEMARK OFF. SOC'Y 991, 999 (2005) ("Signal claims carrying a computer program cover

Given the value of claims to encoded signals, it is perhaps surprising that U.S. and European practices have diverged. In the United States, the Federal Circuit unequivocally forbade such claims in *In re Nuijten*.[61] The patent claim at issue in *Nuijten* was directed to a particular signal "with embedded supplemental data," where the additional data comprised an improved digital watermark.[62] Whereas the court allowed claims directed to the method of and device for embedding the new watermarked signal, it rejected the claim to the signal as not falling within any of the four enumerated statutory categories of process, machine, manufacture, or composition of matter. The court reasoned that the signal did not "possess concrete structure" and was too transient to be considered tangible within the statute's meaning.[63]

In contrast, almost two decades before *Nuijten*, the EPO Board upheld a claim to an electromagnetic signal carrying computer-readable instructions for performing a method.[64] The EPO continues to bless signal-type claims for computer implemented inventions.[65] It also allows "computer program product" claims, which can be construed broadly to include signals.

Although the JPO does not allow signal claims per se,[66] Japanese law takes a broad view of patentable subject matter. It allows claims directed to a computer program product[67] and defines a computer program broadly enough to encompass a program stored on a signal.[68] Japanese law also specifically defines "providing [a computer program] through an electric

---

downloadable software that makes a competitor who makes the signal and offers to sell or sells it an attractive target of an infringement suit."); Jeffrey R. Kuester et al., *A New Frontier in Patents: Patent Claims to Propagated Signals*, 17 J. MARSHALL J. COMPUTER & INFO. L. 75, 86–87 (1998).

[61] 500 F.3d 1346 (Fed. Cir. 2007).

[62] *Id.* at 1351.

[63] *Id.* at 1354–58.

[64] Colour Television Signal, Case T-0163/85 (Tech. Bd. App., Mar. 14, 1989).

[65] *E.g.*, Schiller Medical, Case T-0533/09 (Tech Bd. App., Nov. 2, 2014) (finding that the claimed pulse train constituted patentable subject matter in part because of its tangible nature resulting from the modulation of an electrical signal); EUROPEAN PATENT OFFICE, GUIDELINES FOR EXAMINATION IN THE EPO § 3.91 (Nov. 2017) [hereinafter EPO GUIDELINES] (listing acceptable claim formats, including to a "data carrier signal carrying [a] computer program").

[66] *See* JPO HANDBOOK, *supra* note 57, at ANNEX B, § 1.2.1.2(1) & 1.2.1.3(3).

[67] Japanese Patent Act art. 2(3).

[68] *Id.* art. 2(4) ("A 'computer program, etc.' in this Act means a computer program (a set of instructions given to an electronic computer which are combined in order to produce a specific result, hereinafter the same shall apply in this paragraph) and any other information that is to be processed by an electronic computer equivalent to a computer program.").

telecommunication line" as an act of direct infringement.[69] In addition, the JPO permits some programs to be protected as data structures.[70]

Tangible Computer Memory Is Required in the United States

The ability broadly to claim program products and signals provides patent holders in Japan and Europe with advantages over American patent holders – advantages that the proliferation of 3D printing files will magnify. Without access to signal-type claims, U.S. patentees must resort to drafting patent claims to a computer readable medium (CRM) containing the DMF. This claim format became so ubiquitous in the United States that it earned a nickname, the Beauregard claim.[71] Rather than claim a signal embedded with the computer program, the claim is limited to a concrete medium like a CD or disk. As one would expect, since the EPO allows signal-type claims, it also allows the narrower tangible-media claims.[72]

An example of a hypothetical CRM claim for a 3D printable fuel injector is, "A computer readable storage medium having data stored therein representing instructions executable by a computer, the storage medium comprising instructions to additively manufacture a fuel injector comprising [all the limitations of claim 1 of U.S. Patent Number 4,317,452]."

The drawbacks of a CRM claim in an internet era are clear when one considers that direct infringement generally requires that someone make, use, sell, or offer to sell *the thing claimed*. A patent holder will most commonly want to stop an infringer from offering computer files for download over the Internet. But notice that an offer to sell an internet download is not an offer to sell a tangible medium like a CD or disk; it is an offer to send data as a signal.[73] Thus, there is no direct infringement of a CRM claim for a sale or offer to sell a file for download (though the recipient would be a direct infringer for

---

[69] *Id.* art. 2(3)(i).

[70] *See* JPO HANDBOOK, *supra* note 57, at Annex B, Ch. 1, § 2.1.2.

[71] This name derives from the notable, eponymous case involving that claim format, *In re Beauregard*, 53 F.3d 1583 (Fed. Cir. 1995). Interestingly, because the Patent Office reversed its original opposition to the patentee's claim during the appeal, the Federal Circuit did not affirmatively endorse the format. *Id.* at 1584.

[72] Clipboard Formats I/Microsoft, Case T-0424/03 (Tech. Bd. App., Feb. 23, 2006) (stating that a carrier claim "has technical character since it relates to a computer-readable medium, i.e. a technical product involving a carrier."). Under this decision, simply reciting a computer-readable medium will allow the claim to escape exclusion under Article 52 regardless of what the program does. At the same time, however, the EPO also requires a further technical character, but analyzes that requirement under the rubric of inventive step. *See infra* note 84 and accompanying text.

[73] *See* Brean, *supra* note 14, at 845–46.

"making" the claimed program on its computer's memory). Infringement issues will be explored in more depth in Chapter 5.

Whether claimed as a signal or a CRM, however, patent protection for DMFs face a more fundamental challenge, as the next section discusses.

C. PATENTABLE SUBJECT MATTER AND UNPATENTABLE DMF FILE FORMATS

Even though the United States allows CRM claims, and Japan and the EPC countries allow program product claims (and protect signals), current doctrine will limit patent protections for DMFs depending on the specific DMF category. Of the three types of DMFs, only machine-instruction files clearly fall within patentable subject matter boundaries because they contain the actual computer-readable instructions telling the 3D printer nozzle where to move, etc. Surface-mesh files, on the other hand, simply contain data about the object's surface geometry. Design files are even further removed from the manufacturing process: software must typically convert them into surface-mesh files before additional software converts them into machine-instruction files.

This is an issue of paramount importance for 3D printing technology because people usually buy, sell, and transfer surface-mesh files, not machine-instruction files. Depending on buyers' needs, they also may want the design files, which are the easiest to edit. From an economic perspective, therefore, surface-mesh files and design files are more valuable than machine-instruction files. In contrast, a patent claim is likely viable only if it is drafted toward the machine-instruction file, which is the least valuable format from the patent holder's perspective. As a result, inventors will strive to obtain claims that cover surface-mesh and design files.

Surface-Mesh and Design Files Are Not Patentable Subject Matter in the United States

In the United States, protection for surface-mesh and design files will come, if at all, via CRM claims. CRM claims constitute patentable subject matter as "manufactures" under Section 101 as long as the execution of the code embedded on the medium results in patentable subject matter. The USPTO distinguishes between "functional descriptive material," such as computer programs that "impart functionality when encoded on a computer-readable medium," and "non-functional descriptive material," such as music, literary works, photographs, and "mere arrangement of data" stored on a computer-readable medium.[74] The former are patentable; the latter are not.[75]

Under this rubric, machine-instruction files remain patentable subject matter because they directly control a computer manufacturing process. But surface-mesh and design files would not be patentable subject matter because they simply cause a computer to display an image of the object. In this way, they are similar to computer files containing music, literary works, and photographs, which the USPTO clearly states are not patentable. Music, text, and image files cause a computer to do something (play music, display text, and display an image) and can be edited via a computer, but they do not result in patentable objects or processes.

One could attempt to distinguish surface-mesh and design files from music and photograph files because the former can easily be converted into a format that results in a manufacturing process. It may thus exalt form over function to protect one but not the other. I am sympathetic to that argument, but doctrinally there is no clear pathway to protection – surface-mesh files are a collection of surface data and do no more than display an image. And a slippery slope looms: If surface-mesh files are protected, why not design files, which can be easily converted into surface-mesh files? But design files, being historically nothing more than sophisticated electronic blueprints, have never been patentable subject matter.

This fundamental issue cannot be decided by rote application of doctrine. It should be decided as a matter of policy. It is in some ways reminiscent of the debate about whether computer program source code, as opposed to object code, could constitute patentable subject matter.[76] Source code, like surface-mesh files, is an upstream precursor to the computer-useable object code. But the issue is more salient with 3D printing because the technology shifts significant economic value from tangible objects to surface-mesh and design

---

[74] Examination Guidelines for Computer-Related Inventions, 61 Fed. Reg. 7478, 7481 (Feb. 28, 1996).

[75] Although the result of this dichotomy strikes many as reasonable, the distinction between functional and nonfunctional computer code fails to capture the true distinction in that all code interacts with a computer and causes the computer to do something. *See* Kevin Emerson Collins, *Semiotics 101: Taking the Printed Matter Doctrine Seriously*, 85 IND. L. J. 1379, 1395–96 (2010) (arguing inter alia that if the point of novelty is data whose only use in its claimed form is to serve as a sign, in the sense of informational content to a human, the claim is not patentable subject matter).

[76] *See, e.g.*, Daniel S. Lin, Matthew Sag, & Ronald S. Laurie, *Source Code Versus Object Code: Patent Implications for the Open Source Community*, 18 SANTA CLARA HIGH TECH. L.J. 235 (2001).

files, whereas mass-market software was typically sold in the protectable object code format.[77]

The policy strands are complex and intertwined. On one side, a failure to protect surface-mesh files would significantly weaken patent holder's rights, resulting in a decreased incentive to innovate. Cutting the other way, protecting surface-mesh files with patent claims conflicts with other policy goals. First, it would inhibit others' ability to study and build upon the invention by studying and using the surface-mesh file. Second, as Professor Collins stresses, it may impermissibly allow the patent holder to escape the full scope of the disclosure obligation.[78] Finally, it would also implicate free speech concerns.[79] How to balance these competing interests is not straightforward, and the balancing may change as the conversion from design to surface-mesh to machine-instruction file becomes completely routine and trivial. Most importantly, attempts to balance these interests must pay significant attention to whether 3D printing technology lowers the costs of innovation. I reserve for the moment attempts to balance these interests, picking the task back up primarily in Chapter 10.

Surface-Mesh and Design Files Are Likely Not Patentable Subject Matter in Europe and Japan

The situation in Europe is no better for patent holders. The EPO has crafted an additional test for claims directed to software products (as opposed to system or method claims), which requires the software to produce "further

[77] Another helpful but imperfect analogy can be made to copyright in music, which for years protected only the written sheet music. *See* White-Smith Music Pub. Co. v. Apolo Co., 209 U.S. 1 (1908) (holding that mechanical devices that made music did not infringe copyright in musical compositions). As recording technology developed and proliferated, the economic value shifted from the sheet music to the recorded performances, and yet the law lagged behind in its protection of this new medium. It was not until 1978 that sound recordings were afforded full protection under U.S. copyright law.

[78] Kevin Emerson Collins, *The Structural Implications of Inventors' Disclosure Obligations*, 69 VAND. L. REV. 1785, 1809–13 (2016).

[79] *See, e.g.*, Dan L. Burk, *Patenting Speech*, 79 TEX. L. REV. 99 (2000). *Cf.* Defense Distributed v. U.S. Dept. of State, 838 F.3d 451 (5th Cir. 2016) (upholding the Department of State's order to remove 3D printable files of guns despite First Amendment concerns); Junger v. Daley, 209 F.3d 481, 485 (6th Cir. 2000) (holding that "computer source code is an expressive means for the exchange of information and ideas about computer programming" and thus is protected by the First Amendment); Bernstein v. U.S. Dep't of Justice, 176 F.3d 1132, 1141 (9th Cir. 1999), *withdrawn and reh'g granted*, 192 F.3d 1308 (9th Cir. 1999) (holding "that encryption software, in its source code form and as employed by those in the field of cryptography, must be viewed as expressive for First Amendment purposes"). The *Bernstein* case was never actually considered en banc.

technical effect" that goes "beyond the 'normal' physical interactions between the program (software) and the computer (hardware)."[80] That is, the basic technical effect of software interacting with hardware is not enough, the software must result in some additional technical thing, such as "further effects deriving from the execution (by the hardware) of the instructions given by the computer program."

The further technical effect test should not cause problems for claims to machine-instruction files. After all, they cause hardware – a 3D printer – to manufacture utilitarian objects. In the words of the IBM decision, "a patent may be granted ... where a piece of software manages, by means of a computer, an industrial process or the working of a piece of machinery."[81] A 3D printer certainly qualifies as a piece of machinery. Moreover, from a policy perspective, if patent law will protect the underlying physical object, there is no reason it should not also protect the machine-instruction file.[82]

Surface-mesh and design files, however, run into problems with the further technical effects test. Because they typically do not directly instruct a 3D printer, they will likely be seen in Europe as mere presentations of information. According to the EPO, a "feature relating to a presentation of information defined solely by the content of the information does not have a technical character."[83] Thus, like in the United States, a particular surface-mesh or design file that merely generates an image on a screen will likely not be patentable.

The EPO further complicated the subject matter eligibility analysis by conflating the Article 52 exclusion analysis with the Article 56 inventive step analysis.[84] The inventive step test (roughly parallel to the American nonobviousness requirement) only allows patents for inventions that present

[80] Computer Program Product/IBM, Case T-1173/97 (Tech. Bd. App., July 1, 1998), reasons for decision at ¶ 13.

[81] *Id.* at ¶ 6.5.

[82] *See id.* at ¶ 9.8 (finding it "illogical to grant a patent for both a method and the apparatus adapted for carrying out the same method, but not for the computer program product, which comprises all the features enabling the implementation of the method").

[83] EPO GUIDELINES, *supra* note 65, at § 2.6. *See also* Colour Television Signal, Case T-0163/85 (Tech. Bd. App., Mar. 14, 1989), reasons for decision at ¶ 2 (stating that moving pictures modulated on a standard TV signal are merely information per se).

[84] *See, e.g.*, Programs for Computers, G-0003/08, 33–34 & 40–41 (EPO Enlarged Bd. App., May 12, 2010); Clipboard Formats I/Microsoft, Case T-0424/03 (Tech. Bd. App., Feb. 23, 2006). The UK Court of Appeal has expressed strong reservations about the EPO's approach. Aerotel Ltd. v. Telco/ In re Macrossan's Application [2006] EWCA (Civ) 1371 at [31]. But a subsequent UK court decision has tried to harmonize the approaches to some degree. Astron Clinica Ltd v. Comptroller General of Patents [2008] EWHC 85 (Pat). It will be interesting to see what UK courts might do post-Brexit.

a nontrivial advance over prior inventions. In deciding whether a particular claim involves an inventive step, the EPO only considers features of an invention that contribute to its technical character.[85] Under this test, many business method software claims fail in examination because the business aspect of the claim is not considered in the inventive step analysis, leaving only generic software and/or hardware, which is old.[86]

The technical-character-inventive-step quagmire should not, however, hinder claims to machine-instruction files *as long as* they will print a nonobvious, utilitarian object. With this assumption, the claim would have an inventive step not simply because it is software, but because its instructions will print a nonobvious, utilitarian object. Surface-mesh and design files, however, will not survive the test. Even though they are images of inventive machines, mere images cannot contribute to the inventive step.

As already mentioned, Japanese law is similar in that a claim to 3D printing data only consisting of the "[m]ere presentation of information (where the feature resides solely in the content of the information, and the main object is to present information)," does not constitute patentable subject matter.[87] This precludes claims to surface-mesh and design files, though not machine-instruction files.

In short, in major patent systems around the world, current law will likely not allow patent claims directed to the most economically valuable 3D printing file formats. Allowing claims directly to surface-mesh and design files would provide the strongest protection to inventors of 3D printable inventions. But obtaining such protection would require changes in the law and would involve trade-offs against follow-on innovation, among other things. It may be that the best balance is achieved not through the patentable subject matter doctrine, but through infringement doctrines, which are discussed in Chapters 5 and 6.

A Note on Alice v. CLS Bank

For a time in the United States, even the limited protection offered by Beauregard (CRM) claims appeared to be in jeopardy after the Supreme Court's restrictive decision in *Alice Corp. Pty. Ltd. v. CLS Bank Int'l.*[88] *Alice* involved a claim to a business method, but there were some who feared it

---

[85] *See, e.g.*, Programs for Computers, G-0003/08 at 40–41.
[86] *See, e.g.*, Marsnik & Thomas, *supra* note 54, at 287–97.
[87] JPO HANDBOOK, *supra* note 57, Annex A, Ch. 3, at 23; *see also* METI, *supra* note 59.
[88] 134 S. Ct. 2347 (2014).

would be a death knell for almost all software patents.[89] The dire predictions have not come to pass, and indeed the Federal Circuit has upheld a Beauregard claim.[90]

Although court decisions applying *Alice* are difficult to harmonize and predict, *Alice* should not prevent Beauregard claims to machine-instruction files. Under *Alice*'s first step, a court must determine whether the patent claim is directed to a patent-ineligible concept, such as a method of doing business or an abstract idea. Under this step, it is not enough that a Beauregard claim recites a tangible medium; the claim as a whole can still be directed to an abstract idea if the program stored on the medium relates to an abstract idea such as hedging risk.[91] Nevertheless, machine-instruction files should pass step one because they will be directed to a file that will manufacture a specific, tangible device, and tangible devices are at the core of patentable subject matter.[92] Even if one must proceed to the second step and look for something sufficient to transform the abstract idea into a patent-eligible application, the fact that the claim is directed to a new, nonobvious, and specific device should suffice to make the claim eligible subject matter.

Additionally, the policy concerns articulated by the *Alice* court should not prevent claims to DMFs because they do not pre-empt broad fields of technology. The Court based its ruling in large part on concerns about pre-emption, stating that

> in applying the § 101 exception, we must distinguish between patents that claim the building blocks of human ingenuity and those that integrate the building blocks into something more thereby transforming them into a patent-eligible invention. The former would risk disproportionately tying up the use of the underlying ideas and are therefore ineligible for patent protection. The latter pose no comparable risk of pre-emption, and therefore remain eligible for the monopoly granted under our patent laws.[93]

Because DMF claims are tied to a specific tangible object, they no more pre-empt the building blocks of ingenuity than patent claims to the tangible object.[94]

---

[89] *See, e.g.*, Luke Jensen, *End of the Road for Software Patents?*, N.C. J. L. & Tech. (Oct. 21, 2016), http://ncjolt.org/end-road-software-patents/ ("Many viewed *Alice* as a fatal blow against software patents.").

[90] Amdocs (Isr.) Ltd. v. Openet Telecomm., Inc., 841 F.3d 1288 (Fed. Cir. 2016).

[91] *See, e.g., id.* at 1300 (assuming without deciding that the Beauregard claim was directed to an abstract idea).

[92] *See* Brean, *supra* note 14, at 851–52.

[93] *Alice*, 134 S.Ct. at 2354–55.

[94] Brean, *supra* note 14, at 852.

D. CONCLUSION

Patent systems around the world will protect many inventions related to 3D printing, assuming the various requirements of description, novelty, and inventive step are met. Patent claims directed to printers and printing materials represent eligible subject matter. Further, if someone has invented a new and nonobvious physical object, there is no legal barrier to patenting a machine-instruction DMF of that object in any major patent office. Though no court has decided the issue to date, it is likely that surface-mesh and design file formats will not be patentable.

The lack of protection for these files presents a challenge to innovators of 3D printable inventions. A visit to any 3D printing repository demonstrates that surface-mesh files are the most commonly sold format, and thus the most economically important. Machine-instruction files, on the other hand, are specific to individual 3D printers and thus not widely sold. To more fully protect 3D printable inventions, patent law could treat surface-mesh files as patentable subject matter because they are the locus of economic value. But making that move involves collateral consequences to follow-on innovation, among other things. Chapter 10 takes up the ultimate innovation balancing analysis.

A second, more detailed point allows for quicker resolution. Even though machine-instruction files are patentable, the scope of protection varies across the globe. Europe and Japan consider internet signals to be patentable subject matter, that is, they do not distinguish based on the medium on which a program is stored. U.S. law, in contrast, does not protect internet signals and only protects files if they are claimed as stored on a tangible medium such as a disk. This substantially weakens protection because online vendors do not offer to sell tangible media, but rather ephemeral internet downloads.[95] As will be discussed in Chapters 5 and 6, no matter how many sales such vendors consummate, they will only be liable based on a theory of indirect patent infringement, which requires difficult-to-prove intent and knowledge of the patent. While each buyer will be a direct infringer for "making" the tangible medium, suing diffuse buyers is inefficient.

The American exclusion of signals makes little sense. If the patent system is properly calibrated in protecting files stored on tangible media, it should likewise protect internet transmissions of the relevant files. Making the

---

[95]   This issue did not matter as much with traditional software because it was inevitably given copyright protection against verbatim copying. An internet signal of a program would infringe a copyright in the program. As will be discussed in Chapter 8, some DMFs may not be protected by copyright law.

centralized seller – who initiated and profited from all the sales – a direct infringer would put internet transmissions on the same playing field as now-archaic CDs and floppy disks.

Finally, it is worth reiterating that protection should only extend to DMFs of otherwise patentable physical objects. A DMF of a purely aesthetic sculpture or an old utilitarian object should not enjoy patent protection. No one should be able to remove a known or obvious machine from the public domain simply by claiming a digital version of it.

5

Patents – Direct Infringement, Individual Infringement, and "Digital" Infringement

Chapter Outline:

In a 3D printing world, one of the most problematic infringement scenarios will involve patented goods with many end users. In that case, numerous diffuse actors will each engage in a single act of infringement. Discovering the infringers may be hugely difficult – how does the patentee know who has actually printed the object?[1] The individualized nature of the infringement also presents a problem for patent holders who will need to launch multiple lawsuits, likely in separate jurisdictions where each infringer resides. Then there is the problem of collecting money from individuals or small businesses who may not be able to afford to pay. All this is time consuming and hugely inefficient, and it effectively weakens the value of the patent.

Rather than suing the end users, the patent holder would prefer to stop the entity that is distributing the DMFs. The biggest challenge for patent holders of 3D printable objects is that, as described in Chapter 4, it is probably not possible to obtain a patent claim to the DMF file format most often sold and distributed electronically, namely, the surface-mesh file format. A surface-mesh file contains a surface representation of the object to be printed, but not

---

[1] Even if the patentee looks for those who downloaded the file, discovering their true identities is difficult. *Cf.* Sean B. Karunaratne, Note, *The Case Against Combating BitTorrent Piracy Through Mass John Doe Copyright Infringement Lawsuits*, 111 MICH. L. REV. 283, 286–88 (2012) (describing the copyright litigation process of obtaining IP addresses, filing "John Doe" lawsuits based on the addresses, and then seeking subpoenas to discover the person behind the IP address); Cobbler Nev., LLC v. Gonzalez, 901 F.3d 1142, 1147 (9th Cir. 2018) (holding that the bare allegation that the defendant was the registered subscriber of an IP address associated with infringing activity was insufficient to state a claim for direct or contributory copyright infringement because multiple people live in and visit the facility using the IP address).

the instructions to the 3D printer. The law will likely treat it as if it were a blueprint. Without patent protection for surface-mesh files, patentees cannot sue centralized DMF distributors for direct infringement.

This chapter will focus only on direct infringement. Chapter 6 will focus on indirect infringement. Both will consider infringement in the context of three scenarios, each of which turns on the important rule that literal infringement is determined strictly according to the patent claim's wording. Specifically, they will consider a patent claim to (1) a physical object, (2) a machine-instruction version of a file that will print the physical object, and (3) a surface-mesh version of the file.

In each case it will be assumed that the object printed or described in the file is identical in functional requirements to the thing claimed in the patent. In other words, the only thing that differs is whether the object is a physical or digital instantiation, and if digital, in what format it exists.

A. DIRECT INFRINGEMENT OF A CLAIM TO A TANGIBLE OBJECT

The patent system was founded with tangible objects in mind. Claims to tangible objects like machines are thus at the core of what patent law protects. This subsection imagines a patent containing a valid claim to a tangible machine, such as the fuel injector discussed in Chapter 4. How valuable is such a patent claim in a 3D printing era?

Individual 3D Printing & Direct Infringement

Obviously, 3D printing the patented object constitutes an act of infringement unless an exception applies. "Making" and "using" are acts of infringement whether the device is made by 3D printing or traditional manufacturing means.[2] In the United States, which has no private use exception and virtually no experimental use exception,[3] almost every act of printing and using the object will result in infringement.

---

[2]   In the United States, 35 U.S.C. § 271(a) lists the acts of infringement as making, using, selling, offering to sell, or importing. Other countries have similar listings. *See, e.g.*, Patents Act, 1977, c. 37, § 60(1)(a) (UK) [hereinafter, UK Patents Act] (listing prohibited acts of "makes, disposes of, offers to dispose of, uses or imports the product or keeps").

[3]   *See* Madey v. Duke University, 307 F.3d 1351, 1362 (Fed. Cir. 2002) (holding that the "very narrow and strictly limited experimental use defense" applies only if use of the patented invention is "solely for amusement, to satisfy idle curiosity, or for strictly philosophical inquiry"); Katherine J. Strandburg, *What Does the Public Get? Experimental Use and the Patent Bargain*, 2004 WISC. L. REV. 81.

America's strict liability approach, which will result in widespread, individual infringement liability, can lead to societal tensions. Traditionally, accused infringers were companies who mass-produced infringing goods and had resources to investigate legal issues like patent infringement.[4] But 3D printing brings manufacturing into individuals' hands. This can bring plenty of good, but where patent law comes into play, tricky political questions arise.

Individuals who 3D print a file will be liable for infringement, and thus monetary damages, regardless of whether they knew of the patent or anything about patent law. Imagine the feeling of downloading and printing a file having no clue that the object was patented. At some point later, you are sued for patent infringement. You may feel regret, of course, for unintentionally violating a patent. But you may also feel scandalized[5] – how could you have known? Even large companies feel outraged when sued by so-called patent trolls.[6]

The likely public backlash would be reminiscent of the public's reaction against copyright infringement lawsuits during the peak of the Napster and Grokster era.[7] In fact, patent lawsuits against individuals will likely evoke more outrage than the music copyright suits. Many music downloaders essentially knew they were doing something the law forbade (though they may have disagreed with the law[8]). In contrast, patent law is more obscure. Unlike songs, which are nearly universally protected by copyright, most 3D printable files will print objects not protected by patents. And even if one is aware of patent law generally and that a particular object might be patented, reading and understanding patent claims is virtually impossible for laypeople.[9]

---

[4] *See, e.g.,* Gaia Bernstein, *The Rise of the End User in Patent Litigation*, 55 B.C. L. Rev. 1443, 1444 (2014).

[5] *Cf.* Joe Mullin, *Patent Trolls Want $1,000 – for Using Scanners*, Ars Technica (Jan. 2, 2013, 9:30 AM), http://arstechnica.com/tech-policy/2013/01/patent-trolls-want-1000-for-using-scanners.

[6] *See, e.g.,* Joe Mullin, *Angry Entrepreneur Replies to Patent Troll with Racketeering Lawsuit*, Ars Technica (Sept. 16, 2013, 5:42 PM), https://arstechnica.com/tech-policy/2013/09/angry-entrepreneur-replies-to-patent-troll-with-racketeering-lawsuit/; Lauren K. Ohnesorge, *SAS Lawyer Takes Patent Troll Fight to the White House*, Triangle Bus. J. (Feb. 21, 2014, 7:43 AM), www.bizjournals.com/triangle/news/2014/02/20/sas-lawyer-takes-patent-troll-fight-to.html.

[7] *See, e.g., 12-Year-Old Settles Music Swap Lawsuit*, CNN (Feb. 18, 2004, 1:09 AM), www.cnn.com/2003/TECH/internet/09/09/music.swap.settlement/.

[8] Amy Harmon, *Recording Industry Goes After Students over Music Sharing*, N.Y. Times (Apr. 23, 2003), www.nytimes.com/2003/04/23/us/recording-industry-goes-after-students-over-music-sharing.html ("But students, who often justify their behavior by arguing that CD's are too expensive and that artists do not get the money anyway, may be more hostile toward the music industry than most.").

[9] Timothy R. Holbrook & Lucas S. Osborn, *Digital Patent Infringement in an Era of 3D Printing*, 48 U.C. Davis L. Rev. 1319, 1373–75 (2015).

U.S. scholars have offered various fixes for the perceived problems accompanying widespread individual infringers. One option is to mirror many other countries and excuse private, noncommercial uses of the patented invention.[10] Others have proposed restricting patent infringement lawsuits to those involving a minimum amount in controversy,[11] requiring some level of knowledge or intent when individual infringers are involved, or limiting remedies for innocent individual infringement.[12]

Any potential solution should keep in mind the tremendous costs of litigation, whether or not the lawsuit succeeds. In the United States, unlike many countries, the loser generally does not pay the winner's litigation costs, and the expense of carrying on a suit can ruin individuals. Therefore, an exception should be as clear as possible so that parties can avoid unnecessary litigation.

Some may argue that practical concerns obviate the need for an exemption in most cases. Discovering private infringement and litigating individual lawsuits will be difficult and expensive, not to mention the public ire that will result from such suits. But for those who are sued, the effects can be ruinous in terms of time, stress, and especially litigation costs. Thus, jurisdictions should strongly consider an innocent infringer defense or private, noncommercial use defense.

A private, noncommercial use exception is the approach with the most scholarly attention, probably because it is already the law in many countries, including China, France, Germany, Japan, and the United Kingdom.[13] Under UK law, for example, an act is not infringement if it is (1) done privately and (2) for purposes that are not commercial.[14] Courts have flexibility in setting the scope of these elements. Generally, "private acts" does not mean secret acts, but rather not for the benefit of the public.[15] Noncommercial generally means lacking economic benefit to the user.[16]

---

[10] Davis Doherty, Note, *Downloading Infringement: Patent Law as a Roadblock to the 3D Printing Revolution*, 26 HARV. J. LAW & TECH. 353, 368–69 (2012)

[11] *See* Deven R. Desai & Gerard N. Magliocca, *Patents, Meet Napster: 3D Printing and the Digitization of Things*, 102 GEO. L.J. 1691, 1717 (2014).

[12] Holbrook & Osborn, *supra* note 9, at 1376–77.

[13] For a list of countries with such an exception, see Standing Committee on the Law of Patents, *Exceptions and Limitations to Patent Rights: Private and/or Non-Commercial Use*, WORLD INTELL. PROP. ORG. at ¶ 5 (2014), www.wipo.int/edocs/mdocs/patent_policy/en/scp_20/sc p_20_3.pdf [hereinafter, WIPO, *Exceptions*].

[14] UK Patents Act § 60(5)(a). *See also* Patentgesetz [PatG] [Patents Act] Dec. 16, 1980 § 11(1) (Ger.).

[15] Smith, Kline & French Laboratories Ltd v. Evans Medical Ltd., [1989] FSR 513.

[16] *See* Rosa Maria Ballardini & Nari Lee, *The Private and Non-Commercial Use Defence Revisited: The Case of 3D Printing Technologies*, in 3D PRINTING, INTELLECTUAL

The exception will face challenges in a 3D printing era. While patent owners may have acquiesced in exceptions in the past, 3D printing technology radically changes the calculus. Since the industrial revolution, personal manufacturing has been rare because of the required costs, expertise, and time. But if most people can effortlessly 3D print objects in their homes,[17] the public market for such goods will be decimated, and the patents will be worth little. Indeed, one of the primary policies behind the exception is the belief that private, noncommercial uses do not significantly harm the patent owner.[18] If one consumer makes a patented object at home thereby avoiding paying the patent owner for it, little harm is done. When 3,000,000 consumers do the same thing, the loss to the patentee is great.[19]

So as sympathetic as the innocent infringer is, the law should also spare a thought for the decimated patentee. Patentees who face significant harm from a private, noncommercial use exception will agitate for relief. They may lobby for an end to the exception, pointing in particular to countries' obligations under the TRIPS treaty to limit exceptions to those that do not unreasonably prejudice the rightsholder's interests.[20] Or they may argue that an individual who prints an object saves money, thereby constituting "commercial use."[21] But any successful lobbying on the part of patentees would result in increased individual liability, which itself raises significant fairness concerns. A balance could be struck whereby the exemption only applies where the

Property and Innovation 178 (Rosa Maria Ballardini, Marcus Norrgård, & Jouni Partanen eds., 2017).

[17] The exception may also apply where an individual uses a commercial 3D printing service. Although the 3D print shop makes commercial use *of its printers*, this does not necessarily transform the individual's print job into a commercial use *of the invention*. If an individual rented a 3D printer and kept it in the home, the private, noncommercial use would apply to inventions printed on it. Renting time on another's 3D printer arguably should not be treated any differently.

[18] *See* WIPO, *Exceptions, supra* note 13, at ¶ 7. Some countries statutorily tie the exception to a lack of significant prejudice to the economic interests of the patent holder. Ballardini & Lee, *supra* note 16, at 176–78.

[19] The harm to the patentee can sometimes be greatly reduced if the patentee can sue a centralized distributor of the file for indirect infringement, as is possible in many jurisdictions that provide private noncommercial use exceptions. This possibility is considered in Chapter 6.

[20] TRIPS Agreement art. 30 ("Members may provide limited exceptions to the exclusive rights conferred by a patent, provided that such exceptions do not unreasonably conflict with a normal exploitation of the patent and do not unreasonably prejudice the legitimate interests of the patent owner, taking account of the legitimate interests of third parties.").

[21] *Cf.* Wickard v. Filburn, 317 U.S. 111, 125 (1942) (holding that farmer who grew wheat above permitted quota, but for his own consumption, had a "substantial economic effect on interstate commerce" because he didn't have to buy other wheat).

individual did not have actual knowledge of the patent.[22] It also may be that indirect liability theories can square this circle. But before considering those theories in Chapter 6, additional direct infringement concerns are analyzed.

Intermediary Liability for Direct Infringement – 3D Print Shops

Intermediary liability in the direct infringement context primarily centers around 3D print shops like Shapeways and UPS stores that print tangible objects on behalf of individual consumers. Some of these services allow users to upload a file via the internet and the end product is mailed to the consumer, while others allow users to bring their files in to the store and pick up the printed object when the job is finished. These businesses are attractive when the user needs a sophisticated (and thus expensive) 3D printer. This is also the type of print job that might implicate more complex, and thus more likely to be patented, devices.

Because these print shops actually manufacture the tangible object, they directly infringe for "making" the patented object.[23] They incur the liability despite the fact that, unlike many traditional manufacturers, they are not generally appropriating to themselves the value of the inventions they sell; they are paid for the generic service of manufacturing. (Recall that manufacturing complex shapes is generally no more difficult for 3D printers than manufacturing simple ones.) Nevertheless, U.S. law makes the print shops strictly liable. And any private, noncommercial use exemption would likely not apply to them as they are not printing privately or noncommercially.[24] If they print ten copies of a patented object, they will be liable for ten acts of infringement. Some countries may exempt one-off prints as de minimus infringement, but the United States does not.[25] Print shops (and DMF host websites) can and do attempt to limit liability by making users contractually indemnify against infringement, but this will not prevent lawsuits, and individuals may lack the ability to pay any recovery ordered.

---

[22] Knowledge can come from a stamp on a product (or digital version) indicating the product is patented and listing the patent number. Many jurisdictions require this (or actual notice) as a prerequisite to damages. *See* 35 U.S.C. § 287(a). Note, however, that many DMFs offered online may be infringing and may have no indication they are patented. In that case, the downloader would not have actual knowledge of the patent.

[23] If the print shop merely rented time on its printers for customers to use, the situation would be different – the individual would be the one making the invention.

[24] One could argue that they act as agents of the customers for whom they print and therefore benefit from the customer's private motivation.

[25] Embrex Inc. v. Service Eng'g Corp., 216 F.3d 1343, 1352 (Fed. Cir. 2000) ("[N]o room remains in the law for a *de minimis* excuse.").

And more worrying to the print shop than the damages for accidental infringement are the tremendous costs of litigation.[26] Because the print shop is likely guilty of infringement for printing even a single patented device, it will bear significant costs in a "loser pays" legal system, which is most of the world. Although each party generally bears its own litigation expenses in the United States, the costs remain high. Given this exposure, if patent infringement suits begin to pop up against 3D print shops, they may decide the litigation exposure is too high to justify continuing the business. In that case, society will lose the benefits of 3D print shops.

It may be that print shops and patent holders can cooperate to avoid litigation. Print shops becoming aware of past infringement could pay patent owners a fair price and make good faith efforts to avoid future infringement of the same patent. Good faith patentees might happily pocket the money. But not all patentees will act in good faith. Some may leverage litigation asymmetries to demand higher and higher payments from print shops.[27]

To prevent the threat of litigation from suppressing 3D print shops, the law should provide a safe harbor framework similar to the Digital Millennium Copyright Act (DMCA) in copyright.[28] The safe harbor framework should insulate 3D print shops from liability for printing when they did not know – and, perhaps, had no reason to know – that the items were patented. Patent holders should be provided with contact information to notify print shops of specific patented objects. This system could be complemented with an administrative process to allow patentees to recover for past infringement if they can prove an established market price for the good sold by the patentee (in effect requiring the patentee to practice the invention to recover).

Any safe harbor framework faces challenges. Unlike file repositories like YouTube for videos or Thingiverse for DMFs, many 3D print shops do not host the files to be printed. This prevents patent owners from scanning the host sites for infringement and requesting infringing material to be taken down. Instead, 3D print shops would have to monitor the specific object each customer desired to print. This might be a manual, site-specific process that would quickly become overwhelming unless software could help automate the process.

---

[26]   In the United States, which allows extensive pretrial discovery, the costs of discovery alone can be hundreds of thousands of dollars even for a relatively small case. *See* AIPLA, Report of the Economic Survey 41 (2017).

[27]   So-called patent trolls use these tactics in other situations. *See* Bernstein, *supra* note 4, at 1455–57.

[28]   *See* Doherty, *supra* note 10, at 365–69 (describing a safe harbor framework for DMF file repositories).

Further, any knowledge requirement for a safe harbor would be tricky to balance. Knowledge of a specific patent arguably should be insufficient to trigger liability, because the laypeople staffing each print shop will generally lack the ability to interpret patent claims. Hiring a patent lawyer to review and analyze each print job at each shop would be prohibitively expensive. Given the potential information overload faced by print shops, a "should have known" standard would be unwieldy, and even an actual knowledge standard should be interpreted with due regard for the realities of the print shop business and the complexities of patent claim interpretation. Unlike repositories, patent owners cannot point to specific files that should be removed from the inventory, because the "inventory" depends entirely on the daily customers' requests.

Thus, a knowledge requirement should be calibrated to capture the most egregious, repeat infringers, but not to bog down good faith enterprises. That is, to be liable for traditional infringement remedies, a shop owner would need to know of a specific patent and continue knowingly to print objects that come within that scope. A knowledge-of-infringement standard would equate with the standard for indirect infringement in the United States, which recognizes that a good faith belief in noninfringement (as opposed to patent invalidity) is a defense to a charge of indirect infringement.[29] To be clear, even if it did not know of the patent, the 3D print shop would owe an administratively determined remedy based on the printed object's market price.

The burdens on 3D print shops could be lessened if the safe harbor framework included a centralized file database to which patent holders (and other IP holders) could upload files of patented objects. 3D print shops could compare files brought by clients with those in the database. If the comparison revealed a match, the 3D print shop could refuse to print the object or require more information from the client. Utilizing the comparison database could be a prerequisite for safe harbor protection. The database and comparison software should be funded by a consortium of interested parties and be freely available to all 3D print shops, to alleviate costs to start-ups and small businesses.

A safe harbor database would help 3D print shop owners perform their due diligence, but such a system would not be perfect or cheap. Similar content scanning software in the copyright arena faces persistent attempts at avoidance and is criticized for removing false positives.[30] Because intentional copyists

---

[29] Commil USA, LLC v. Cisco Systems, Inc., 135 S. Ct. 1920, 1926 (2015).
[30] *See, e.g., Prevent Your Youtube Video from Getting Removed*, Rantic (Jan. 17, 2015), www .rantic.com/articles/prevent-youtube-video-getting-removed/.

could often significantly alter the shape of an object in a DMF file without changing its utilitarian functionality, avoidance of automated comparison schemes may be even easier in the patent sphere than in copyright. And users might modify the files for reasons other than avoidance; they may simply want to make the objects more aesthetically pleasing. Users will not be the only ones trying to game a database system. Reports have arisen of copyright owners misusing the DMCA takedown procedures,[31] and patent owners may similarly overreach by uploading multiple files, some of which arguably are not in the scope of the patent. Others could upload files to the database that are not protected by patents or other IP, either out of ill motives or lack of legal sophistication.[32] Although the system will not be perfect, it should help facilitate a valuable service from 3D print shops.

In sum, a patent claim drawn toward a physical object is infringed whenever someone 3D prints the object. This threat of liability brings genuine concerns for patent holders, individuals who 3D print, and 3D print shops. Accommodating all the legitimate concerns will be no easy task. It appears that a limited exemption for individuals and a limited safe harbor for 3D print shops would best balance the competing interests, though lawmakers should be wary of eviscerating the value of patents without due consideration. Chapter 10 takes up a deeper analysis of the patent system's role in innovation and provides a framework to further analyze the merits of these proposals.

Thus far we have considered only instances of tangibly printing the patented object. What about making a DMF of the patented object – will that infringe a claim to a tangible object? Under the doctrine of *literal* infringement, an accused device must have each and every element recited in the claim and the elements must be arranged in the same way.[33] Because a digital object is different from a tangible object, there would be no literal infringement.

---

[31] Jennifer M. Urban & Laura Quilter, *Efficient Process or "Chilling Effects"? Takedown Notices Under Section 512 of the Digital Millennium Copyright Act*, 22 SANTA CLARA COMPUTER & HIGH TECH. L.J. 621, 681–88 (2006); *Takedown Hall of Shame*, ELECTRONIC FRONTIER FOUNDATION, www.eff.org/takedowns. Of course, abuses can run both directions. *See* Peter S. Menell, *Jumping the Grooveshark: A Case Study in DMCA Safe Harbor Abuse*, available at https://ssrn.com/abstract=1975579.

[32] *Cf.* Michael Weinberg, *What's the Deal with Copyright and 3D Printing?*, PUBLIC KNOWLEDGE 7–8 (Jan. 2013), www.publicknowledge.org/news-blog/blogs/whats-the-deal-with-copyright-and-3d-printing (discussing a legally unsophisticated individual's probably erroneous DMCA takedown request based on a 3D printable file).

[33] *See, e.g.*, Festo Corp. v. Shoketsu Kinzoku Kogyo Kabushiki Co., 535 U.S. 722, 732 (2002).

B. DIRECT INFRINGEMENT UNDER THE DOCTRINE OF EQUIVALENTS

Although liability clearly attaches when someone physically prints a patented object, patent holders would prefer to stop the digital precursor to the tangible object. Indirect infringement theories, discussed in Chapter 6, can provide patent holders with power to stop some infringement, but they have significant drawbacks. Consequently, patent holders will strive to develop direct infringement theories against DMFs even when their patent claims are directed to a physical device.[34] These theories will be novel, but precursors to them can be found in existing legal precedent.

The first option is to assert infringement under the doctrine of equivalents, which is an exception to the strict rule of literal infringement, which requires every limitation from the claim to be present in the accused device.[35] The rigidity of literal infringement can lead to perceived injustice if a competitor can make minor changes to a device and avoid infringement. The doctrine of equivalents states that modifications will still infringe if the differences between the patent claim and the accused device are insubstantial.[36] In addition, the doctrine allows a patent to capture technologies that arise after the patent's issuance, which can serve as substitutes for elements claimed in the patent.[37]

Under the insubstantial differences test, a patentee could argue that a DMF is equivalent to the tangible object. The initial reaction to this assertion might be incredulousness, because the doctrine of equivalents is typically applied where a competitor has substituted one component of a patented device for a different component (e.g., a screw in place of a nail). It does not generally allow a patent holder to prevent a competitor from making, using, or selling something categorically different from what is claimed.

And yet, in a world with mature 3D printing technology, how different is a DMF from the tangible object? Of course, the file does not have the same functionality as the object. But the doctrine of equivalents is a flexible doctrine that seeks to maintain the value of a patent in the face of technological

---

[34]   Many patents will not have claims directed to digital versions of objects because they issued before most people were aware of the threat of DMF-based infringement. In addition, as will be seen, even claims to DMFs have limited enforcement power.

[35]   *See, e.g.,* Festo, 535 U.S. at 732.

[36]   *Id.;* Actavis UK Limited v. Eli Lilly & Co. [2017] UKSC 48; Protocol on the Interpretation of Article 69 of The European Patent Convention, EUROPEAN PATENT OFFICE art. 2 (1973), *available at* www.epo.org/law-practice/legal-texts/html/epc/2016/e/ma2a.html.

[37]   *See* Christopher A. Cotropia, *"After-Arising" Technologies and Tailoring Patent Scope,* 61 N.Y. U. ANN. SURV. AM. L. 151, 174–75 (2005).

change.[38] If making the object is a trivial push of a button, and patentees cannot otherwise effectively protect against the proliferation of DMFs, perhaps the digital version would be considered insubstantially different from its tangible counterpart.[39] This is especially true if we regard 3D printing as an after-arising technology.

C. A THEORY OF "DIGITAL" PATENT INFRINGEMENT

The second theory patent holders could use to combat digital versions of tangibly claimed devices is "digital patent infringement," a term coined by Professor Tim Holbrook and me in our article introducing the theory.[40] This theory bucks the historical trend that requires or assumes direct infringement must involve physical instantiations of inventions. It recognizes that digital technologies like 3D printing erode the barrier between the tangible world of atoms and the intangible world of bits and asks how patent law should react to a world where buying and selling a DMF of an object is regarded as buying or selling the physical object.

Sales & Offers to Sell

Under current doctrine, direct infringement can be conceptually divided into acts that necessarily contemplate a tangible version of the invention, such as making and using an invention, and acts that appropriate the economic value of the invention, such as selling and offering to sell.[41] Under this framework, the law need not require a physical instantiation for offers and sales of the claimed invention because the economic value of the invention can be appropriated before physicality arises.

---

[38]   *See generally* Timothy R. Holbrook, *Equivalency and Patent Law's Possession Paradox*, 23 HARV. J.L. & TECH. 1, 36–37 (2009) (arguing fairness as the most persuasive normative basis for doctrine of equivalents); Michael J. Meurer & Craig Allen Nard, *Invention, Refinement and Patent Claim Scope: A New Perspective on the Doctrine of Equivalents*, 93 GEO. L.J. 1947, 1956–60 (2005) (tracing a fairness rationale for the doctrine of equivalents).

[39]   Lucas S. Osborn, *Regulating Three-Dimensional Printing: The Converging Worlds of Bits and Atoms*, 51 SAN DIEGO L. REV. 553, 587 (2014).

[40]   Holbrook & Osborn, *supra* note 9.

[41]   Timothy R. Holbrook, *Liability for the "Threat of a Sale": Assessing Patent Infringement for Offering to Sell an Invention and Implications for the On-Sale Patentability Bar and Other Forms of Infringement*, 43 SANTA CLARA L. REV. 751, 805–15 (2003) [hereinafter *Threat of a Sale*]. Pursuant to the TRIPS Agreement each signatory country should include sales and offers to sell as directly infringing acts. *See, e.g.*, 35 U.S.C. § 271(a) ("offers to sell, or sells"); UK Patents Act § 60(1) ("disposes of, offers to dispose of").

Consider the non-patent example of an e-book. When someone buys the file for the e-book, they consider themselves as owning "the book." As 3D printing matures, society may begin similarly to regard the sale of a DMF of an object as a sale of the object. Tangibility will take a back seat to economic considerations and technological advances.

Indeed, court decisions have already begun to appreciate the economic impact of offers and sales of inventions even when no physical incarnation exists. The leading case in the United States on this point is *Transocean Offshore Deepwater Drilling, Inc. v. Maersk Contractors USA, Inc.*[42] In *Transocean*, Maersk offered to sell a yet-to-be-constructed offshore oil rig, an offer the buyer accepted.[43] The Federal Circuit held that, even without a physical rig in existence at the time of the offer and sale, the seller infringed based on the diagrams and descriptions contained in the offer to sell.[44] Moreover, the court reached its decision despite the fact that the rig ultimately delivered was based on a modified, noninfringing design to which the parties agreed after the formal offer and acceptance.[45]

The court based its decision on an economic understanding of patent infringement for sales and offers, stating that the "underlying purpose of holding someone who offers to sell liable for infringement is to prevent 'generating interest in a potential infringing product to the commercial detriment of the rightful patentee.'"[46] Because an offer to sell or sale of an item that has yet to be constructed can harm the patentee, the court allowed a claim for infringement based solely on a paper contract. It rejected the defendant's argument that "the entire apparatus must have been constructed and ready for use in order to have been sold."[47]

As the first decision in the United States to find infringement under section 271(a) based on the offer and sale of a yet-to-be-manufactured device,[48] it received a large amount of scholarly attention.[49] The focus on the commercial

---

[42] 617 F.3d 1296 (Fed. Cir. 2010).

[43] *Id.* at 1307.

[44] *Id.* at 1310 n.4.

[45] *Id.*

[46] *Id.* at 1309 (quoting 3D Sys., Inc. v. Aarotech Labs., Inc., 160 F.3d 1373, 1379 (Fed. Cir. 1998)).

[47] *Id.* at 1311.

[48] The U.S. Supreme Court analogously held that an offer to sell an unconstructed item can constitute prior art against patent applications for the same invention. Pfaff v. Wells Elecs., Inc., 525 U.S. 55, 67–68 (1998).

[49] *See, e.g.,* Daniel Harris Brean, *Asserting Patents to Combat Infringement via 3D Printing: It's No "Use,"* 23 FORDHAM INTELL. PROP. MEDIA & ENT. L.J. 771, 792–93 (2013); Holbrook & Osborn, *supra* note 9, at 1358–64; Timothy R. Holbrook, *Territoriality and Tangibility After Transocean,* 61 EMORY L.J. 1087, 1106 (2012); Melissa Y. Lerner, *You Can Run, but You Can't*

harm to the patentee by a sale or offer has important implications for the sale and offer of DMFs. An offer to sell a DMF of a patented object would directly generate "interest in a potential infringing product to the commercial detriment of the rightful patentee" because the buyer can manufacture the product with ease. The offer would also tend to cause price erosion from competition even if no one purchases the file.[50]

Additionally, an actual sale of the DMF would typically displace completely the sale of the tangible item. In fact, with societal interest in environmentally responsible, localized manufacturing, not to mention cost efficiencies to sellers, it is not difficult to imagine that centralized sales and delivery of physical objects will become antiquated for 3D printable goods. In that world, extending *Transocean*'s rationale to digital patent infringement of DMFs seems natural. It would admittedly require an extension because in *Transocean*, the offer and sale were for delivery of a tangible object.[51] But the extension is not a large one because one or both parties to a traditional sale can delegate the actual manufacture of tangible objects to a third party. In the sale of a DMF, the parties are in a sense delegating the manufacturing to a 3D printer. Manufacturing is completely commoditized; the value is in the file.[52]

Hide: The Expansion of Direct Infringement and the Evisceration of Preventive Contracting in Maersk, 93 J. PAT. & TRADEMARK OFF. SOC'Y 207, 232 (2011); Lucas S. Osborn, *The Leaky Common Law: An "Offer to Sell" as a Policy Tool in Patent Law and Beyond*, 53 SANTA CLARA L. REV. 143, 172–76, 199–200 (2013).

[50] Price erosion refers to the downward price pressure on patented goods when a competitor signals to the market that it will offer a competing (often infringing) good, since the market expects the patentee to lower its price to compete with the infringer.

[51] Though it is worth emphasizing that the tangible rig delivered was modified during manufacture to avoid infringement, but the court found liability, stating, "[t]he potentially infringing article is the rig sold in the contract, not the altered rig that Maersk USA delivered to the U.S." *Transocean*, 617 F.3d at 1311.

[52] In the context of infringement for exporting components, however, the U.S. Supreme Court has been unimpressed with claims that defendants come "close enough" to infringing. The Court has held that a sale in the United States of uncombined components of a machine was not infringement. *See* Deepsouth Packing Co. v. Laitram Corp., 406 U.S. 518, 527 (1972) ("[The patent holder's] argument that Deepsouth sells the machines – based primarily on Deepsouth's sales rhetoric and related indicia such as price – cannot carry the day unless it can be shown that Deepsouth is selling the 'patented invention.' The sales question thus resolves itself into the question of manufacture"). *Deepsouth* is discussed *infra* at notes 74–81. The Court has also been unimpressed with the ease of copying software. *See* Microsoft Corp. v. AT&T Corp., 550 U.S. 437, 450–51 (2007) ("Because it is so easy to encode software's instructions onto a medium that can be read by a computer, AT&T intimates, that extra step should not play a decisive role under § 271(f). But the extra step is what renders the software a usable, combinable part of a computer; easy or not, the copy-producing step is essential."). The *Microsoft* Court was considering a different context in several respects, including extraterritoriality concerns and the definition of the term "component," but the Court's literalism bodes ill for claims to digital patent infringement.

Some European jurisdictions also provide precursors to a digital patent infringement doctrine. Some countries are willing to find direct infringement of entire system claims based on a party supplying only a portion of the system.[53] Although supplying part of a combination normally triggers indirect infringement, courts are probably motivated by practical and fairness concerns when finding direct infringement for these divided infringement scenarios. Similar concerns suggest recognizing a doctrine of digital patent infringement, because the offeror/seller is causing harm to the patentee.

Free Files for Everyone

It is important to note a potential gap in patent holders' protection against sales and offers to sell with digital patent infringement. As seen with copyrighted music, digital copying is effortless. In addition, with 3D printing technology people who cannot access someone's file can mimic the object using a CAD program or by 3D scanning it. The low imitation costs will result in some imitators offering their DMFs for free.[54] Giving away a file does not constitute an offer to sell or a sale, but only a gift. Would a gift trigger liability as a sale or offer to sell?

In the United States, the Federal Circuit has interpreted the phrase "offer to sell" "according to the norms of traditional contractual analysis."[55] Particularly, an offer must constitute a "manifestation of willingness to enter into a bargain, so made as to justify another person in understanding that his assent to that bargain is invited and will conclude it."[56] This definition is potentially narrow on two fronts. First, U.S. courts have interpreted it to exclude most advertisements,[57] although other countries disagree or use broader phrases.[58]

---

[53] *See, e.g.*, Mario Franzoni, *The Italian Practice, in* Interpretations of Patents in Europe 164 (2006); Bundesgerichtshof [BGH] [Federal Court of Justice], BlPMZ 51, 322 (Ger.); OLG Düsseldorf, April 27, 2017, I-2 U 23/14 (Ger.); *Divided Patent Infringement in Germany*, McDermott, Will, & Emery, https://s3.amazonaws.com/documents.lexology .com/2dc6db95-4ee6-4678-9a8d-d429bafo64b4.pdf at pages 4–5.

[54] Holbrook & Osborn, *supra* note 9, at 1363–64.

[55] Rotec Indus., Inc. v. Mitsubishi Corp., 215 F.3d 1246, 1254–55 (Fed. Cir. 2000).

[56] *Id.* at 1257 (quoting Restatement (Second) of Contracts § 24 (1979)).

[57] *See, e.g.*, Holbrook, *Threat of a Sale, supra* note 41, at 791–92; Osborn, *Offer to Sell, supra* note 49.

[58] *See, e.g.*, Gerber Garment Technology Inc. v. Lectra Systems Ltd., [1995] 13 R.P.C. 383, 411–12 (Eng.) (expressing "no hesitation in rejecting" the argument that the term offer included only contract law offers, and instead interpreting it to include advertisements because such acts "disturb[] the patentee's monopoly"); Marketa Trimble, Global Patents: Limits of

Second, and more importantly, the terms "sale," "sell," and "bargain" can exclude truly donative transfers. The Federal Circuit recognized this in *HollyAnne Corp. v. TFT, Inc.*,[59] stating that "a mere offer to donate, where a donation is never made, cannot be an offer for sale" under section 271(a).[60] The court further opined, in dictum, that "[a]rguably, even numerous offers to donate could not be considered an infringing act under section 271(a) because Congress made offers to sell infringing acts and not offers to donate, despite the obvious commercial uses of a donation."[61]

Because all TRIPS signatories must include sales and offers to sell as forms of direct infringement, other countries face a similar interpretive issue. The UK statute uses the terms "dispose" and "offers to dispose,"[62] and the CPC uses "putting on the market,"[63] but it is unclear if the different wording signals a different meaning.[64] No UK decision has squarely addressed the issue, but at least one commentator notes that "doubts arise as to whether [dispose of] would extend to gifts."[65] It is interesting to note, however, that the UK Patents Act distinguishes between selling and disposing, indicating a difference in scope.[66] In other countries the statute, or its interpretation, may be more expansive.[67]

TRANSNATIONAL ENFORCEMENT § 3.3, 100 .106 (2012) (quoting OLG Düsseldorf, Dec. 21, 2006, I-2 U 58/05, GRUR-RR 2007, 261) (stating that the term offer under German law "must be understood in the economic sense and does not coincide with the legal term of a contract offer" but rather includes advertising and related commercial marketing).

[59] 199 F.3d 1304 (Fed. Cir. 1999).

[60] *Id.* at 1309. The case was decided on personal jurisdiction grounds, but the statement was likely necessary to the holding.

[61] *HollyAnne*, 199 F.3d at 1309 n.7.

[62] UK Patents Act § 60(1).

[63] Convention for the European Patent for the Common Market (Community Patent Convention), 1976 O.J. (L 17) 1, art. 25(a), http://legis.obi.gr/espacedvd/legal_texts/LAWS_E/eu_cvn01.htm.

[64] Kalman v. PCL Packaging (UK) Ltd., [1982] FSR 406 (Eng.) (stating that "dispose of" in § 60(1)(a) and the equivalent expression "putting on the market" in CPC article 29(a) (since renumbered as article 25(a)) must at least include selling, and holding that mere carriers did not themselves "dispose of" the goods that they carried). Though it has since repealed its implementation of the CPC, the United Kingdom had at one time adopted the CPC. *See* UK Patents Act § 86 (repealed 2004).

[65] CATHERINE COLSTON & KIRSTY MIDDLETON, MODERN INTELLECTUAL PROPERTY LAW 193 (2005).

[66] *See* UK Patents Act § 55(1)(a)(ii) (allowing, in certain circumstances, the government to "sell or offer to sell [another's patented product] for foreign defence purposes or for the production or supply of specified drugs and medicines, or *dispose* or offer to *dispose* of it (*otherwise than by selling it*) for any purpose whatever") (emphasis added).

[67] *See, e.g.*, Patent Act, 1995, art. 53(1)(a) (Netherlands) (listing as infringement "to make, use, put on the market or resell, hire out or *deliver* the patented product, *or otherwise deal in it in or*

An exclusion for donative transfers leaves a loophole for some actions that would otherwise constitute direct digital infringement. And, worryingly for patent holders, this loophole involves a centralized act that exposes the file to a huge audience.

There may be ways to alleviate these pressures on patent holders. For instance, a sale need not involve money. The Uniform Commercial Code in the United States defines a "sale" as "the passing of title from the seller to the buyer for a price."[68] Price, in turn, does not necessarily mean money, but includes any consideration.[69] Consideration would exist, for example, if owners of DMFs insisted that downloaders agree to contract terms, such as creative commons licenses popular with many files.[70] Courts could get creative and find consideration in more tenuous avenues, such as advertising revenue for web hosts and the likelihood of future benefits for individuals who post files without charge. Alternatively, they may enlarge the normal meaning of sale for policy reasons.[71]

Extraterritoriality

Liability for sales and offers can raise territoriality issues, because patents generally only have effect within the granting country's borders. But offers and sales can take place in one country and have effects in others. Though these concerns are important for 3D printing technology, they do not affect the technology in any unique way, and thus are not covered herein.[72]

Making & Using

In contrast to liability for selling, the normative case for creating digital patent infringement based on making or using a DMF is less clear. My hesitancy to

---

for his business") (emphasis added). Note, however, the Dutch limitation that the delivery or dealing must be "in or for his business," which may exclude nonbusiness donative transfers.

[68]   U.C.C. § 2–106 (Am. Law. Inst. & Unif. Law Comm'n 1977).

[69]   See Price, BLACK'S LAW DICTIONARY (10th ed. 2014) ("The amount of money or other consideration asked for or given in exchange for something else; the cost at which something is bought or sold"); Hudson Iron Co. v. Alger, 54 N.Y. 173, 176–78 (Ct. App. N.Y. 1873) (defining price to include more than only money).

[70]   See, e.g., Commons Licenses Explained, MAKERBOT (Dec. 11, 2015), www.makerbot.com/sto ries/news/thingiverse-creative-commons-licenses-explained/.

[71]   Cf. LifeScan Scot., Ltd. v. Shasta Techs., LLC, 734 F.3d 1361, 1374–77 (Fed. Cir. 2013) (finding patent rights exhausted under the so called first sale doctrine even though item was distributed for free).

[72]   Numerous resources exist examining the issue in both the direct and indirect infringement context. See, e.g., TRIMBLE, supra note 58; Heinz Goddar, Cross-Border Contributory Patent Infringement in Germany, 7 WASH J.L. TECH. & ARTS 135 (2011); Timothy R. Holbrook, Territoriality, supra note 49.

extend digital infringement to making or using is due to the widespread liability that would result for unintentional and unsuspecting individuals, as described in Section A of this chapter when discussing individual printing. Doctrinally, there is no case analogous to *Transocean* that involves liability without tangibility for making or using. Certainly, creating traditional blueprints of an object does not result in patent infringement.[73]

Courts might be guided by cases involving unassembled components, where a seller makes all the components but does not assemble them and leaves the final step to the buyer. The most famous U.S. case with such facts is *Deepsouth Packing Co. v. Laitram Corp.*[74] *Deepsouth* involved an accused infringer who manufactured the components of the patented invention and shipped them abroad for assembly. In a 5–4 decision, the Court concluded that the accused infringer had not "made" the invention within the United States under section 271(a) of the Patent Act.[75] The Court's majority was clear that making requires making the exact thing claimed.[76] This was despite the fact that the patent holder at the time also did not have recourse to an indirect infringement theory, because U.S. indirect infringement law requires an underlying act of direct infringement in the United States, and these machines were assembled abroad.[77]

Deepsouth gives little hope to patent holders looking to stretch the meaning of "make" to include digital patent infringement.[78] It is possible, however, to minimize *Deepsouth*'s importance. First, it was decided "in light of this Nation's historical antipathy to monopoly,"[79] by which it meant to equate patent rights with monopoly. Today's Court might have a more balanced view of patent rights. Second, the Court was concerned to limit the extraterritorial effects of patents,[80] a concern that may be less limiting in a more globalized

---

[73] *Cf.* Microsoft Corp. v. AT&T Corp., 550 U.S. 437, 450 (2007) (stating in the context of § 271(f) that a "blueprint may contain precise instructions for the construction and combination of the components of a patented device, but it is not itself a combinable component").

[74] 406 U.S. 518 (1972).

[75] *Id.* at 531.

[76] *Id.* at 528–29.

[77] Congress subsequently created direct liability for these kinds of exports under 35 U.S.C. § 271(f).

[78] It also calls into question digital patent infringement for selling, since it treated selling and making similarly. *Id.* at 527 ("[The patent holder's] argument that Deepsouth sells the machines – based primarily on Deepsouth's sales rhetoric and related indicia such as price – cannot carry the day unless it can be shown that Deepsouth is selling the 'patented invention.' The sales question thus resolves itself into the question of manufacture."). But the Court's reasoning is questionable on economic grounds, and the case preceded the addition of "offer to sell" as an act of direct infringement.

[79] *Id.* at 530.

[80] *Id.* at 531.

economy. Finally, and most importantly, Congress legislatively overrode *Deepsouth* by enacting section 271(f), though of course that statute only proves that Congress desired liability for exports when all the requirements for indirect infringement, including intent to infringe, were otherwise met.[81]

Intriguingly, the Federal Circuit distinguished *Deepsouth* over a decade later in *Paper Converting Machine Co. v. Magna-Graphics Corp.*[82] That case dealt not with export of components, but with supplying in the United States unassembled components prior to the patent's expiration.[83] Relying on this distinction and that the accused infringer *tested* the components before shipping them, the Federal Circuit concluded that the activity constituted infringement for "using" (but not making) and distinguished *Deepsouth* as being limited to "making" and the extraterritorial issue.[84] *Paper Converting* was controversial from the start, and its attempted distinction from *Deepsouth* was and is unsatisfying.[85] Accordingly, courts have since marginalized it.[86] Its emphasis on using rather than making limits its usefulness in the digital context, but it is precedent patent holders can point to.

Normatively, this chapter has already suggested how widespread infringement by individuals for actual printing might be problematic. This problem would increase if direct liability attached to files. In addition, if making a file were an act of direct infringement, intermediaries that merely host DMFs might face liability similar to, but in some ways greater than, that of the 3D print shops. Even though users upload the files, depending on the architecture, the website may make copies of them. These host sites might wither in the face of high liability exposure. Even if litigation exposure is justified when sites commercialize DMFs through sales (a contention not free from doubt), it is less defensible when they passively host DMFs. For these reasons, it may be better policy to avoid creating liability based on merely making or using a file. Alternatively, safe harbors similar to those discussed for print shops should be adopted.

---

[81] *See* 35 U.S.C. §271(f).

[82] 745 F.2d 11 (Fed. Cir. 1984).

[83] *Id.* at 15–16.

[84] *Id.* at 16–20.

[85] *See, e.g.,* J. Dwyer Murphy, Case Note, Paper Converting Machine Company v. Magna-Graphics Corporation: *Increased Protection Against Making and Using Combination Patents*, 34 Am. U. L. Rev. 761, 773–78 (1985).

[86] *See* Joy Techs., Inc. v. Flakt, Inc., 6 F.3d 770, 775–76 (Fed. Cir. 1993) (concluding that *Paper Converting* is inapplicable to method claims); De Graffenried v. United States, 25 Cl. Ct. 209, 214 (1992); Conner Peripherals, Inc. v. W. Digital Corp., No. C-93-20117-RMW-EAI, 1993 WL 645932, at *12 (N.D. Cal. Aug. 16, 1993) (noting that the narrow purpose of *Paper Converting* was to preserve the patent term).

An additional consideration that might militate against creating liability for making or using files is the beneficial effects of tinkering with and designing around patented products.[87] In some contexts, studying or manipulating a DMF of an invention would allow a follow-on innovator to learn about, test, and design around a patented object.[88] Unlike other countries, the United States has an extremely limited experimental use exception, and fear of liability might prevent such digital uses.[89]

D. DIRECT INFRINGEMENT OF A CLAIM TO A DMF

Section C considered the scenario where a patent claim covered only the tangible embodiment of the patented device. In the past, most patent holders were unaware of 3D printing technology and did not draft patent claims with it in mind. At a minimum, therefore, the digital patent infringement theory discussed above can serve as a bridge for patent holders until they begin to obtain claims to digital versions of their tangible inventions.

But recall from Chapter 4 that a patent claim to a machine-instruction file constitutes patentable subject matter, but a claim to a surface-mesh file does not. The inability to obtain a claim to a surface-mesh file limits the patentee's ability to stop the format most commonly transferred and sold. As the following analysis shows, patent claims to machine-instruction files may not offer patentees much benefit above a claim to the tangible object. So, if patentees cannot obtain patent claims to surface-mesh files, a digital patent infringement theory may play a vital role for innovation policy.

Patent Claim to a Machine-Instruction (Gcode) File

A machine-instruction file is a direct precursor to actual printing, so a patent claim to that format raises virtually all the same issues as a claim to the tangible object. There is no need, therefore, to rehash this chapter's analysis. In short, if

---

[87] *See* State Indus., Inc. v. A.O. Smith Corp., 751 F.2d 1226, 1236 (Fed. Cir. 1985) ("One of the benefits of a patent system is its so-called 'negative incentive' to 'design around' a competitor's products, even when they are patented, thus bringing a steady flow of innovations to the marketplace.").

[88] *See* B. Thomas Watson, *Carbons into Bytes: Patented Chemical Compound Protection in the Virtual World*, 12 DUKE L. & TECH. REV. 25, 28–29 (2014) (describing the use of molecular modeling to avoid infringing a patent to a chemical).

[89] *Cf.* Evans Misati & Kiyoshi Adachi, *The Research and Experimentation Exceptions in Patent Law: Jurisdictional Variations and the WIPO Development Agenda*, INT'L CTR. FOR TRADE AND SUSTAINABLE DEV. (2010), http://unctad.org/en/Docs/iprs_in20102_en.pdf.

a patent contains a claim to a machine-instruction file, anyone who makes the file infringes the claim. But users do not typically trade in the machine-instruction format because it is specific to a given 3D printer's settings. Generally, the only people who would make that format are those who are about to actually print it on their own printer.

Instead, people buy and sell surface-mesh files. Everyone trading in the surface-mesh file format would not be guilty of directly infringing a claim to a machine-instruction format. That is, not unless a court were to consider a variation on the theory of digital patent infringement or to regard machine-instruction files as equivalents.

Given how similar a surface-mesh file and a machine-instruction file of the same object are, it would be correspondingly easier to regard the two as substantially similar under the doctrine of equivalents. Further, converting surface-mesh files into machine-instruction files can be easy,[90] suggesting they are functionally equivalent from the skilled user's perspective. On the other hand, at a more granular level, the technical function of the two files is substantially different, with one describing only surface characteristics and the other containing precise movement instructions for a 3D printer. Thus, as is generally the case with equivalents, whether the file formats would be regarded as equivalents depends in large part on the granularity of the test used.[91]

Given the ease with which file types can be converted, a judge might also be more willing to apply a theory of digital patent infringement. Refusing to recognize infringement on the basis of an easily interchangeable file format seems to enthrone form over function. Then again, the Supreme Court in the United States has taken a highly formalistic view toward infringement issues.[92]

---

[90] Though with more complex objects, skilled personnel often must manually perfect the machine-instruction file. *See, e.g.,* Dibya Chakravorty, *2018 3D Printer G-Code Commands – 2019 Programming,* ALL3DP (Feb. 22, 2019), https://all3dp.com/g-code-tutorial-3d-printer-gcode-commands/.

[91] The United States uses at least two tests, one being the general insubstantial differences test, and the other being the more granular function-way-result test. Warner-Jenkinson Co. v. Hilton Davis Chem. Co., 520 U.S. 17, 39–40 (1997). Each is typically applied on an element-by-element basis, making wholesale comparisons of files atypical. The function-way-result test asks whether the alleged equivalent has substantially the same function, performs the function in substantially the same way, to achieve substantially the same result. *Id.* Under this test, the surface-mesh file would likely not qualify as an equivalent of the machine-instruction file because at least the function and the result are different.

[92] *See supra* note 52 (discussing the *Deepsouth* and *Microsoft* decisions).

Patent Claim to a Surface-Mesh (STL) File

As discussed in Chapter 4, surface-mesh files likely do not constitute patentable subject matter. But if they did, they would dramatically increase the amount of direct infringement. Many concerns that arise from direct infringement of claims to tangible objects have corollaries here, albeit in magnified form, so discussion will be brief. The amount of unintentional infringement would increase to include all who simply create, sell,[93] use, or download a surface-mesh file. If these claims were allowable, there would be no need for a digital infringement theory because traditional infringement theories would capture those who deal in surface-mesh files. The amount of accidental infringement arising in such a regime would counsel all the more urgently for an exception like the private, noncommercial use exception.

This type of claim would dramatically impact 3D file repositories that host files but do not print them on behalf of others. Depending on the website's architecture, they might become direct infringers for making the files they store, and thus face huge liability exposure.[94] As with the 3D print shops described above, repositories in the United States would likely need some sort of safe harbor to allow their business model to continue. Unlike the United States, Europe already provides for a safe harbor with its e-Commerce Directive.[95] Article 14 of the Directive generally provides safe harbor for hosting services that do not know of infringing material or that remove infringing material about which they know. Although the Directive is primarily applied in the context of copyright infringement, its wording is neutral as to IP and thus can apply to patents as well.

One final note. In the past, commentators have suggested that patent claims to files transferable over the Internet raise the potential for internet service providers to be found liable for direct infringement for making or importing the patented file.[96] Some of these concerns represent a misunderstanding of how internet file transfers occur. In general, files are broken into small packets

[93] In the United States, the computer-readable-medium claim would not be directly infringed by a sale or offer of a digital download. Signal claims, however, would result in direct infringement for digital downloads. *See supra* Chapter 4.

[94] It may be that the users who upload the files make the copies, but it is not clear. Peer-to-peer architecture could remove a centralized actor from the equation.

[95] European Parliament & Council Directive 2000/31 on Certain Legal Aspects of Information Society Services, in Particular Electronic Commerce, in the Internal Market, 2000 O.J. (L 178) 1 (EC) art. 14 [hereinafter e-Commerce Directive].

[96] *See, e.g.*, Stephen G. Kunin & Bradley D. Lytle, *Patent Eligibility of Signal Claims*, 87 J. PAT. & TRADEMARK OFF. SOC'Y 991, 1002 (2005) ("A major concern with propagated signal claims is the effect on 'innocent infringers' such as ISPs and telecommunications companies."); Keith E. Witek, *Software Patent Infringement on the Internet and on Modern Computer*

(on the order of 1.5KB), and each individual piece is sent over the Internet and is not reassembled until it reaches the destination computer.[97] Thus, the ISP with its equipment does not make or use the complete invention, it only makes and sends individual, non-assembled pieces. Sending all the components that make up an invention can incur liability in the United States under section 271 (f)(1), but that requires knowledge and intent, which ISPs generally will not have.[98]

E. CONCLUSION

This chapter demonstrates that current direct infringement doctrine might make very few people happy where 3D printable goods are involved. On one side, individuals and 3D print shops who accidentally infringe may be exposed to legal costs that are wildly out of proportion to any harm they have done. One the other side, patent holders will be unable to capture as direct infringers the actors who are at the root of any infringement: the distributors of surface-mesh files. This chapter included some recommendations about how to address these concerns. But before thinking further about changes in the law, the doctrine of indirect infringement must be considered to see whether it fills some of the protection gaps. Chapter 6 addresses this issue.

Systems – Who Is Liable for Damages?, 14 SANTA CLARA HIGH TECH. L.J. 303, 337 (1998) (noting that serial copies may constitute direct infringement under 35 U.S.C. § 271(f)).

[97] *See, e.g.,* Witek, *supra* note 96, at 351–56; Rus Shuler, *How Does the Internet Work?*, POMEROY IT SOLUTIONS (last updated 2002), https://web.stanford.edu/class/msande91si/www-spr04/re adings/week1/InternetWhitepaper.htm.

[98] *See* Witek, *supra* note 96, at 337, 380–81.

6

Patents – Indirect Infringement and Intermediaries

Chapter Outline:

This chapter analyzes patent infringement liability based on an indirect infringement theory. Indirect infringement is generally helpful to capture centralized actors who assist others who are directly infringing. The direct infringers may be too difficult to discover, too diffuse to efficiently sue, or too impecunious to pay any judgment.[1] The hallmark of indirect infringement is assisting others in infringing. "Assistance" could theoretically encompass a potentially large amount of activity. Anyone who sells a 3D printer has in one sense assisted a buyer who printed an infringing article. So too has the 3D printing "ink" maker, the electricity provider that helped power the 3D printer, and the shipping company that transported the 3D printer from the manufacturer. But holding all these attenuated actors liable would be absurd, so the law has several ways to cabin the scope of liability.

The law essentially requires culpability on the part of the indirect infringer. For technologies, like 3D printers, which have clear noninfringing uses, the law does not want to hamper technological development by imposing liability on manufacturers for uses over which they have no control. Unlike with the strict liability of direct infringement, the law of many jurisdictions requires the indirect infringer to have knowledge of the patent and to knowingly take actions that assist others in infringement. Further, general knowledge that downstream infringement will occur is generally not sufficient; knowledge must be specific.

---

[1] Although these concerns predate the digital age, it certainly exacerbates them. *See* Wallace v. Holmes, 29 F. Cas. 74, 80 (C.C.D. Conn. 1871) (noting that without a claim for indirect infringement, "the complainants would be driven to the task of searching out the individual purchasers for use who actually place the chimney on the burner and use it – a consequence which, considering the small value of each separate lamp, and the trouble and expense of prosecution, would make the complainants helpless and remediless.").

Who indirectly infringes a patent depends on the claims in the patent. If the patent claim is to a tangible object, those who supply DMFs may be liable as indirect infringers because they are assisting those who print the object, which is an act of direct infringement. Similarly, if the patent claim is to a machine-instruction file, those who provide surface-mesh or design files can be liable as indirect infringers. Finally, if the patent claim is to a surface-mesh file, almost all the relevant actors will be direct infringers, obviating the need for indirect infringement theories.

Indirect infringers come in all shapes and sizes, but two of the most common with 3D printing technology will be website repositories that host files for others to download and DMF file creators who share those files with others. This group of accused infringers could include individuals who have comparatively little business knowledge, legal experience, and money. Or they could be businesses with more knowledge, experience, and money, though this will vary with the size of the business.

A. INDIRECT INFRINGEMENT IN THE UNITED STATES

In the United States, indirect infringement is codified and separated into two categories. The first, active inducement under Section 271(b), makes liability attach to "[w]hoever actively induces infringement of a patent."[2] Though the statute's wording is succinct, the common law has supplied several details. First, the Supreme Court interprets the statute as requiring "some intent,"[3] which in turn requires "knowledge that the induced acts constitute patent infringement."[4] To have knowledge that actions constitute patent infringement, one must know of, or be willfully blind to, the existence of a specific patent.[5] The Court has explained that willful blindness is more culpable than negligence or even recklessness. It requires at least that "(1) the defendant must subjectively believe that there is a high probability that a fact exists and (2) the defendant must take deliberate actions to avoid learning of that fact."[6] Finally, "[t]he addition of the adverb 'actively' suggests that the inducement must involve the taking of affirmative steps to bring about the desired result."[7] The Supreme Court has not elaborated much on the term "actively."

---

[2] 35 U.S.C. § 271(b).
[3] Global-Tech Appliances, Inc. v. SEB S.A., 563 U.S. 754, 760 (2011) (quoting 35 U.S.C. § 271(b)).
[4] *Id.* at 766.
[5] *Id.* at 765–68.
[6] *Id.* at 769.
[7] *Id.* at 760.

The second kind of statutory indirect infringement in the United States is labeled "contributory" infringement in section 271(c).[8] The statute fixes a much more specific and unique meaning to the term contributory infringement when compared to general tort law. The section provides:

> Whoever offers to sell or sells within the United States or imports into the United States a component of a patented machine, manufacture, combination or composition, or a material or apparatus for use in practicing a patented process, constituting a material part of the invention, knowing the same to be especially made or especially adapted for use in an infringement of such patent, and not a staple article or commodity of commerce suitable for substantial noninfringing use, shall be liable as a contributory infringer.[9]

Breaking down this lengthy statute reveals several elements. First, liability is limited only to selling, offering to sell, or importing in the United States. Thus, making and using components does not trigger contributory infringement. Second, supplying a component triggers liability, but the component must (1) be a material part of the invention and (2) not have substantial noninfringing use. Finally, the accused must know that the component is "especially made or especially adapted for use in an infringement of such patent."[10] As with inducement, knowledge means knowing "that the combination for which [the] component was especially designed was both patented and infringing."[11]

Knowledge & Intent

The knowledge/intent requirement under both types of indirect infringement represents a significant hurdle for patent owners. People have no obligation to search for patents owned by others, and even a patentee's marking of its patented products with the relevant patent number(s) does not trigger any knowledge on the part of third parties[12] (unless, presumably, they see the markings).[13] So, the onus is generally on the patentee specifically and directly to notify the accused party of patents it believes are infringed.

---

[8]   35 U.S.C. § 271(c).

[9]   *Id.*

[10]   Aro Mfg. Co. v. Convertible Top Replacement Co., 377 U.S. 476, 487 (1964).

[11]   *Id.* at 488.

[12]   *See, e.g.,* Mendenhall v. Astec Indus., Inc., 14 U.S.P.Q.2d 1134, 1137 (E.D. Tenn. 1988) ("While [the patentee] argued vigorously ... that the word 'knowingly' as used in [Section 271(c)] included constructive knowledge of the patent, it was unable to produce any case law to support that position."), *aff'd per curium,* 891 F.2d 299 (Fed. Cir. 1989).

[13]   Patent marking remains important for patent holders. It is a prerequisite to obtaining damages unless the infringer has actual notice of the patent. 35 U.S.C. § 287(a). And of course, if an

The notice requirement insulates a lot of activity that would otherwise be indirect infringement. Individuals who create or copy DMFs and websites that host such files may have no idea that they are covered by patents. Unlike copyrighted music, where it could be assumed that any popular music was covered by a copyright, it is difficult to discover if a particular object is patented. Even if someone wanted to find out if a file would print a patented object, searching for patents is a highly specialized task requiring significant legal knowledge. The burden on the searcher would be great, especially where the actor is an individual with few resources or a website repository that hosts numerous files.

Patentees, therefore, will need to police activities closely and send notice letters to anyone implicating their rights. But the policing burden will be immense in a 3D printing world. Traditionally, patentees were on the lookout for a single large, wealthy actor who was aiding another in mass-producing infringing goods.[14] In the 3D printing era, potential indirect infringers include countless websites and individuals. From the patentee's perspective, infringement litigation will be transformed from a single, pitched battle into guerrilla warfare.

Moreover, patent holders can never guess where an infringing file might appear, and thus may have to continuously update their searches. Without automation, the costs of such searching would overwhelm them. Patent holders could try to anticipate infringement and pre-emptively send letters to notify popular websites of their patent portfolios, leaving it to the websites to police for infringing files. But this strategy is unlikely to constitute effective notice. In the direct infringement context where the patented products are not marked, courts have required patent holders to point to a specific accused product.[15] Specifying a product currently being infringed would seem even more important for indirect infringement cases where product marking is not sufficient notice.[16]

---

accused indirect infringer is actually aware of the marking, it will constitute notice. *Cf.* Global-Tech Appliances, Inc. v. SEB S.A., 563 U.S. 754, 770–71 (2011) (holding that the indirect infringer was willfully blind to patent when, inter alia, it purposely chose to copy an overseas version of patented product to avoid seeing U.S. patent marking).

[14] *See* Jason A. Rantanen, *An Objective View of Fault in Patent Infringement*, 60 AM. U. L. REV. 1575, 1580 (2011) ("Accused inducers of infringement are not individuals and small companies but giant, multi-national corporations.").

[15] Gart v. Logitech, Inc., 254 F.3d 1334, 1345 (Fed. Cir. 2001) (requiring "affirmative communication [to the alleged infringer] of a specific charge of infringement by a specific accused product or device") (internal citation omitted); Amsted Indus. Inc., v. Buckeye Steel Castings Co., 24 F.3d 178, 187 (Fed. Cir. 1994) (stating that mere "notice of the patent's existence or ownership" is not "notice of the infringement").

[16] *Cf.* Fujitsu Ltd. v. Netgear, Inc., 620 F.3d 1321, 1331–32 (Fed. Cir. 2010) (discussing but not relying on district court's use of § 287(a) cases to inform adequate notice standard for indirect infringement). Just as marking is insufficient, letters should be insufficient because the

Once notice is provided, the accused presumably has some obligation to study the patent. Refusing to study it could amount to willful blindness. But knowledge of the patent by itself is not enough because the Supreme Court has made clear that a person cannot be liable if "he did not know the acts were infringing."[17] If an accused party studies a patent and in good faith concludes it does not infringe, it shields itself from indirect liability.[18] (In contrast, the Court has held that a good faith belief in the patent's invalidity does not shield the actor from indirect liability.)[19]

Not many cases have explored how a party can form a good faith belief of noninfringement. The gold standard is to obtain a competent opinion from a patent lawyer detailing why the accused product does not infringe.[20] Opinions of counsel, however, are expensive, and their costs can hurt small businesses and individuals.[21] Deep-pocketed web repositories may be able to invest in a few of them but may choose to save the money and instead remove the accused file. Less wealthy repositories and individuals, though, are unlikely to be able to afford an opinion, and may seek less expensive substitutes.

What besides a formal opinion of counsel will insulate someone from indirect infringement? This question has not often arisen in patent litigation, but in the willful infringement context courts are skeptical when in-house counsel provide opinions[22] or when oral, rather than written, opinions are relied upon.[23] Courts are even more skeptical when sophisticated businesses

---

recipient would quickly be overwhelmed by letters from numerous patent holders regarding potentially thousands of patents.

[17] *Commil USA, LLC v. Cisco Sys., Inc.*, 135 S. Ct. 1920, 1928 (2015).

[18] *Global-Tech Appliances, Inc. v. SEB S.A.*, 563 U.S. 754, 766 (2011).

[19] *Commil USA, LLC*, 135 S. Ct. at 1928. Commentators have criticized the Court's differential treatment of invalidity and noninfringement defenses. Timothy R. Holbrook, *The Supreme Court's Quiet Revolution in Induced Patent Infringement*, 91 NOTRE DAME L. REV. 1007, 1033–37 (2016).

[20] *Cf.* Bettcher Indus., Inc. v. Bunzl USA, Inc., 661 F.3d 629, 649 (Fed. Cir. 2011) (finding opinion of counsel regarding noninfringement "admissible, at least with respect to [defendant's] state of mind and its bearing on indirect infringement").

[21] *See* Halo Elecs., Inc. v. Pulse Elecs., Inc., 136 S. Ct. 1923, 1936 (2016) (Breyer, J., concurring) ("It may well be expensive to obtain an opinion of counsel ... Such costs can prevent an innovator from getting a small business up and running.").

[22] *See, e.g.*, Underwater Devices Inc. v. Morrison-Knudsen Co., 717 F.2d 1380, 1390 (Fed. Cir. 1983) ("[Defendant] knew that the attorney from whom it sought advice was its own in-house counsel. While this fact alone does not demonstrate [defendant's] lack of good faith, it is a fact to be weighed.") (citations omitted).

[23] Omega Patents, LLC v. CalAmp Corp., No. 6:13-cv-1950-Orl-40DCI, 2017 U.S. Dist. LEXIS 55846, at *15 (M.D. Fla. Apr. 6, 2017) (stating that it was "incomprehensible that counsel would refrain from issuing a written opinion of noninfringement").

rely on non-attorneys.[24] But reliance on nonlawyers is not foreclosed.[25] Furthermore, where small businesses or individuals are concerned, some members of the Supreme Court have indicated that such skepticism is not always warranted, stating, "an owner of a small firm, or a scientist, engineer, or technician working there, might, without being 'wanton' or 'reckless,' reasonably determine that its product does not infringe a particular patent, or that that patent is probably invalid."[26]

Courts may follow Justice Breyer's lead and adopt a sliding standard based on the accused's resources. While there is no excuse for ignoring patent assertions or making perfunctory inquiries, perhaps a court would be satisfied if an individual or small business in good faith studies the patent closely, refers to freely available internet sources regarding patent law, and concludes that it does not infringe the patent. One problem with this approach is that patent law is so esoteric that laypeople are probably destined to make many serious errors in analysis.[27] Such flexibility may appear fair to the good faith actor but would be open to abuse by less scrupulous individuals who could feign effort. Yet the risk of a modicum of abuse may be worth the price of allowing small businesses and individuals to continue in their entrepreneurial pursuits.[28]

In the end, many accused infringers may decide it is easier simply to remove accused files than face the time, effort, and expense of investigating the accusation. Removal of offending files is a good thing, but that assumes all accusatory letters are in good faith. In the copyright arena there have been

---

[24] *See, e.g.,* CPG Prods. Corp. v. Pegasus Luggage, Inc., 776 F.2d 1007, 1014–15 (Fed. Cir. 1985) (finding advice of noninfringement by corporate president, who was "not a lawyer and admittedly [had] little knowledge of patent law," did not insulate accused from willful infringement); Arctic Cat Inc. v. Bombardier Recreational Prods., Inc., 198 F. Supp. 3d 1343, 1348 (S.D. Fla. 2016) (discussing unfavorably a one-sentence opinion given by a non-attorney patent agent); Dominion Res. Inc. v. Alstom Grid, Inc., No. 15–224, 2016 WL 5674713, at *22 (E.D. Pa. Oct. 3, 2016) (refusing to find a good faith belief in noninfringement because the belief was "based entirely on the opinion of people without expertise in reading patent claims."), *rev'd-in-part on other grounds,* 725 Fed. Appx. 980 (Fed. Cir. 2018).

[25] *See, e.g.,* Nickson Indus., Inc. v. Rol Mfg. Co., 847 F.2d 795, 800 (Fed. Cir. 1988) (crediting nonlawyer's opinion); Rolls-Royce Ltd. v. GTE Valeron Corp., 800 F.2d 1101, 1109–10 (Fed. Cir. 1986) (same).

[26] Halo Elecs., Inc. v. Pulse Elecs., Inc., 136 S. Ct. 1923, 1936 (2016) (Breyer, J., concurring). The *Halo* case involved willful infringement, not indirect infringement, but many of the concerns are the same. Though Chapter 5 did not explore the issue, whether to enhance baseline damages for direct or indirect infringement based on willful infringement under 35 U.S.C. § 285 raises many of the same issues.

[27] *See* Timothy R. Holbrook & Lucas S. Osborn, *Digital Patent Infringement in an Era of 3D Printing,* 48 U.C. Davis L. Rev. 1319, 1341 (2015).

[28] *Cf. Halo Elecs., Inc.,* 136 S. Ct. at 1937–38 (Breyer, J., concurring) (noting that excessive patent infringement assertions can stifle innovation).

criticisms of overreaching takedown notices, and similar effects could occur with patents.[29] At the same time, state laws now offer protections against bad faith assertions of patent infringement,[30] which will help deter patentees from overreaching.

Requirement for Direct Infringement

In the United States, a claim for indirect infringement can only succeed if there is some provable underlying direct infringement.[31] The patentee will therefore need to prove that someone downloaded or streamed the accused's file and actually printed it. This will cause patentees headaches, because finding out who has downloaded a file can involve significant time and effort.[32] Additionally, if direct infringement requires actually printing the file, the patentee will need to prove this action occurred.[33] This might be exceptionally challenging if there are multiple sources for the same file and it is not easy to trace a particular direct infringement back to a particular source.

Aside from the difficulty of proving underlying direct infringement, there is the obvious disadvantage of having to wait for it to occur. An uploader of the DMF is not liable the moment the file is uploaded; liability only attaches once the file is printed (where the claim requires a tangible machine). When files can be copied and shared quickly and costlessly, delays in forcing a file to be removed can be harmful. Although nothing prevents a patentee from drafting a letter demanding removal before the direct infringement occurs, the letter should be worded to reflect the law accurately.

---

[29] See Jennifer M. Urban & Laura Quilter, *Efficient Process or "Chilling Effects"? Takedown Notices Under Section 512 of the Digital Millennium Copyright Act*, 22 SANTA CLARA COMPUTER & HIGH TECH. L.J. 621, 681–88 (2006).

[30] *See* Paul R. Gugliuzza, *Patent Trolls and Preemption*, 101 VA. L. REV. 1579, 1590–1600 (2015).

[31] Limelight Networks, Inc. v. Akamai Techs., Inc., 134 S. Ct. 2111, 2115 (2014); Aro Mfg. Co. v. Convertible Top Replacement Co., 365 U.S. 336, 341 (1961) ("[T]here can be no contributory infringement in the absence of a direct infringement.").

[32] *Cf.* Sean B. Karunaratne, Note, *The Case Against Combating BitTorrent Piracy Through Mass John Doe Copyright Infringement Lawsuits*, 111 MICH. L. REV. 283, 286–88 (2012) (describing the copyright litigation process of obtaining IP addresses, filing "John Doe" lawsuits based on the addresses, and then seeking subpoenas to discover the person behind the IP address).

[33] In some instances, circumstantial evidence of direct infringement will suffice. Linear Tech. Corp. v. Impala Linear Corp., 379 F.3d 1311, 1326–27 (Fed. Cir. 2004) (vacating summary judgment in part based on circumstantial evidence of direct infringement). But the law is fuzzy as to what evidence suffices. *See* Holbrook & Osborn, *supra* note 27, at 1336–37.

Active Inducement

Inducement under section 271(b) requires that the inducement is "active," which "suggests that the inducement must involve the taking of affirmative steps to bring about the desired result."[34] What constitutes the affirmative steps? At a minimum the inducer needs to have transferred or hosted the DMF with a specific intent that it be printed.[35] But is a further affirmative step required? For example, it is possible that someone might upload or host a file for others to view, but not print. It seems fair to presume in general, though, that anyone who hosts or uploads a file intends that others print it. It should be possible, however, for that presumption to be rebutted where a different intent is clearly indicated.[36]

Common sense and case law suggest that supplying DMFs can constitute active inducement where the other elements are met. By analogy, courts have held that providing design or engineering work for another may constitute active inducement.[37] With mature 3D printing technology, there will be little more one can do to help another person infringe than to supply a DMF. Going one small step further – pushing the print button for the person – would constitute direct infringement.

Offer to Sell/Dispose Issue Under Section 271(c)

Shifting from inducement to contributory infringement, it is important to note that contributory infringement, unlike inducement, is only triggered by offers

---

[34] Global-Tech Appliances, Inc. v. SEB S.A., 563 U.S. 754, 760 (2011).

[35] DSU Med. Corp. v. JMS Co., 471 F.3d 1293, 1306 (Fed. Cir. 2006) (en banc as to Section III.B of the opinion) (holding en banc that inducement requires that the alleged infringer knowingly induced infringement and possessed "specific intent" to encourage another's infringement).

[36] But courts should be careful against faux warnings. *Cf.* Cross Med. Prods., Inc. v. Medtronic Sofamor Danek, Inc., 424 F.3d 1293, 1312–14 (Fed. Cir. 2005) (finding a genuine issue of material fact around the accused inducer's specific intent because defendant's "field bulletins" instructed users to configure the device in a noninfringing manner, but an employee of the defendant testified that he instructed users to configure the device however "they feel comfortable," which might involve an infringing configuration); Lifescan, Inc. v. Can-Am Care Corp., 859 F. Supp. 392, 396 (N.D. Cal. 1994) (finding a genuine issue of material fact existed regarding inducement because the "fact that [the accused] provides the warning [against configuring in an infringing manner] to consumers does not equate with the fact that the consumers, in fact, understand and heed the warning.").

[37] *See* Water Techs. Corp. v. Calco, Ltd., 850 F.2d 660, 668–69 (Fed. Cir. 1988) (finding intent based, inter alia, on defendant "having given all of the resin formulas to Calco, helped Calco make the infringing resins, and prepared consumer use instructions."); Nat'l Tractor Pullers Ass'n v. Watkins, 205 U.S.P.Q. 892 (N.D. Ill. 1980) (finding that adoption by national association of rules for tractor pulling contests requiring use of patented invention qualified as inducement); Baut v. Pethick Constr. Co., 262 F. Supp. 350 (M.D. Pa. 1966) (holding general contractor, subcontractor, and architect all liable for the infringement).

to sell, sales, or imports of prohibited components. As discussed in Chapter 5, an offer to sell excludes most advertisements and offers for gratuitous transfers.[38] The inability to capture donative transfers represents a potential loophole under section 271(c) just like under section 271(a).

What Is a "Component"?

Contributory infringement under section 271(c) requires a component to be sold, offered, or imported. Normally, a component refers to a part that is less than the whole of the patented object, like an engine for a car. But DMFs are not tangible pieces of a finished product. Can files ever be components of an invention? Courts have answered yes, but only where the patent claims a method involving software[39] or affirmatively claims a computer with software loaded thereon.[40]

An interesting question for patentees wanting to capture DMF versions of tangible objects is whether a DMF of the entire object might be considered a "component" of the printed version. This argument faces steep challenges, not least that it goes against the normal meaning of the term component. In addition, the Supreme Court has seemingly foreclosed this argument in a case involving a master copy of a piece of software that was used to make numerous copies on CDs.[41] The patentee argued the master copy could be a component of the claimed computer-plus-software combination, but the Court rejected this contention because the master copy was a precursor to the copy used to install the software. The Court stated,

> A machine for making sprockets might be used by a manufacturer to produce tens of thousands of sprockets an hour. That does not make the machine a "component" of the tens of thousands of devices in which the sprockets are incorporated, at least not under any ordinary understanding of the term "component." Congress, of course, might have included within § 271(f)'s compass, for example, not only combinable "components" of a patented invention, but also "information, instructions, or tools from which those components readily may be generated." It did not.[42]

---

[38] *See supra* Chapter 5, notes 54–71 and accompanying text.

[39] *See* Lucent Techs., Inc. v. Gateway, Inc., 580 F.3d 1301, 1320–21 (Fed. Cir. 2009) (holding that various software products, including Microsoft Outlook, contributorily infringed a patented method concerning a calendar date-picker function).

[40] *E.g.*, Microsoft Corp. v. AT&T Corp., 550 U.S. 437, 449–51 (2007).

[41] *Id.* at 453–54. The *Microsoft* case involved 35 U.S.C. § 271(f) rather than § 271(c), but both use the term "component" in the same way and the term should be interpreted similarly in each provision.

[42] *Id.* at 451.

This dictum does not squarely address whether a DMF precursor of the entire device might be a component, because the Court was stating that a machine that makes components is not itself a component.[43] Nevertheless, the thrust of the language is not encouraging to patentees. In language even more relevant to DMFs, the Court analogized software to a blueprint and opined that "[a] blueprint may contain precise instructions for the construction and combination of the components of a patented device, but it is not itself a combinable component."[44] This language, albeit dictum, likely dooms any argument that a DMF of an object is a component of the object.

B. INDIRECT INFRINGEMENT IN EUROPE, JAPAN, AND ELSEWHERE

Countries vary in the contours of indirect infringement, but some of the basics are the same in many countries. For example, section 60(2) of the UK Patents Act, which is similar to many provisions in other European countries,[45] provides that one can be indirectly liable for patent infringement if

> he supplies or offers to supply in the United Kingdom ... with any of the means, relating to an essential element of the invention, for putting the invention into effect when he knows, or it is obvious to a reasonable person in the circumstances, that those means are suitable for putting, and are intended to put, the invention into effect in the United Kingdom.

Means and Elements

This section may at first appear to parallel U.S. law for contributory infringement where an "essential element" is roughly equivalent to a "material component." But the wording differs, potentially significantly, because the prohibited act is not supplying an essential element, it is supplying "means, relating to an essential element." It may be that the wording was chosen to ensure that indirect infringement arises when someone supplies a product to be used to perform a patented method (which, after all, is a series of intangible steps).[46]

---

[43] *See id.* at 450–51. In a 3D printing example, the machine making the component would be a 3D printer.

[44] *Id.* at 451.

[45] Most European countries have very similar infringement provisions because they are based on the 1975 Community Patent Convention. *See* Convention for the European Patent for the Common Market, *reprinted in* 1976 O.J. (No. L 17) 1.

[46] *Cf.* Marc Mimler, *3D Printing, the Internet and Patent Law – A History Repeating?*, in BIG DATA, CHALLENGES AND OPPORTUNITIES 55, 63 (2013).

That the phrase can be applied to method claims strongly suggests that the "means" need not be the same thing as the "element." It is surprising, therefore, to this author,[47] that commentators are wary of opining that DMFs can constitute "means."[48] As a matter of plain reading, the statute distinguishes between the means and an element. If one interprets "means" to refer to the exact same thing as the "element," the wording is superfluous. The better, natural reading is that the means supplied need not physically be part of the invention, whereas an element would impliedly be physically part of a patented device. This interpretation is critical for patentees who want DMFs to constitute "means" even though they are not elements of the patented invention.

Most cases involving section 60(2) have involved scenarios where the means supplied were tangible ingredients or parts of the patented combination as opposed to digital precursors of the ingredients/invention.[49] In addition, commentators point out that some courts have suggested that pure instructions or plans do not constitute means in the sense of the statute.[50] DMFs, however, differ from mere words or blueprints because they enable infringement much more directly and without human intervention. Indeed, assuming mature 3D printing technology, one might wonder what more effective means one could supply to aid someone than a DMF. Pushing a print button is far easier than assembling a kit of components.[51]

Although most cases involved tangible elements of an invention, courts have been attentive to the statute's wording. In *Actavis UK Ltd v. Eli Lilly & Co.*,[52] the Court of Appeal emphasized that the "language of section 60(2) does not require the supply of an element of the claim, but a means *relating to*

---

[47]   Who admittedly is not as familiar with patent cases in European jurisdictions as with those in the United States.

[48]   Rosa Maria Ballardini et al., *Enforcing Patent in the Era of 3D Printing*, 10 J. OF INTELL. PROP. L. PRAC. 850, 863 (2015) (presenting arguments in both directions); Simon Bradshaw et al., *The Intellectual Property Implications of Low-Cost 3D Printing*. 7 SCRIPTED 5, 27 (2010) (stating that it "is not obvious that a [DMF] counts" as the required means and stating that legislative clarification may be required); Dinusha Mendis, *"The Clone Wars": Episode 1*, EURO. INTELL. PROP. REV. 155, 161 (2013) (stating that it is "not very clear" whether a DMF would constitute the required means but ultimately concluding it could).

[49]   *Cf.* Ballardini et al., *supra* note 48, at 858. A quintessential case of indirect infringement is one in which a defendant has supplied a kit containing all the parts for the direct infringer to assemble. But a DMF is not the same thing as a kit of tangible components.

[50]   *See id.* at 858; Mimler, *supra* note 46, at 64; Geertrui Van Overwalle & Reinout Leys, *3D Printing and Patent Law: A Disruptive Technology Disrupting Patent Law?*, 48 INT'L REV. OF INTELL. PROP. & COMPETITION L. 504, 523 (2017).

[51]   For authority, the author cites his experiences assembling children's toys and IKEA furniture.

[52]   [2015] EWCA (Civ) 555, *aff'd* [2017] UKSC 48.

an essential element."[53] The patent claim at issue in *Actavis* required peme-trexed ions and sodium ions in a solution, but Actavis only supplied a solid that contained pemetrexed dipotassium, but no sodium. Actavis argued it did not supply pemetrexed ions (meaning dissolved in a solution) because it supplied a solid, and even if a third party dissolved it in water, the required sodium would be missing. The court rejected this argument, observing that the solid could be dissolved in saline, which would include the sodium ions.[54]

The case stands for the proposition that something can constitute a "means relating to an element" even if some further manipulation of the means is required to produce the claimed element. In *Actavis*, the solid chemical needed to be manipulated (dissolved) to transform into its ionic (dissolved) form. That is somewhat different from the manipulation required to turn a DMF into a tangible object, but, as a matter of the statute's wording, it can be viewed as a difference in degree.

Some commentators point to another UK case, *Menashe Business Mercantile Ltd v. William Hill Organisation Ltd*,[55] as holding that software can constitute a means under section 60(2).[56] But the case is not directly on point. First, the software was one of the explicitly claimed elements, whereas a DMF is not if the claim is to a physical object.[57] Second, the parties and court assumed without deciding that the software could be a "means."[58] The court focused instead on whether supplying the software put the invention into effect *in the United Kingdom* even though part of the system was in another country.[59] A passive acquiescence in the parties' stipulation is far from an endorsement of it. For these reasons, *Menashe* is of limited significance on the issue of DMFs as a means.

---

[53] *Id.* at [89].

[54] *Id.* at [83]. The Supreme Court specifically affirmed this point. [2017] UKSC 48 at [109]–[110].

[55] [2002] EWHC 397, *aff'd* [2002] EWCA (Civ) 1702. The Court of Appeal adopted the assumption that software could be a means but did not analyze it.

[56] *See, e.g.*, Ballardini et al., *supra* note 48, at 858 (stating that software qualified as a means in *Menashe*); Mimler, *supra* note 46, at 63 (stating that "the Court of Appeal found that software . . . could be such means").

[57] *Menashe*, EWHC 397 at [1]. Note however, that when the software was provided by CD, *see id.* at [2], the software would likely be copied from the CD and stored on the computer such that the CD would no longer be used in the system. (This can be deduced because the software could also be downloaded from the Internet. *Id.*) In that case, the CD that was supplied is left over, so to speak, and would not be continuously used in the claimed system. This would be analogous to a DMF file that is supplied as a means and is left over after printing and is not part of the claimed invention.

[58] *Id.* at [3].

[59] *Id.* at [3]–[4].

The *Menashe* decisions could, however, speak more broadly to DMFs through their flexible treatment of the statute in light of new technology. The Court of Appeal was unimpressed with the argument that the claimed system was not put into effect in the United Kingdom because the host computer was outside the country. The court stated:

> In the age that we live in, it does not matter where the host computer is situated. It could be in the United Kingdom, on a satellite, or even on the border between two countries. Its location is not important to the user of the invention nor to the claimed gaming system. In that respect, there is a real difference between the claimed gaming system and an ordinary machine. For my part I believe that it would be wrong to apply the old ideas of location to inventions of the type under consideration in this case. A person who is situated in the United Kingdom who obtains in the United Kingdom a CD and then uses his terminal to address a host computer is not bothered where the host computer is located. It is of no relevance to him, the user, nor the patentee as to whether or not it is situated in the United Kingdom.[60]

The notion of not applying "old ideas" in light of new technological realities counsels for a broader construction of "means" as applied to DMFs.

But how broadly should a court construe the means relating to an essential element when it comes to DMFs? A machine-instruction file is the means most directly related to the physical object, and it certainly aids in putting the invention into effect. But parties do not typically trade in machine-instruction files. Instead, they usually supply surface-mesh files, which are one degree further removed from the tangible object. Courts must be attentive to facts and policy as they choose whether a file format constitutes a means. For instance, dissolving a chemical was easy in *Actavis* despite the fact that its chemical structure is altered. Similarly, to the extent that technology makes the translation between DMF formats easy, surface-mesh and design files should be considered "means."

The threshold issue of DMFs as means is a pressing issue to sellers of patented, 3D printable goods. If end users can print the objects in their homes, they likely will not directly infringe based on the private, noncommercial use exception. But if DMFs cannot constitute means for indirect infringement, patent holders will also have no ability to stop the true source and enabler of the excused infringement. In other words, their patents may be commercially worthless. To avoid decimating patent rights, courts should regard DMFs as means for purposes of indirect infringement.

[60] *Id.* at [32].

Element

In the statute, the means supplied must relate to "an essential element of the invention." Typically, the element is an important part of the patented combination. Where the DMF will print the entire invention, however, the file is a "means relating to" the *whole* invention, not just a part of it.[61] Should this fact preclude application of indirect infringement? From a policy perspective, the answer must be no, unless the DMF constitutes direct infringement under a theory espoused in Chapter 5. It makes no sense that a DMF of a component of a patented machine could indirectly infringe, but that a DMF of the whole machine would not trigger liability.[62]

Knowledge & Intent

Most European countries' indirect infringement statutes require the accused to offer or supply the means "when he knows, or it is obvious to a reasonable person in the circumstances, that those means are suitable for putting, and are intended to put, the invention into effect."[63] In Europe, a question of fundamental importance remains unanswered with respect to the knowledge/intent requirement. Does the statute require (1) merely knowledge of the underlying conduct for which the means are suitable, or (2) that knowledge plus knowledge that those acts infringe a patent (i.e., a mentally culpable state)? Stated another way, is the relevant knowledge/intent merely intent to perform the actions themselves, or rather to perform acts knowing they constitute infringement of a specific patent? Commentators analyzing 3D printing and indirect infringement have not addressed this question.[64]

The former standard would be favorable to the patentee because proving a defendant's knowledge of the patent can be difficult. At the same time, that standard would open the door to a lot of "innocent" indirect infringement. The United States struggled with this same issue, but eventually decided that the more demanding requirement of knowledge of infringement should

---

[61] Of course, one could make a DMF that would print only a component or element of the invention.

[62] *Cf.* Grimme v. Scott, [2010] EWCA (Civ) 1110, [103] ("Moreover we can see no rational basis for the 'whole machine' point. Why should a device to which a part can be readily added to make it fall within the claim be a 'means essential' but a device from which a part can readily be removed or replaced to make it fall within the claim not be such a means?"). In *Grimme*, the means supplied was a complete machine from which a part (the wheels) could be removed and replaced with different wheels to make an infringing machine.

[63] *See, e.g.*, UK Patent Act § 60(2).

[64] *See, e.g.*, Ballardini et al., *supra* note 48, at 860–62; Mimler, *supra* note 46, at 65.

govern.[65] The issue transcends 3D printing and is important across all technologies, so this book does not propose a course. Suffice to say that in the 3D printing arena, the more lenient knowledge standard would lead to widespread liability that would be problematic for reasons similar to those discussed with direct infringement. These reasons include legally unsophisticated actors having to search for and interpret highly technical patent documents and being exposed to large litigation costs.

In addition, there is ambiguity as to whose intent is relevant – the supplier or the recipient. UK courts have focused on the latter.[66] It can be proved, for example, "where the supplier proposes or recommends or even indicates the possibility of such use in his promotional material,"[67] but such recommendation is not required.[68] Other countries, in contrast, place the focus on the intent of the supplier.[69]

Direct Infringement Not Required

In Europe, indirect infringement is seen not only as a way to capture the centralized actor, but also to do so before the direct infringement can occur.[70] This provides the patentee with the advantage of being able to sue sooner in time than in the United States, where direct infringement is required. It also relieves patent holders in Europe from the burdens of proving the underlying infringement.

The lack of requirement for direct infringement also interreacts in an important way with the private, noncommercial use exception to direct infringement. Chapter 5 detailed how 3D printing technology might turn the private, noncommercial use exception into a significant threat to a patentee's ability to profit from its patented technology. But the indirect infringement statutes in most European countries should ease the patentee's worries. Those statutes specify that an indirect infringement cause of action exists even if the recipient of the means for infringing can benefit from the private use exception.[71] They do this in a roundabout way, but the effect is clear. For example, recall that the UK Patents Act exempts individuals

---

[65] *See* Rantanen, *supra* note 14, at 1596–1604.
[66] Grimme v. Scott, [2010] EWCA (Civ) 1110.
[67] *Id.* at [131].
[68] *See* KCI Licensing Inc v. Smith & Nephew Plc, [2010] EWCA (Civ) 1260.
[69] Ballardini et al., *supra* note 48, at 860–62.
[70] Mimler, *supra* note 46, at 62.
[71] *See, e.g., id.* at 65–66.

engaged in private, noncommercial use in section 60(5)(a). Following that exemption, section 60(6) states:

> For the purposes of subsection (2) above a person who does an act in relation to an invention which is prevented only by virtue of paragraph (a), (b) or (c) of subsection (5) above from constituting an infringement of a patent for the invention shall not be treated as a person entitled to work the invention.

Section 60(2), in turn, triggers indirect infringement for one who "supplies or offers to supply in the United Kingdom a person other than a licensee or *other person entitled to work the invention* with any of the means" for infringement. Thus, by specifically defining the private, noncommercial user as one *not* "entitled to work the invention," the law makes clear that indirect liability can be found against one who supplies to those individuals.

Japanese Law

Japanese law prohibits "acts of producing, assigning, etc., importing or offering for assignment, etc. any product to be used . . . for the producing of the said [patented] product as a business" where the subsidiary product either has exclusive use for the invention, or (oversimplifying) where the supplier has knowledge of the infringement.[72] Professor Nari Lee reports that the term "product" can be translated as something close to the meaning of "component" in U.S. law.[73] Depending on the precise meaning of that term, patentees may face a problem similar to U.S. patentees under section 271(c), namely that a DMF is a digital precursor to a machine and does not become part of it. This narrow interpretation would impermissibly weaken patentees' rights in relation to 3D printable goods. If, on the other hand, "product" is construed more broadly, DMFs would seem to qualify because they can clearly be used for producing the patented object.

C. CONCLUSION

Indirect infringement can play a vital role for patentees looking to enforce their rights in 3D printable goods. The doctrine allows patentees to focus on the centralized root of infringement – the DMF. Interpretive issues remain around the world, and I believe that they should be resolved in a manner that

---

[72]   *See* Japanese Patent Act art. 101(i)–(ii).
[73]   *See, e.g.*, Nari Lee, *Fragmented Infringement of Computer Program Patents in the Global Economy*, 48 IDEA 345, 374 n.114 (2007).

captures at least the most egregious actors who repeatedly and knowingly facilitate infringement via DMF distribution. The availability of indirect infringement theories suggests that direct infringement exceptions for private, noncommercial uses will not eviscerate patents' value and should be adopted.

A requirement that the accused indirect infringer must have knowledge of the patent and some culpability for infringement represents a hurdle for patent holders, but not an insurmountable one. The requirement allows innocent actors to avoid liability at the expense of increasing patentees' policing costs. But these might be acceptable trade-offs compared to the alternative. In both the direct and indirect infringement situations, 3D printing technology will open the door to an increased number of legally unsophisticated actors. If the law ensnares too many accidental infringers, a backlash may result against perceived unfairness. That is not to say that patent law should always bend to normative pressures, but rather to point out the political and equitable realities at stake.

In the end, patent law is primarily about optimally incentivizing innovation. Therefore, questions about individual and group preferences must be considered in light of broader concerns about innovation policy, an issue taken up more fully in Chapter 10. Innovation policies surrounding IP law, however, include more than merely patent law. Therefore, the following three chapters consider the laws and policies governing trademarks, copyrights, and design rights.

7

3D Printing and Trademarks: The Dissociation Between Design and Manufacturing

Chapter Outline:

One of the most disruptive aspects of 3D printing technology is the radical separation of design and manufacturing. For any 3D printable good, manufacturing is commoditized. Manufacturing is an afterthought, something that might take place in the home or at a print shop. Design of the product, however, will continue to need skill and know-how even if 3D printing technology lowers barriers and catalyzes more participation in design.[1] If a product is poorly designed (as opposed to poorly manufactured) such that it functions poorly, the DMF and the resulting physical product will carry those design flaws.

The consequences of this radical separation between design and manufacturing, coupled with the physitization of goods, will be profound for trademark law and theory. A trademark's traditional core function is as an indicator of origin for a tangible object. Through the mark the proprietor claims responsibility for quality and the consumer relies on it as an indication of quality.[2] In the past, trademark owners oversaw and controlled both the design and manufacture of products, even if they outsourced one or both of those tasks to others. But 3D printing technology dissociates manufacturing quality from the proprietor and transfers it to the owner of the DMF, who controls

---

[1]   User-friendly and free CAD programs allow more people access to design technology, and the ability to modify existing DMF files allows people to tweak designs without investing the time to create them from scratch.

[2]   *See, e.g.,* FRANK I. SCHECHTER, THE HISTORICAL FOUNDATIONS OF THE LAW RELATING TO TRADE-MARKS 20–63 (1925); FRANCIS H. UPTON, A TREATISE ON THE LAW OF TRADE MARKS 22 (1860) (stating that the fundamental policy of trademark law was "to protect the manufacturer, who by his skill and industry, has produced an article of merchandise, that has found favor with the public, and which he has designated by a particular name or mark.").

manufacturing by choosing a 3D printer. Whatever logo appears on the final good and its digital counterpart tells the DMF owner nothing about who stood behind the manufacturing of the product; the DMF owner dictated that process.

What role then do trademarks play for 3D printed goods? This book has argued that much of the value of 3D printable goods now resides in DMFs, so maybe, as with patents and copyrights, trademark law should ensure robust protection for marks appearing within digital versions of the goods. But trademarks play a very different role than patents and copyrights, which aim to incentivize production of useful and creative works, respectively. Trademark law does not seek to incentivize the creation of marks, nor does it seek to incentivize the production of certain categories of works. Understanding the role of trademarks and how they function in a 3D printing world is key to understanding how trademark law should apply to DMFs. And, of course, the expanding role of trademarks is at the center of a deep debate that directly impacts how DMFs interact with trademark law.

As with previous chapters, this chapter focuses primarily on the novel issues raised by trademark law's interactions with 3D printing. Some difficult trademark issues are no more difficult when 3D printing enters the picture. Thus, any tangible 3D printed product that bears an unauthorized mark and is sold in the marketplace will raise the same issues as if the good were manufactured by another method. Similarly, the boundaries of trade dress and three-dimensional trademarks, while interesting, are no different when a product is 3D printed.[3] The important issues of the boundaries between patent law and trademark law (the utilitarian functionality doctrine) and between design/copyright law and trademark law (the aesthetic functionality doctrine) are perhaps highlighted by 3D printing technology, but the same analysis applies whether or not the goods are 3D printable.[4]

One important but basic issue deserves emphasis. Unlike with patented and copyrighted objects, the mere 3D printing of an object bearing another's trademark does not by itself incur infringement liability. In other words, individual manufacturing for personal use does not trigger liability. In the few times the issue has arisen in U.S. case law, the analysis has focused on the

[3] For a discussion of 3D shapes, 3D printing, and trademark law, see Amanda Scardamaglia, *Flashpoints in 3D Printing and Trade Mark Law*, 23 J. L. INFO. & SCI. 30, 36–45 (2015).
[4] For a recent, interesting case involving the trademark/copyright interface, specifically whether famous works of art whose copyrights have expired can be used as trademarks, see *Municipality of Oslo*, Case E-5/16, 2017 E.F.T.A. Ct. Rep. 55 (2017).

lack of use in commerce.[5] A similar approach would follow in the European Union and elsewhere.[6] The relevance of this legal rule is obvious: 3D printing will drastically increase the amount of personal manufacturing.

Of course, if a user 3D prints an object bearing an unauthorized trademark and sells that physical object, a traditional trademark infringement analysis would apply. The difficult issue is how to apply trademark law to transfers of digital versions of goods bearing another's trademark.[7]

A. THE ORIGIN FUNCTION OF TRADEMARKS AND CONSUMER PROTECTION

The primary function of a trademark is to indicate the origin of a product or service.[8] Though the specific identity of the originator need not be known, by indicating the origin of the goods, a mark "reduces the customer's costs of shopping and making purchasing decisions" and "helps assure a producer that it (and not an imitating competitor) will reap the financial, reputation-related rewards associated with a desirable product."[9]

3D printing technology dissociates manufacturing from trademarks. Manufacturing of 3D printable goods will become commoditized such that

---

[5] *See* Hunn v. Dan Wilson Homes, Inc., 789 F.3d 573, 588 (5th Cir. 2015), *cert. denied*, 136 S. Ct. 592 (2015) (holding there can be no false designation of origin claim where plaintiff's actions (submitting allegedly misleading architectural plans to city) were entirely local and thus did not meet the requirement "that the allegedly false designation enter into and/or have an effect on interstate commerce"); Cognotec Servs. Ltd. v. Morgan Guar. Tr. Co. of N.Y., 862 F. Supp. 45, 51 (S.D.N.Y. 1994) ("Cognotec has failed to allege that any of the infringing materials were disseminated 'in commerce.' Indeed, the amended complaint makes clear that Morgan developed a program to use internally for its currency customers. In other words, Morgan's program is not disseminated 'in commerce' as is required by a § 43(a) claim.") (citation omitted); Obolensky v. G.P. Putnam's Sons, 628 F. Supp. 1552, 1556 (S.D.N.Y. 1986), *aff'd*, 795 F.2d 1005 (2d Cir. 1986) (holding that, even assuming defendant publisher's book catalogs falsely indicated that plaintiff's book had been published by defendant, there could be no liability under § 43(a) where defendant did not publish or ship the book because the goods did not enter into commerce).

[6] *See* Case C-206/01, Arsenal Football Club PLC v. Reed, 2002 E.C.R. I-10273, [40] (noting that the complained of use was "use in the course of trade, since it takes place in the context of commercial activity with a view to economic advantage and not as a private matter"); Dinusha Mendis, *"The Clone Wars": Episode 1*, EURO. INTELL. PROP. REV. 155, 162 (2013) (discussing EU law); Scardamaglia, *supra* note 3, at 45 (discussing Australian law).

[7] This chapter's references to trademarks include trade dress.

[8] *See, e.g.*, 15 U.S.C. § 1127 (defining a trademark as something that is used "to identify and distinguish ... goods ... and to indicate the source of the goods"); Case C-206/01, Arsenal Football Club PLC v. Reed, 2002 E.C.R. I-10273, [48] ("[T]he essential function of a trade mark is to guarantee the identity of origin ... ").

[9] Qualitex Co. v. Jacobson Prods. Co., 514 U.S. 159, 163–64 (1995).

people no longer equate trademarks with indicators of their manufacturing origin. Lawmakers will need carefully to consider how the technology upsets trademarks' historical source indication function.

Of course, it may be that some trademark owners continue to manufacture their own goods (whether via 3D printing or traditional methods) and sell those in the market. In that case, trademark law can apply in the same manner as before at the point of sale. But where instead a DMF is offered for sale, trademarks play a very different role.

To understand the function of trademarks in the sale of a DMF, imagine a website like MyMiniFactory, Turbosquid, or Thingiverse that offers numerous DMFs for download (some for free, some for a price). The website allows you to search for files of interest. If you want to download a cell phone case for your iPhone, you could type "iPhone case" in the search bar. A list of relevant results appears, with images of the DMF and a short description for each possible match.

The first line of the description might be, for example, "iPhone 7 case." A second line of each description includes the "by" line, which identifies the username of the person or company who uploaded the file. Clicking on any given result takes you to a more detailed page with information such as whether the person who uploaded the file remixed the design from someone else or instead represents that they created the file from scratch.

Now let's assume you are a big fan of the Nike brand. You want a cell phone case for your iPhone that includes the Nike "swoosh" trademark. So, you type "iphone case nike" into the search bar.[10] You browse the search results, all of which contain a title line with some variation of "nike iphone case" and a "by" line indicating a user who uploaded the file. Each result also has an image of the DMF with the Nike trademark plainly visible.

Suppose you focus on a particular file uploaded by "User123." What origin-indicating role, if any, do the words "nike" and "iphone" play in a given search result? Does the appearance of "iphone" in the title line tell you the source of the DMF? Of course not. It is a description of what phone the case will fit. It is a nominative fair use – one that refers to Apple's product and is necessary to describe the seller's product as conforming to the shape of Apple's iPhone.[11]

---

[10]   I performed that exact search on Thingiverse's website on Oct. 28, 2018, and received twenty-one results for 3D printable cases for iPhones with one of Nike's logos on it, either the swoosh, the word "Nike," or the Air Jordan symbol.

[11]   *See, e.g.,* Toyota Motor Sales, U.S.A., Inc. v. Tabari, 610 F.3d 1171, 1175 (9th Cir. 2010); European Parliament & Council Directive 2015/2436 to Approximate the Laws of the Member States Relating to Trade Marks, 2015 O.J. (L 336) 1 (EC) art. 14(1)(c) (permitting use of the trademark "where it is necessary to indicate the intended purpose of a product or

The appearance of the word "nike" in the title is more likely to encounter objections. Of course, the appearance in the title tells the searcher something important about the product that will be printed. Namely, that it has a Nike symbol on it. In that sense, the word is merely descriptive. Whether it is permissible or not is likely tied to whether it is permissible to include the Nike swoosh logo on the digital version of the phone case.

Thus, the question becomes, what source-indicating function, if any, does the Nike swoosh logo appearing within the image of the DMF serve? The answer has to be "none." The website context makes plain who the source of the DMF is: that information is unambiguously provided by indicating the username of the user who uploaded the file (here, User123). In addition to the username of the uploader, the entire website context indicates that Nike is not the company who uploaded the file. The name of the website, Thingiverse, is prominently displayed along with the search results, making clear that the overall host of the files is Thingiverse, not Nike. Further, the formatting of the search results, with usernames attached to each result, tells the searcher that each file is uploaded by individual users of the Thingiverse community. If needed, this can be made even clearer with appropriate disclaimers on the website and accompanying each file.[12]

Now, it may be that User123 did not actually design the DMF. User123 may have made a copy of someone else's DMF and uploaded it. If this is true, User123 is not the *designer* of the object in the file. The analysis doesn't change even if the DMF is created by someone who is copying a tangible object – something Nike actually manufactures, such as a shoe. In that case, Nike *is* the designer of the underlying object. But no Thingiverse user thinks that Nike is the source of the actual file, because the website specifically shows that User123 uploaded the file. The trademark appearing on the digital version simply tell users what the object in the DMF is designed to *look like*, rather than who made the file.

Whether User123 created a DMF in CAD to imitate a physical object or made a digital copy of another's DMF, User123 is nevertheless the source of the *actual copy* that was uploaded to Thingiverse. This last point is of immense importance to understanding the role of trademarks in DMFs. It also illustrates the difference between design and manufacturing.

<hr/>

service, in particular as accessories or spare parts") [hereinafter TM Directive]. For convenience I will cite to the TM Directive only and not to the regulation.

[12] *See, e.g.*, Home Box Office, Inc. v. Showtime/The Movie Channel, Inc., 832 F.2d 1311, 1315 (2d Cir. 1987). ("In many circumstances a disclaimer can avoid the problem of objectionable infringement by significantly reducing or eliminating consumer confusion by making clear the source of a product.")

Design, broadly understood in its engineering and aesthetic sense, refers to intellectual origins – the conceptualization of the shape, appearance, and function of an object. If the design is novel or original, a product embodying it may enjoy design rights or copyright protection. If it is useful and nonobvious, the product may enjoy patent protection. But trademarks as source indicators do not protect intellectual origins. They indicate the source of a good or service. And on websites hosting or selling DMFs, the source is the user who uploaded the copy of the file.

In the digital context, of course, copying a file is effortless. But nothing about the source indication function of a trademark takes account of the ease or difficulty involved in making the good. The focus is on whether the consumer is confused about the source of the good (here, a file), whether copied or not.

Dastar *and Tangible Goods*

Cases on both sides of the Atlantic support a careful and thoughtful approach to the source indication function of marks in situations analogous to DMFs. In the United States, the Supreme Court's decision in *Dastar Corp. v. Twentieth Century Fox Film Corp.*[13] announced a rule that, if not read narrowly, will have dramatic effects not only on DMFs, but also on all digital goods.[14] The case involved Dastar, an accused infringer that had copied extensive footage from Fox's *Crusade in Europe* television series and reused large portions of it in its own videos. Dastar credited itself as the producer and distributor without providing any attribution to Fox.[15] Fox would have had a claim for copyright infringement, but the copyright in the *Crusade* series had lapsed.[16] Instead, Fox alleged Dastar violated section 43(a) of the Lanham Act by reverse passing off Fox's content as its own, thus causing confusion as to origin.[17]

The Supreme Court rejected Fox's claim and held that "origin of goods" in the Lanham Act refers only to the "producer of the tangible goods that are offered for sale, and not to the author of any idea, concept, or communication

---

[13] 539 U.S. 23 (2003).
[14] *See generally* Mark P. McKenna & Lucas S. Osborn, *Trademarks and Digital Goods*, 92 Notre Dame L. Rev. 1425 (2017); Mark P. McKenna, *Dastar's Next Stand*, 19 J. Intell. Prop.L. 357 (2012).
[15] *Dastar*, 539 U.S. at 26–27.
[16] *Id.* at 37.
[17] *Id.* at 28. In the United States, infringement based on registered marks and unregistered marks are governed by federal law (the Lanham Act). Thus, claims for reverse passing off (and passing off, where the defendant manufactures the goods and represents them to be from the trademark holder) require application of the Lanham Act.

embodied in those goods."[18] One of the Court's purposes in distinguishing between tangible goods and intellectual concepts was to prevent trademark claims from becoming "a species of mutant copyright law" that would conflict with the federal copyright regime.[19]

Even though the case involved a work whose copyright term had ended, *Dastar* was not limited to copyright concerns. The justices also worried that section 43(a) might be used to "create[] a species of perpetual patent . . ."[20] Thus, the ideas embodied in, and intellectual origins of, goods are irrelevant to trademark law, and such concerns should be channeled to copyright law, patent law, or design law, if anywhere. The Court did not rule out that some consumers might care about a product's intellectual origins (e.g., such as the videos' authorship or a shoe's design), but the Court held that such concerns are not the province of *trademark* law. The Court stated:

> In sum, reading the phrase "origin of goods" in the Lanham Act in accordance with the Act's common-law foundations (which were *not* designed to protect originality or creativity), and in light of the copyright and patent laws (which *were*), we conclude that the phrase refers to the producer of the tangible goods that are offered for sale, and not to the author of any idea, concept, or communication embodied in those goods.[21]

Under this rule, it doesn't matter who originally created the Nike swoosh or who designed the shoe or cell phone case. In *Dastar*, third parties originally filmed the scenes, Fox's predecessor combined them into the *Crusade* series, and Dastar copied the series. Similarly, in our hypothetical, Nike originated the swoosh and designed the physical shoe, an unknown CAD user created the digital version of the shoe, and User123 copied that file. Anyone viewing the DMF will understand that the digital object looks like a Nike shoe, but *Dastar* mandates a focus on the source of the tangible good sold in the marketplace, not on the source of the content or ideas embodied in the good.[22] As the Court stated:

> If anyone has a claim to being the *original* creator of the material used in both the Crusade television series and the Campaigns videotapes, it would be

---

[18] *Id.* at 37.

[19] *Id.* at 34 ("[A]llowing a cause of action under § 43(a) for [a representation that Dastar originated the creative work in the videos] would create a species of mutant copyright law that limits the public's 'federal right to "copy and to use,"' expired copyrights.") (quoting Bonito Boats, Inc. v. Thunder Craft Boats, Inc., 489 U.S. 141, 165 (1989)).

[20] *Id.* at 37.

[21] *Id.*

[22] *Dastar* applies equally to claims of reverse passing off, traditional passing off, and infringement of registered marks. *See* McKenna & Osborn, *supra* note 14, at 1433–35.

those groups [that shot the original footage], rather than Fox. We do not think the Lanham Act requires this search for the source of the Nile and all its tributaries.[23]

Hence, it does not matter that Nike is the source of certain shoe designs.

At the same time, the Court's focus on tangibility poses conceptual challenges for DMFs, which are intangible as to their data.[24] But as long as courts focus on digital files as the relevant good and follow *Dastar's* command to ignore the content of the file for trademark purposes, the application is straightforward. Digital data resides on tangible storage media, and even when the tangible medium is not transferred (as in a typical internet download, which simply transfers data), the file can nevertheless be treated as a good because the person downloading it treats it as a good.[25] The question then becomes, who is the origin or source of that file?

Most courts have failed to treat digital files appropriately under *Dastar* because they fail to understand that the person who makes a copy of a file is the origin (manufacturer) of *that copy*. Making the copy is easy, but *Dastar* demands treating a particular copy as the relevant good. After all, it was not difficult for Dastar to copy Fox's *Crusade* series, but the court treated Dastar's copy as unique from Fox's copy. Thus, even if User123 copied a DMF of a Nike shoe from Nike, User123 is the source of the specific copy that is uploaded to the website. Hence, it is not trademark infringement for User123 to claim to be the source of the uploaded file.

Dastar's rule to ignore content should apply even to registered trademarks, such as the Nike swoosh, appearing within the digital file. Why? Because the symbol indicates not the source of the digital file, but rather an idea or concept devoid of meaningful source indication. Though it is possible to try to distinguish *Dastar* as a case not involving a registered mark, courts have not gone this route. Were it otherwise, trademarks could be embedded in content to create mutant copyrights or patents. As the Seventh Circuit observed:

> [A] movie theater may freely exhibit a copy of Universal Studios' 1925 silent film, *The Phantom of the Opera*, which is now in the public domain, without fear of committing trademark infringement simply because Universal's registered trademark will be displayed when the film is played.[26]

---

[23] *Dastar*, 539 U.S. at 35–36.

[24] For a catalogue of lower court errors when applying *Dastar* to digital files (and a few correct analyses), see McKenna & Osborn, *supra* note 14, at 1439–51.

[25] *See id.* at 1450–53.

[26] Phx. Entm't Partners v. Rumsey, 829 F.3d 817, 829–30 (7th Cir. 2016).

In other words, trademarks inside of content do not suggest the origin of the copy. Courts could insist that those who copy content must remove any registered trademarks before distributing the content, but apparently they feel – rightly in my view – that the effort required to do so is unnecessary given the unlikelihood of confusion. Even if a few consumers were confused, the desire to protect the public domain was, to the Court, an overriding concern that justified a bright-line rule.

Lastly, *Dastar* is not limited to content that was once protected by copyrights or patents. Instead, the Court was intensely concerned with promoting a public domain in goods that never enjoy IP protection, thereby encouraging competition, creativity, and culture. The opinion invoked language from the Court's earlier, public domain–favoring cases and reiterated a solicitous view of copying, stating, "[i]n general, unless an intellectual property right such as a patent or copyright protects an item, it will be subject to copying."[27]

In sum, under *Dastar*, trademarks appearing "inside" of DMFs (i.e., appearing on the digital version of the object) cannot be considered to indicate source or origin. The only relevant indicia of origin will appear "outside" of the file. At the same time, even outside the file, context matters. Labeling a digital file of a shoe that looks like a Nike shoe as a "Nike shoe" does not indicate source. It describes content. (How else can one easily describe what the file will print?) On the other hand, if the user labeled the file as "created by Nike" or "officially licensed by Nike," traditional origin-indicating functions would arise.

The Origin Function in Europe

In the United States, *Dastar*'s rule allows courts to avoid the traditional likelihood of confusion analysis in favor of a bright-line rule. Europe does not have a similar rule. This may be in part attributable to Europe's greater emphasis on registrations and how those registrations shape the parties' rights in trademarks.[28]

---

[27] Dastar, 539 U.S. at 34 (quoting TrafFix Devices, Inc. v. Mktg. Displays, Inc., 532 U.S. 23, 29 (2001)). For more on the Supreme Court's endorsement of copying as a form of competition, see Sheldon W. Halpern, *A High Likelihood of Confusion*: Wal-Mart, TrafFix, Moseley, *and* Dastar – *The Supreme Court's New Trademark Jurisprudence*, 61 N.Y.U. ANN. SURV. AM. L. 237, 270–71 (2005). *See also* Lucas S. Osborn, *Trademark Boundaries and 3D Printing*, 50 AKRON L. REV. 865, 877–80 (2017).

[28] *See* Mark P. McKenna & Lucas S. Osborn, *Digital Goods and Trademark Law: A Comparative Perspective, in* RESEARCH HANDBOOK ON INTELLECTUAL PROPERTY AND DIGITAL TECHNOLOGIES (2018). In many countries, unregistered marks may be protected via the doctrine of passing off. In U.S. law, unregistered marks are covered by the Lanham Act and are

Thus, for example, if a trademark owner held a registration for tangible shoes, a digital representation of the shoes would not constitute infringement under a double identity analysis (identical mark and identical goods).[29] The analysis would proceed under article 10(2)(b) of the TM Directive, with a court looking at the likelihood of confusion factors. Under that analysis, the lack of confusion as to the file's origin would be clear for most DMFs for the reasons explained above (the origin is the user who uploaded the file).

Even if a company obtains a registration for digital versions of particular objects, which would require that it has or will use the mark in relation to digital files,[30] European courts have proven to be more attentive than some U.S. courts to commercial realities. The most relevant case is *Adam Opel AG v. Autec*, in which the Court of Justice of the European Union (CJEU) considered a trademark's essential function of guaranteeing to consumers the origin of the goods.[31] Autec manufactured a remote-control scale-model replica of an Opel Astra, which bore the Opel logo in the same manner as the full-sized car. Adam Opel owned registrations for the trademark not only for full-sized cars, but also for toys, thus implicating the double-identity provision (identical mark on identical goods).[32]

Despite the double-identity situation, the CJEU stressed that liability "must be reserved to cases in which a third party's use of the sign affects or is liable to affect the functions of the trade mark, in particular its essential function of guaranteeing to consumers the origin of the goods."[33] The CJEU noted the German court's finding that German consumers understand that scale models must be made to look like the real cars and thus would "understand that the Opel logo appearing on Autec's products indicates that this is a reduced-scale reproduction of an Opel car."[34]

The CJEU left the ultimate decision to the referring court, but stated that the origin function would not be affected if the lower court found that "the relevant public does not perceive the [allegedly infringing use] as an indication that those products come from Adam Opel or an undertaking

---

treated roughly the same as registered marks in terms of scope of protection. *See* 15 U.S.C. § 1125(a) (protecting unregistered marks).

[29]   TM Directive art. 10(2)(a).

[30]   *Id.* arts. 16–17.

[31]   Case 48/05, Adam Opel AG v. Autec AG, 2007 E.C.R. 1–01017. *See also* Bundesgerichtshof [BGH] [Nuremberg Higher Regional Court] Jan. 14, 2010, Case I ZR 88/08 (Ger.) (deciding the case in light of the CJEU's decision).

[32]   Adam Opel, 2007 E.C.R. at [20].

[33]   *Id.* at [21]. The court did not consider other trademark functions because Opel did not raise them. *Id.* at [25].

[34]   *Id.* at [23].

economically linked to it."[35] The German Federal Supreme Court (Bundesgerichtshof) eventually held that origin function was not affected by the use of the logo on the model.

The *Opel* decision provides a framework from which to analyze DMFs containing trademarks. To the extent that consumers of DMFs understand that marks appearing on digital versions of objects do not indicate origin, which is especially likely where websites are clear as to origin, courts should follow that consumer understanding. This would profoundly limit the role of trademarks appearing inside of DMFs.

B. OTHER TRADEMARK RATIONALES

In addition to the origin indication function of trademarks, a second commonly accepted rationale is the producer incentive rationale. The rationale posits that trademark law incentivizes companies to invest in the manufacture of quality goods by allowing the trademark holder to control use of the mark in certain circumstances, thereby protecting consumers' associations between the quality of goods and the producer.[36]

The traditional version of the producer incentive rationale fits comfortably alongside the consumer confusion rationale. If consumers are confused at the point of sale as to who manufactured a good, then producers have less incentive to invest in quality manufacturing because they will not reap the reputational rewards of good quality when the market is flooded with low-quality fakes. In recent years, however, courts have interpreted the rationale more aggressively to strengthen and expand trademark protection.

Aggressively interpreted, the rationale can quickly become a one-way ratchet for stronger trademark rights rather than socially optimal rights.[37] After all, anything that strengthens the mark strengthens consumers' associations with the mark, thereby further ensuring the mark owner reaps

---

[35] *Id.* at [24].

[36] *See* Qualitex Co. v. Jacobson Prods. Co., 514 U.S. 159, 164 (1995) (stating that trademark law lowers consumer search costs because it "quickly and easily assures a potential customer that *this* item – the item with this mark – is made by the same producer as other similarly marked items that he or she liked (or disliked) in the past. At the same time, the law helps assure a producer that it (and not an imitating competitor) will reap the financial, reputation-related rewards associated with a desirable product. The law thereby 'encourage[s] the production of quality products' .... ") (quoting 1 J. MCCARTHY, MCCARTHY ON TRADEMARKS AND UNFAIR COMPETITION § 2.01[2] (3d ed. 1994))).

[37] *See, e.g.,* Mark A. Lemley, *Property, Intellectual Property, and Free Riding*, 83 TEX. L. REV. 1031, 1046–69 (2005).

reputational rewards. A strong producer incentive rationale therefore tends to propertize trademarks.

In one sense, the producer incentive rationale will be of limited significance for 3D printed goods because the production of tangible goods is commoditized. It is not that there cannot be high- and low-quality production with 3D printing (the quality of production depends on the 3D printer used). Rather, it is that production is in the hands of the end user who can match production quality with individual need.

On the other hand, trademark holders may benefit from incentives to invest in quality DMFs. But courts must be careful to apply any such incentive with care lest it trample on other IP rights. The quality of a DMF can have many facets, only some of which implicate trademark policy. For example, trademark incentives should not include innovation quality, because that is the realm of patents. Nor should aesthetic quality be included, because that is the realm of design patents and copyright. But there remains the need to create good, safe, user-friendly product designs, and trademarks can play a role in ensuring that trademark holders reap rewards for such quality.

Beyond the producer incentive rationale, in recent years trademark protection has grown in scope and power to include post-sale confusion, affiliation and sponsorship confusion, and dilution.[38] These rationales are considered in turn.

Post-Sale Confusion

The typical internet website offering DMFs for downloads in some ways resembles a "flea market" setting. At flea markets, many goods bear unauthorized trademarks and yet no one is confused as to their authenticity because everyone knows they are not made by or with the permission of the trademark holder. In those cases, no one is confused about the origin of the products. How then do courts find trademark infringement?

One answer is post-sale confusion, a theory that although point-of-sale consumers are not confused as to the origin of the goods, third party observers who see the goods used in public will be confused as to their origin. For example, if I buy fake Nike Air Jordan basketball shoes knowing they are knockoffs, third parties will see my shoes when I wear them and may attribute

---

[38] *See, e.g.,* Mark A. Lemley, *The Modern Lanham Act and the Death of Common Sense,* 108 YALE L.J. 1687, 1706–07 (1999); Glynn S. Lunney, Jr., *Trademark Monopolies,* 48 EMORY L.J. 367 (1999); Irina Pak, *The Expansion of Trademark Rights in Europe,* 3 IP THEORY 158 (2013).

any poor quality in the shoe to Nike. Under this theory, disclaimers at the point of sale do not matter.

U.S. courts have widely adopted this theory, even if they apply it inconsistently.[39] The CJEU tepidly introduced the theory in *Arsenal v. Reed*,[40] but it has not followed up with much clarity[41] and national courts have been inconsistent and slow in adopting it.[42] Scholarship has grown increasingly critical of the doctrine.[43]

Post-sale confusion, however, will have virtually no relevance with DMFs because of the wedge 3D printing drives between design and manufacturing. In the first place, a purchaser of a DMF will not use the file in public, and thus third parties cannot be confused by it. The file will reside on the purchaser's computer.[44] The purchaser might 3D print the file and use the tangible item (e.g., a shoe) in public, but that will not result in any confusion about the origin of *the file*, which is the good that was sold. To hold that hypothetical third party confusion as to the tangible shoe is indicative of confusion about the DMF would stretch an already tenuous doctrine beyond its breaking point. After all, if I buy blueprints describing how to make a tangible counterfeit pair of Nike shoes and use them to manufacture ten pairs of infringing shoes, any confusion as to the ten pairs of shoes does not count back to the blueprints. Indirect infringement is the trademark owner's only recourse against the blueprint seller.

Secondly, 3D printing technology radically alters the public's understanding of manufacturing and design for 3D printed goods. Third parties will no longer expect tangible goods necessarily to be manufactured by or on behalf of the brand owner, and thus it will become even more unreasonable to assume

---

[39]   *See, e.g.*, Lois Sportswear, U.S.A. Inc. v. Levi Strauss & Co., 799 F.2d 867, 872–73 (2d Cir. 1986).

[40]   Case C-206/01, Arsenal Football Club PLC v. Reed, 2002 E.C.R. I-10273, [57] ("[S]ome consumers, in particular if they come across the goods after they have been sold by Mr Reed and taken away from the stall where the notice appears, may interpret the sign as designating Arsenal [soccer club] as the undertaking of origin of the goods.").

[41]   *See* Opinion of Advocate General Kokott, Case C-412/05, Alcon v. OHIM, 2006 E.C.R. I-3573 ("Other points in time, at which confusion on the part of the consumers might be more likely because they display a lesser level of attention, are by contrast of secondary importance.").

[42]   *See* P. Sean Morris, *Guess What Gucci? Post-Sale Confusion Exists in Europe*, 47 Val. U. L. Rev. 1 (2012).

[43]   *E.g.*, Connie D. Powell, *We all Know It's a Knock Off – Re-Evaluating the Need for the Post-Sale Confusion Doctrine in Trademark Law*, 14 N.C. J.L. & Tech. 1 (2012); Jeremy N. Sheff, *Veblen Brands*, 96 Minn. L. Rev. 769, 776 (2012) (proposing that "post-sale confusion doctrine should be discarded entirely").

[44]   If the purchaser chooses to upload the file to a repository, the uploaded file is a separate copy than the purchased copy. Any confusion as to origin of the uploaded copy will be determined by the context of the website, not by the internal contents of the file.

that consumers infer anything material about the brand owner by looking at other people's uses of trademark-bearing goods.[45]

Affiliation & Sponsorship Confusion

Post-sale confusion is not the only expansion of trademark rights to occur in the last few decades. With the increase in trademark licensing, courts began to push confusion beyond origin into the realm of sponsorship and affiliation confusion,[46] a movement now codified in the United States and the European Union.[47] Under this type of confusion, even if a consumer is not confused about the actual origin of the good, it may be confused about whether the seller has some affiliation with the trademark owner. The doctrine makes sense when consumers actually believe there is some affiliation and actually care about that affiliation in a way that affects their purchasing decision. But there is a difference between wanting a good because I believe it is formally affiliated with (i.e., licensed by) a trademark owner and wanting a good merely because it displays a trademark. In the latter case, I don't care about source or affiliation.[48] It is true that the trademark has value in that situation, but the value only belongs to the trademark owner if the law says it does.

In other words, if courts interpret affiliation and sponsorship confusion broadly, a one-way ratchet occurs: The law assumes that consumers are confused about affiliation anytime they see a mark because marks are valuable and must be protected, and thus marks become more valuable and courts find infringement more often.[49] Consumers, eventually absorbing the law's stance, become conditioned to expect virtually any trademark usage to indicate sponsorship or affiliation with the mark owner.[50] By this circular route, marks are strengthened and confusion is manufactured.

---

[45] *See* Deven R. Desai & Gerard N. Magliocca, *Patents, Meet Napster: 3D Printing and the Digitization of Things*, 102 Geo. L.J. 1691, 1711 (2014); James Grace, Note,*The End of Post-Sale Confusion: How Consumer 3D Printing Will Diminish the Function of Trademarks*, 28 Harv. J. L. & Tech. 263, 278 (2014).

[46] *See, e.g.*, Triangle Publ'ns, Inc. v. Rohrlich, 167 F.2d 969, 972–73 (2d Cir. 1948).

[47] Trademark Law Revision Act of 1988, Pub. L. No. 100–667, tit. I, sec. 132, § 43(a), 102 Stat. 3935, 3946 (1989); TM Directive art. 10(2)(b) ("[T]he likelihood of confusion includes the likelihood of association between the sign and the trade mark.").

[48] *See generally*, Stacey L. Dogan & Mark A. Lemley, *The Merchandising Right: Fragile Theory or Fait Accompli?*, 54 Emory L.J. 461 (2005).

[49] Felix Cohen, *Transcendental Nonsense and the Functional Approach*, 35 Colum. L. Rev. 809, 815 (1935) ("The vicious circle inherent in this reasoning is plain. It purports to base legal protection upon economic value, when, as a matter of actual fact, the economic value of a sales device depends upon the extent to which it will be legally protected.").

[50] Lunney, *supra* note 38, at 396–97.

The European Union has recently expanded trademark rights even further. In *L'Oréal SA v. Bellure NV*, the CJEU clearly endorsed the existence of undefined but potentially expansive additional trademark functions, which include the quality, communication, advertisement, and investment functions.[51] According to the CJEU, these functions are protected even under article 10(2)(a) and (b) of the TM Directive, despite the fact that they would seem to be functions usually fulfilled by marks with a reputation (i.e., famous marks protected against dilution).[52] The role these new functions will play in EU jurisprudence is not fully clear, but it is likely they portend an additional expansion of trademark rights.

Without doubt, the issue of stronger versus weaker trademark rights transcends issues with 3D printing. The stronger, property-centric views of trademark law can always be extended to make DMFs bearing unauthorized trademarks acts of direct infringement. For example, one court found confusion based simply on the buyer's knowledge "that the source and origin of the *trademark symbols* were" with the trademark holder.[53] In that view, mere recognition of the mark is enough.

Among the many critiques of these expansions, one that is particularly relevant to 3D printing technology is that they run against the thrust of leading cases. If one can recast a claim to confusion about origin as a claim about sponsorship or affiliation, *Dastar* would be eviscerated.[54] Fox could point to its video content as confusing consumers as to sponsorship, and trademark owners could point to trademarks inside of public domain movies for the same

---

[51] Case C-487/07, L'Oréal SA v. Bellure NV, 2009 E.C.R. I-05185, [58]; Joined Cases C-236/08 to C-238/08, Google France, 2010 E.C.R. I-02417, [91]–[98] (analyzing the effect on the advertising function of the mark).

[52] Martin Senftleben, *Adapting EU Trade Mark Law to New Technologies – Back to Basics?*, in Constructing European Intellectual Property: Achievements and New Perspectives 137 (Christophe Geiger, ed.) (2013) (discussing *L'Oréal* as it related to then-denominated article 5(1)(a)).

[53] Bos. Prof'l Hockey Ass'n v. Dall. Cap & Emblem Mfg., Inc., 510 F.2d 1004, 1012 (5th Cir.), *cert. denied*, 423 U.S. 868 (1975) (emphasis added). The court went on to say that the "argument that confusion must be as to the source of the manufacture of the emblem itself is unpersuasive, where the trademark, originated by the team, is the triggering mechanism for the sale of the emblem." *Id.* Courts have generally disagreed with this perspective, including the Fifth Circuit itself. *See, e.g.*, Int'l Order of Job's Daughters v. Lindeburg & Co., 633 F.2d 912, 918–19 (9th Cir. 1980) (characterizing *Bos. Hockey* as "an extraordinary extension" of trademark protection and stating that "our reading of the Lanham Act and its legislative history reveals no congressional design to bestow such broad property rights on trademark owners"); Ky. Fried Chicken Corp. v. Diversified Packaging Corp., 549 F.2d 368 (5th Cir. 1977) (rejecting "any notion that a trademark is an owner's 'property' to be protected irrespective of its role in the protection of our markets").

[54] McKenna, *supra* note 14, at 376–80.

reason. Likewise, the *Opel* case would be severely limited if the trademark holder could simply point to some other trademark interest that was supposedly harmed by the model car.[55]

Dastar and *Opel* represent important cases for focusing attention on what trademark law is supposed to do. They harken back to a more limited role for trademarks where reusing content and even marks in commercial endeavors that compete with the trademark holder can be permissible as long as consumers are not genuinely confused. Like the trademark on Autec's model car, the trademarks appearing in DMFs by themselves do not indicate sponsorship, affiliation, advertisement, or quality. Rather, they indicate verisimilitude in the case of DMFs that will print goods identical to the trademark owners, or they represent expressions of affinity for brands where the mark is placed on DMFs for noncompeting goods. This sort of imitation is not necessarily bad in a competitive economy.[56]

Of course, the expansions of trademark rights demonstrate that other views of trademark norms compete for adherents. Those favoring broader rights have enjoyed their most visible success with the advent of protections against dilution.

Dilution

Both the United States and the European Union make dilution actionable.[57] Dilution has always been controversial, but with it established as the law of Europe and America, the arguments of those opposed to it have increasingly focused on cabining its scope. On the threshold issue of what counts as a famous mark (or mark with a reputation in EU parlance) the United States is more stringent. It excludes niche fame and instead requires the mark to be "widely recognized by the general consuming public of the United States as

---

[55] The *Opel* opinion did, however, emphasize that it was only considering the origin function. Case 48/05, Adam Opel AG v. Autec AG, 2007 E.C.R. 1–01017, [25]. The subsequent German opinion found no harm to other functions of the mark. Bundesgerichtshof [BGH] [Nuremberg Higher Regional Court] Jan. 14, 2010, Case I ZR 88/08 (Ger.).

[56] *See, e.g.*, Groeneveld Transp. Efficiency, Inc. v. Lubecore Int'l, Inc., 730 F.3d 494, 512 (6th Cir. 2013) ("No harm is done to this incentive structure, however, by the copying of a product design that does not confuse consumers as to the product's source . . . [T]rademark law, like the law of unfair competition of which it is a part, focuses not on copying per se, but on confusion."); Dogan & Lemley, *supra* note 48.

[57] 15 U.S.C. § 1125(c); TM Directive, art. 10(2)(c). The 2015 TM Directive made dilution protection mandatory, whereas the previous directive left the issue to member states. Canada recognizes "depreciation of goodwill," which is roughly analogous to dilution. Australia does not appear to have dilution as a part of its law, although there is some ambiguity. *See* Scardamaglia, *supra* note 3, at 49.

a designation of source of the goods or services of the mark's owner."[58] Europe, on the other hand, allows niche fame both in terms of geography and specialized audiences.[59]

Obviously, a broad scope of dilution would prevent most uses of others' trademarks within DMFs. If recognition of a mark is all that is required to constitute blurring,[60] then uses inside of DMFs will inevitably constitute blurring unless an exception applies. But it is possible to demand more exacting proof of blurring and tarnishment. For example, after the CJEU opinion in *Adam Opel*, the German court held there was no dilution of the Opel mark for vehicles (the mark was not famous as to toys) because there was no unfair advantage taken of or detriment caused to the repute of the mark.[61]

In addition, dilution laws provide exceptions that can be expansively applied. The U.S. law excludes "any fair use ... other than as a designation of source for the person's own goods or services" and "any noncommercial use of a mark."[62] The EU TM Directive limits dilution to cases "where use of that sign without due cause takes unfair advantage of, or is detrimental to, the distinctive character or the repute of the trade mark."[63] The CJEU has, however, interpreted the exception narrowly, seemingly condemning all free riding, regardless of harm to the trademark holder.[64] The decision has invited a flurry of objections.[65]

The myriad arguments against dilution and overly strong trademark protection need not be recounted here. It is enough to recognize that stronger forms

---

[58] 15 U.S.C. § 1125(c)(2)(A).

[59] *See* Case C-375/97, Gen. Motors Corp. v. Yplon SA, 1999 I-05421, [24] (allowing fame among "a more specialized public, for example traders in a specific sector"); Case C-301/07, PAGO Int'l GmbH v. Tirol Milch registrierte Genossenschaft mbH, 2009 I-09429, [29] (stating that a reputation in one member state is sufficient).

[60] For a case contemplating mere recognition to be sufficient, see Case C-408/01, Adidas-Salomon AG v. Fitnessworld Trading Ltd., 2003 I-12537, [29].

[61] Bundesgerichtshof [BGH] [Nuremberg Higher Regional Court] Jan. 14, 2010, Case I ZR 88/08 (Ger.).

[62] 15 U.S.C. § 1125(c)(3).

[63] TM Directive art. 10(2)(c).

[64] *See* Case C-487/07, L'Oréal SA v. Bellure NV, 2009 E.C.R. I-05185, [41] ("As regards the concept of 'taking unfair advantage of the distinctive character or the repute of the trade mark', also referred to as 'parasitism' or 'free-riding', that concept relates *not to the detriment caused to the mark but to the advantage taken* by the third party as a result of the use of the identical or similar sign. It covers, in particular, cases where, by reason of a transfer of the image of the mark or of the characteristics which it projects to the goods identified by the identical or similar sign, there is clear exploitation on the coat-tails of the mark with a reputation.") (emphasis added).

[65] *See, e.g.*, Dev Gangjee & Robert Burrell, *Because You're Worth It*: L'Oréal *and the Prohibition on Free Riding*, 73 MOD. L. REV. 282 (2010); Senftleben, *supra* note 52.

of trademark protections will make most trademark uses within digital files actionable, whereas a more traditional, consumer confusion focus would permit many such uses. Lazy observations about free riding do not advance the discourse in a market economy where imitation is seen as beneficial[66] and free expression, even expression implicating trademarks, is regarded as an important value.[67]

In addition, expressive uses of trademarks will only increase with 3D printing. Consumers will be able to personalize their goods and create new goods.[68] Some trademark owners have embraced user-generated content.[69] Others will surely resist it.

DMFs do not create the tensions between confusion-based and property-based views of trademark law, but they certainly contribute to them. By separating and democratizing design from manufacturing, the technology can demystify brands by giving individuals increased access to the means of design and production. In this way, the technology puts increasing pressure on the assertion that brands deserve stronger legal protection merely because they have become more valuable and further elucidates the fact that brands owe their value in large part to broader legal protections.

Intermediaries and Contributory Infringement

Thus far this chapter has focused primarily on 3D printing uses that do not cause confusion among the purchasing public. The technology will, however, facilitate nefarious uses, including the deceptive sales of tangible goods. Contributory infringement liability represents an important route for holding

---

[66] Lord Justice Jacob cogently made this point in the *L'Oréal* case itself at the appeal stage. L'Oréal SA v. Bellure NV 2007 E.W.C.A. Civ. 968, [27] ("'[The phrase 'free riding'] is, to me at least, subtly and dangerously emotive: it carries the unwritten message that it ought to be stopped. That is far from being necessarily so. The needs of proper competition and lawful free trade will involve an element at least of 'free riding.' The problem for trade mark law is where to draw the line between permissible and impermissible 'free riding.' Using the epithet does not solve the problem.").

[67] *See, e.g.*, Katya Assaf, *Brand Fetishism*, 43 CONN. L. REV. 83 (2010); Jeffrey L. Harrison, *Trademark Law and Status Signaling: Tattoos for the Privileged*, 59 FLA. L. REV. 195 (2007). Not to mention the importance of parody, comment, and remixing. *See* Osborn, *supra* note 27, at 895–99.

[68] *See, e.g.*, Osborn, *supra* note 27, at 895–98.

[69] Brian Krassenstein, *Hasbro & Shapeways Team up for New Toy Business Model via SuperFanArt*, 3DPRINT.COM (Jul. 21, 2014), https://3dprint.com/9740/hasbro-shapeways-3d-print-toys/ (describing a forum cosponsored by Shapeways and brand owner Hasbro for fan creations based on trademarked designs). It is worth noting that the partnership ended roughly a year after it debuted.

purveyors of DMFs bearing another's trademark accountable for downstream harms they facilitate. Under the U.S. Supreme Court's opinion in *Inwood Laboratories, Inc. v. Ives Laboratories, Inc.*, if a party "intentionally induces another to infringe a trademark, or if it continues to supply its product to one whom it knows or has reason to know is engaging in trademark infringement, the manufacturer or distributor is contributorily responsible for any harm done as a result of the deceit."[70]

Indirect infringement in the United States requires an underlying act of direct infringement.[71] If someone who obtains a DMF prints tangible copies bearing another's mark and sells those goods as if they were from the mark owner, direct infringement results. The DMF supplier should be held liable if it knew or had reason to know that the specific buyer would engage in this activity.

But as with patent law, indirect infringement will be absent in many cases. If the DMF is never printed or is only printed for purely personal use, no direct infringement results.[72] Moreover, the distributor must have particular knowledge (or reason to know) that the specific downstream entity will engage in trademark infringement. Many times this will be difficult to prove, especially with websites that host third-party DMFs, because they will have little knowledge of specific files on their sites or what the downstream users will do with them.

Courts will need to develop the contours of indirect infringement for online intermediaries. The *Inwood* case involved the manufacture and direct distribution of tangible goods.[73] In *Tiffany (NJ) Inc. v. eBay, Inc.*,[74] the Court of Appeals for the Second Circuit applied *Inwood* to an intermediary if it has "more than a general knowledge or reason to know that its service is being used to sell counterfeit goods" and instead had "contemporary knowledge of" *specific* acts that "are infringing or will infringe in the future."[75] Generalized knowledge that some online listings were counterfeit was not sufficient to find liability. The defendant, eBay, removed any specific listings it learned were infringing and thus avoided liability.

---

[70] Inwood Labs., Inc. v. Ives Labs., Inc., 456 U.S. 844, 854 (1982).

[71] *Id.*

[72] *See supra* note 5.

[73] Inwood Labs, Inc., 456 U.S. at 844.

[74] 600 F.3d 93 (2d Cir. 2010).

[75] *Id.* at 107. The court also stated that knowledge is satisfied by willful blindness to the infringement. *Id.* at 109–10. Other courts have followed the *Tiffany* analysis. *See, e.g.,* Spy Phone Labs LLC v. Google Inc., No. 15-cv-3756, 2016 WL 6025469 (N.D. Cal. Oct. 14, 2016); Rosetta Stone Ltd. v. Google Inc., 730 F. Supp. 2d 531 (E.D. Va. 2010).

The approach in *Tiffany* provides important safeguards for DMF intermediaries who remove items if they know infringement will result. But will courts limit *Tiffany* to its facts? eBay devoted millions of dollars, sophisticated technology, and significant employee effort to policing infringement on its site.[76] Many websites lack such funds, and typically have no idea what DMF purchasers plan to do with the files.[77] Courts should be flexible in their application of indirect liability, using it to capture actors who continually and knowingly supply files to those who they know are committing infringement.

The contours of contributory liability in other countries will be an important issue as well.[78] In Europe, under the e-Commerce Directive (in addition to the laws of member states), online intermediaries can avoid liability for content posted by others if

(a) the provider does not have actual knowledge of illegal activity or information and, as regards claims for damages, is not aware of facts or circumstances from which the illegal activity or information is apparent; or

(b) the provider, upon obtaining such knowledge or awareness, acts expeditiously to remove or to disable access to the information.[79]

Unlike what might be the situation in the United States after *Tiffany*, in the European Union, "Member States shall not impose a general obligation on providers ... to monitor the information which they transmit or store, nor a general obligation actively to seek facts or circumstances indicating illegal activity."[80]

---

[76] *Id.* at 97–100 (detailing, inter alia, eBay's $20 million per year and 4,000 employees devoted to promoting trust and safety on its website, including 200 employees devoted exclusively to combating infringement).

[77] Not to mention that intermediaries will face charges of direct infringement for DMFs bearing trademarks. For example, BMW recently sued the internet intermediary TurboSquid for selling digital models (which were not 3D printable) of BMW vehicles. Complaint at 1, BMW of N. Am., LLC v. TurboSquid, Inc., No. 2:16-CV-02500 (D.N.J. May 3, 2016). The case was dismissed, presumably after the parties reached some settlement. This chapter has demonstrated that such uses may not be directly infringing, but cautious intermediaries may choose to monitor their websites for and remove any infringing items. Technology may help, but at a cost.

[78] One scholar of 3D printing and IP has described Australia's law in this area as "murky." Scardamaglia, *supra* note 3, at 47 n.68 (citing ROBERT BURRELL & MICHAEL HANDLER, AUSTRALIAN TRADE MARK LAW 512 (2010)). Canada does not expressly recognize secondary trademark liability, but the effect may be achieved through a claim in negligence. James Plotkin, *The Impact of 3D Printing on Canadian Trademark Law: Selected Issues and Potential Solutions*, 33 CANADIAN INTELL. P. REV. 63, 89–90 (2017).

[79] e-Commerce Directive art 14(1).

[80] *Id.* art. 15(1).

eBay's practices have provided opportunities for courts on both sides of the Atlantic to develop the law of intermediary liability. In *L'Oréal SA v. eBay International AG*,[81] the CJEU stated that online intermediaries cannot rely on Article 14(1) of the e-Commerce Directive's exemption if they have "provided assistance which entails, in particular, optimising the presentation of the offers for sale in question or promoting those offers."[82] Future case law will need to clarify what activities constitute providing assistance. For instance, DMF websites sometimes emphasize certain "featured" files or sort files by popularity.

Passing Off & Unfair Competition

Many countries have doctrines that complement infringement for registered trademarks, such as the law of passing off and unfair competition.[83] Passing off exists in many common law countries to protect unregistered marks, and typically requires "that the offended party has goodwill ... ; that there has been misrepresentation as to the origin of goods; and that actual damage to the offended party has resulted."[84] The focus on misrepresentation of origin, which has not been expanded as in trademark law, suggests that passing off claims for DMFs will be treated roughly as traditional, origin-focused trademark claims.

Many civil law countries have a robust, if difficult to predict, doctrine of unfair competition.[85] Unfair competition in these countries is broader in scope than passing off, which requires deception as an element, whereas unfair competition focuses on unfairness.[86] Unfairness is an unwieldy horse on which to ride, and countries have considered many types of copying ("slavish imitation") to constitute unfair competition.[87] This attitude recalls the instinctive if poorly thought-out aversion to "free riding" discussed in relation to the *L'Oréal* case. After all, all imitation is "competition." Something more must make it "unfair."

---

[81] Case C-324/09, 2011 E.C.R. I-06011.
[82] *Id.* at [116].
[83] The doctrine of extra-contractual liability under the civil law of Quebec represents another complementary law. *See* Plotkin, *supra* note 78, at 84–86.
[84] Simon Bradshaw et al., *The Intellectual Property Implications of Low-Cost 3D Printing*. 7 SCRIPTED 5, 29 (2010).
[85] *See, e.g.*, Brunhilde Steckler, *Unfair Trade Practices Under German Law: "Slavish Imitation" of Commercial and Industrial Activities*, 7 EURO. INTELL. PROP. REV. 390 (1996).
[86] *See generally*, Mary LaFrance, *Passing Off and Unfair Competition: Conflict and Convergence in Competition Law*, MICH. ST. L. REV. 1413 (2011).
[87] *Id.* at 1421–23.

C. CONCLUSION

Physitization changes consumer perceptions about the origins of tangible goods, which directly implicates trademark law's traditional, core concern. Recent expansions in trademark protections leave room for trademark law to regulate trademarks appearing inside of digital files, but it is not at all clear that this is necessary or desirable. The issue is not an existential threat to utilitarian competition policy because it is easy to remove trademarks placed on digital versions of objects (or not include them in the first place when designing in CAD). At the same time, requiring removal of marks from digital objects is at best an annoyance and may unnecessarily slow competition.

On the aesthetic and expressive side of the equation, however, trademarks represent objects of desire in their own right, apart from the products on which they appear. As long as consumers are not confused, allowing people to design and share trademark-bearing 3D printable files for phone cases, shoes, clothes, and furniture increases consumer welfare.

Unlike the sale of physical goods, the sale (or free transfer) of DMFs will not result in post-sale confusion of the thing (file) sold or transferred, removing a doctrine long relied on by trademark holders battling knockoffs. It is difficult to see why the law should invest the time and effort to police imitative but non-confusing uses,[88] though as mentioned there is disagreement on this point.

In many ways, therefore, trademark law can have reduced significance for 3D printable goods. In other ways, however, trademark law can gain in importance. In a cacophonous sea of DMF offerings, trademark usage *external* to the DMFs provides consumers with important information about the source and affiliation of the digital files. For example, websites and usernames associated with quality DMFs will represent important repositories of goodwill on which consumers will rely.

---

[88] *See, e.g.*, Barton Beebe, *Intellectual Property Law and the Sumptuary Code*, 123 HARV. L. REV. 809, 851–59 (2010) (arguing that trademark law acts as a sumptuary code that allows trademark owners to control uses of status goods to preserve a system of consumption-based differentiation).

8

Creativity and Utility: 3D Printable Files and the Boundary Between Copyright and Patent Protection

Chapter Outline:

Copyright disputes over DMFs have been taking place for years.[1] Katy Perry's accusation of copyright infringement against a DMF of "left shark" (a Super Bowl meme), the Estate of Marcel Duchamp's assertion of IP rights against a 3D printable chess set modeled after a work by Duchamp, and Augustana College's assertion that an artist needed its permission to create DMFs from a public domain sculpture on its campus all reveal the prevalence of copyright law in 3D printing.[2]

Of all parts of IP, the copyright system is best prepared for 3D printing because it has faced digitization issues before. Indeed, for decades it has adapted to multiple shifts in media, such as music media progressing from sheet music to records to tapes to CDs to MP3s. There are, however, issues endemic to copyright law that will cause frustration in a world where legally unsophisticated individuals can create and share a vast array of works. These include difficulty in understanding what copyright covers, when it expires,

---

[1] Matthew Rimmer, *The Maker Movement: Copyright Law, Remix Culture and 3D Printing*, 41 W. AUSTL. L. REV. 51 (2017) (describing several copyright-based disputes involving 3D printing).

[2] *See id.*

infringement issues, and what constitutes fair use (fair dealing).[3] Other important and delicate issues include the application of moral rights to DMFs,[4] the line between industrial design (design patent) and copyright law, or any number of issues that, while intractable, are made no more difficult by 3D printing technology. This chapter will not focus on these issues because they are not novel enough – they have clear analogues in other works.

On the other hand, 3D printing technology raises one issue not raised by the digitization of music, images, or books: the boundary between copyright and patent law. DMFs can be displayed as drawings and text, and thus potentially implicate copyright law. But they simultaneously serve as direct manufacturing precursors to tangible objects, and when a DMF will print a utilitarian object, patent policy is implicated. DMFs now embody much of the economic value of the corresponding utilitarian objects they will manufacture, raising important questions about what role, if any, copyright should play for the files.

This chapter analyzes the balance between patent law and copyright law and emphasizes the existing doctrinal landscape that, if properly interpreted, will channel works between patent and copyright law. This chapter begins with some U.S. copyright law basics to explore its application to DMFs. This doctrinal overview is helpful to the nonexpert and is necessary to clear up misconceptions in the U.S. literature. Analysis then proceeds to address the copyright status of DMFs that depict purely utilitarian objects, first from a U.S. perspective and then from other countries' perspectives.

The bulk of the analysis will be on DMFs that will manufacture utilitarian objects not protected by copyright law. I will refer to these objects as "purely utilitarian" or sometimes simply as "utilitarian" objects, but both terms are

---

[3]   Helpful explorations of these topics in the 3D printing context can be found. *See, e.g.,* Simon Bradshaw et al., *The Intellectual Property Implications of Low-Cost 3D Printing.* 7 SCRIPTED 5, 24 (2010); Thomas Margoni, *Not for Designers: On the Inadequacies of EU Design Law and How to Fix It,* 4 J. INTELL. PROP., INFO. TECH., & E-COM. L. 225 (2013) (EU law); Matthew Rimmer, *Makers Empire: Australian Copyright Law, 3D Printing, and the 'Ideas Boom',* in 3D PRINTING AND BEYOND: INTELLECTUAL PROPERTY AND REGULATION (Dinusha Mendis, Mark Lemley, & Matthew Rimmer eds., 2019) (Australian law); Michael Weinberg, *What's the Deal with Copyright and 3D Printing?,* PUBLIC KNOWLEDGE (Jan. 2013), www.publicknowledge.org/files/What%27s%20the%20Deal%20with%20Copyright_%2 oFinal%20version2.pdf (U.S. law).

[4]   Many helpful analyses of the role of moral rights in digital environments exist. For early works, see Jane C. Ginsburg, *Have Moral Rights Come of (Digital) Age in the United States?,* 19 CARDOZO ARTS & ENT. L.J. 1, 17 (2001) and J. Carlos Fernández-Molina & Eduardo Peis, *The Moral Rights of Authors in the Age of Digital Information,* 52 J. AM. SOC'Y. INFO. SCI. & TECH. 109 (2001). For a more recent work, which includes a rich discussion of many works, see Peter K. Yu, *Moral Rights 2.0,* 1 TEX. A&M L. REV. 873 (2014).

inexact. What I am actually referring to are tangible objects that receive no copyright protection because they are, in a sense, too utilitarian. Such objects may contain ingenuity or even aesthetic appeal, but, to police the boundary between copyright law and patent law, copyright law does not protect them. In some countries, this issue is phrased in terms of whether the object has "separable" creativity, while others simply include a heightened standard of creativity for utilitarian articles.[5]

This chapter will not analyze separability tests or other tests that determine whether a tangible object should receive copyright protection. Instead, it will *assume* the physical utilitarian object does not receive protection under a country's copyright law and will proceed to analyze whether the DMF that will print the object receives copyright protection. This will focus attention on the novel copyright law aspect raised by physitization.

A. U.S. LAW: DMFS ARE NOT A SEPARATE CATEGORY OF COPYRIGHTABLE "WORKS," AND WHETHER FILES ARE "USEFUL ARTICLES" IS IRRELEVANT

The U.S. copyright statute provides a non-exhaustive list of protected works that includes literary works, musical works, motion pictures, sound recordings, and "pictorial, graphic, and sculptural works" (PGS works).[6] The statute in turn defines PGS works in part as "two-dimensional and three-dimensional works of fine, graphic, and applied art, photographs, prints and art reproductions, maps, globes, charts, diagrams, models, and technical drawings, including architectural plans."[7]

To analyze the basic application of the statute, imagine an original, beautiful, and creative sculpture that an artist carved from a block of marble. Copyright law protects the sculpture as a PGS work, but the law uses some nonintuitive vocabulary that must be grasped. The sculptural "work" protected by the statute is an intangible thing.[8] Copyright law labels *any* tangible instantiation of a work, *including the original*, as a "copy."

---

[5] *See, e.g.*, Star Athletica, L.L.C. v. Varsity Brands, Inc., 137 S. Ct. 1002 (2017) (applying a separability test); Case C-168/09, Flos SpA v. Semeraro Casa e Famiglia SpA, 2011 E.C.R. I-00181 (referencing the Italian scindabilità doctrine); Lucasfilm Ltd v. Ainsworth, [2011] UKSC 39 (analyzing what constitutes a sculpture under UK law).
[6] 17 U.S.C. § 102(a).
[7] *Id.* at § 101.
[8] *Id.* at § 102 ("Copyright protection subsists ... in original works of authorship fixed in any tangible medium of expression ... "); *see also* Mark P. McKenna & Lucas S. Osborn, *Trademarks and Digital Goods*, 92 NOTRE DAME L. REV. 1425, 1459 (2017) ("[C]opyright attaches to the intangible work of authorship, *not* to the tangible copy in which it is fixed.").

Copies are defined as "material objects . . . in which a work is fixed by any method now known or later developed, and from which the work can be perceived, reproduced, or otherwise communicated, either directly or with the aid of a machine or device."[9] So the original sculpture as carved by the artist is a copy because that is where the intangible sculptural work was fixed such that it was perceptible.

To understand how copyright law applies to DMFs, imagine that the artist did not sculpt the marble. Instead, imagine the artist had a mental image of the same sculptural work and created a 3D model of it in a CAD program. The artist then converted the design file into a surface-mesh file and converted that into a machine-instruction file, which was then 3D printed. The end result is a physical sculpture, which is clearly protected as a copy under the statute.

But what about the DMFs? As should be clear, DMFs are not "works." Rather, the DMF that will print the tangible sculpture is a "copy" of the sculptural work, just like a MOV file is a copy of a motion picture. Tracking the statutory definition of a copy, a machine-instruction file is a material object (namely the tangible computer memory) in which the sculptural work is fixed (i.e., stored), and from which the work can be perceived (i.e., seen) with the aid of a machine (i.e., a 3D printer).

It is also important to understand that a DMF simultaneously can be a copy of other types of works. For example, because a computer can use a machine-instruction file to depict a two-dimensional image on a computer screen or on a printed sheet of paper, the file is also a copy of a pictorial work. The same is true for the surface-mesh version and the design version. Moreover, because a DMF of a sculpture can be depicted in a text (code) form as described in Chapter 2, it also constitutes a literary work whose text inherently embodies the originality of the sculpture it can print.

Even though DMFs are not copyrightable works, it is common, if inexact, to say that DMFs are protected by copyright. A more precise statement would be that a DMF is a copy of a protected work.[10] People who make unauthorized copies of that DMF commit copyright infringement by violating the copyright holder's reproduction right. But that is a mouthful, so it is common to elide the phrase and simply state that a file is protected by copyright.

The early 3D printing literature, however, evidences problematic confusion about DMFs and copyrightable works. Some commentators have mistakenly

[9] 17 U.S.C. § 101.
[10] 17 U.S.C. § 102(a). ("Copyright protection subsists, in accordance with this title, in original works of authorship fixed in any tangible medium of expression, now known or later developed, from which they can be perceived, reproduced, or otherwise communicated, either directly or with the aid of a machine or device.")

sought to analyze whether DMFs constitute works.[11] They do not. They are copies of PGS and literary works. At best, this confused analysis leads to pointless, complicated tests.[12] At worst, it compounds into other errors.

For example, the confusion that DMFs constitute their own category of works has led some authors to erroneously query whether DMFs constitute "useful articles."[13] They do not. A useful article is "an article having an intrinsic utilitarian function that is not merely to portray the appearance of the article or to convey information."[14] For example, a fuel injector is a useful article. To prevent copyright protection from extending to useful articles, the statute states:

> [PGS] works shall include works of artistic craftsmanship insofar as their form *but not their mechanical or utilitarian aspects* are concerned; the design of a useful article, as defined in this section, shall be considered a pictorial, graphic, or sculptural work only if, and only to the extent that, such design incorporates pictorial, graphic, or sculptural features that can be identified separately from, and are capable of existing independently of, the utilitarian aspects of the article.[15]

In short, if a tangible object has a utilitarian function that is not merely to portray the appearance of the article (which is what a sculpture does) or to convey information (which is what printed words do), the utilitarian aspects of that object cannot be protected by copyright.

---

[11]   *See* Kyle Dolinsky, Note, *CAD's Cradle: Untangling Copyrightability, Derivative Works, and Fair Use in 3D Printing*, 71 WASH. & LEE L. REV. 591, 628–57 (2014) (performing a search for the appropriate analogy to DMFs among other works that copyright protects and concluding that DMFs are not perfectly analogous to architectural plans or technical drawings); Nathan Reitinger, Comment, *CAD's Parallel to Technical Drawings: Copyright in the Fabricated World*, 97 J. PAT. & TRADEMARK OFF. SOC'Y 111, 133 (2015) (analyzing how to "assert a copyright on the CAD file itself"); Brian Rideout, *Printing the Impossible Triangle: The Copyright Implications of Three-Dimensional Printing*, 5 J. BUS. ENTREPRENEURSHIP & L. 161, 168 (2011) (erroneously concluding that DMFs are not "copyrightable software" because they are "more of a blueprint"); Sarah Swanson, Note, *3D Printing: A Lesson in History: How to Mold the World of Copyright*, 43 SOUTHWESTERN L. REV. 483, 489 (2014) ("Another option is to create a new category of protection or qualify the object and digital blueprint as a new medium.").

[12]   *Cf.* Dolinsky, *supra* note 11, at 642–51 (proposing a "composite test for copyrightability of CAD files").

[13]   *See* Dolinsky, *supra* note 11, at 633–34 (stating that it is unclear whether DMFs constitute useful articles); Darrell G. Mottley, *Intellectual Property Issues in the Network Cloud: Virtual Models and Digital Three-Dimensional Printers*, 9 J. BUS. & TECH. L. 151, 159–161 (2014) (analyzing DMFs as useful articles); Reitinger, *supra* note 11, at 136 (analyzing DMFs as useful articles).

[14]   17 U.S.C. § 101.

[15]   *Id.* (emphasis added).

Further, when the copyright statute uses the phrase "the design of a useful article," it is referring to things that might otherwise be copyrightable works. It is not referring to substrates that contain copies of works. Pages containing the words in a book, canvases that support the brushstrokes of paintings, and computer memory that holds digital code for a song are all useful articles, but they are not determinative of the question of whether literary works, pictorial works, and sound recordings, respectively, constitute protectable works. Hence, it is a red herring to ask whether DMFs are useful articles.[16]

Rather, the copyright question is whether the object the DMF will manufacture or depict constitutes a useful article.[17] If the 3D printed object is purely a useful article, it is not protected by copyright. On the other hand, if the 3D printed object is an aesthetic sculpture, it is copyrightable subject matter (and any DMF that would print it or display an image of it is protected by copyright).

B. U.S. LAW: PICTORIAL WORKS AND DMFS OF UTILITARIAN OBJECTS – THE BOUNDARY BETWEEN COPYRIGHT AND PATENT PROTECTION

This section analyzes a more contentious issue, one on which copyright scholars disagree.[18] The issue is whether a DMF depicting a purely utilitarian

---

[16]   In the sense used by the Court in Star Athletica, L.L.C. v. Varsity Brands, Inc., 137 S. Ct. 1002 (2017), the computer memory is of course a useful article, but the code on the memory is easily separable. Many believe the *Star Athletica* Court needlessly complicated matters by using a separability analysis to separate the shapes on the cheerleading outfits from the underlying useful article (the blank outfits). Under that framework, just about every case needs a separability analysis because a painting rests on the useful article of a canvas and printed words rest on the useful article of paper. It would be easier to say that the cheerleading case involved a design *on* a useful article, rather than a design *of* a useful article.

[17]   See, e.g., 2 WILLIAM F. PATRY, PATRY ON COPYRIGHT § 3:145 (March 2017) (stating that one must ask "if the design for which protection is sought is a PGS work, is the three-dimensional article that it is the design of, according to the statutory definition, a 'useful article.'"). Interestingly, Mr. Patry changed the language of this query in the 2018 update. He now asks, "[I]f the design for which protection is sought is a PGS work, is the article in which it is embodied a 'useful article' as defined in the statute?" This change is probably to be consistent with the *Star Athletica* mode of analysis.

[18]   When I say that copyright scholars disagree as to my specific argument, I am referring to numerous personal conversations with copyright commentators who have seen me present my research. My specific arguments regarding the design of a useful article are novel, so no one has had the opportunity to respond to them in writing. I have no formal count but would estimate that about half agree with my analysis and half do not. In the broader sense, copyright scholars often disagree about the appropriateness of copyright protection for works that are largely utilitarian in nature. See, e.g., Peter S. Menell, *Tailoring Legal Protection for Computer*

object can enjoy copyright protection as a copy of a pictorial work.[19] To reify the issue, consider a DMF of a shovel that has no artistic features.

It is clear that the 3D printed shovel does not enjoy copyright protection because it is a useful article.[20] It has the intrinsic utilitarian function of helping to dig holes. Because the shovel does not qualify as a sculptural work, the DMF of the shovel is not a copy of a sculptural work.

But recall that a DMF can constitute a copy of more than one kind of work. It can be a copy of a sculptural work, a pictorial work, and a literary work (and if it would print a building, an architectural work). Hence, the next issue concerns the DMF as a pictorial work: Since the DMF can, with the aid of a computer, generate a drawing of the shovel, is it protectable as a copy of a pictorial work?

I have elsewhere argued that exact engineering drawings consisting only of the shape of a useful article are not protectable.[21] Others offer the opposite view.[22] The issue is debatable as a matter of statutory interpretation, Supreme Court case law, and policy. This subsection sorts through these arguments.

The "Design" of a Useful Article

Although the fact is rarely appreciated, the Copyright Act does not necessarily exclude only tangible useful articles from copyright protection. Instead, it

---

Software, 39 STAN. L. REV. 1329 (1987) (arguing for sui generis protection for programs); A. Samuel Oddi, *An Uneasier Case for Copyright Than for Patent Protection of Computer Programs*, 72 NEB. L. REV. 351 (1993) (arguing that programs should be protected by patent law, not copyright law); J. H. Reichman, *Computer Programs as Applied Scientific Know-How: Implications of Copyright Protection for Commercialized University Research*, 42 VAND. L. REV. 639 (1989); Pamela Samuelson et al., *A Manifesto Concerning the Legal Protection of Computer Programs*, 94 COLUM. L. REV. 2308 (1994) (critiquing copyright protection of software and arguing for sui generis protection for programs).

[19] To reiterate what was stated in the introduction to this chapter, this section does not analyze DMFs that will manufacture objects that contain a separable mixture of utilitarian and aesthetic features. If the tangible object is protected by copyright law, so is the corresponding DMF.

[20] A useful article is "an article having an intrinsic utilitarian function that is not merely to portray the appearance of the article or to convey information." 17 U.S.C. § 101.

[21] Lucas S. Osborn, *Intellectual Property Channeling for Digital Goods*, 39 CARDOZO L. REV. 1303 (2018) [hereinafter, Osborn, *IP Channeling*]; Lucas S. Osborn, *The Limits of Creativity in Copyright: Digital Manufacturing Files and Lockout Codes*, 4 TEX. A&M J. PROP. L. 25, 41–52 (2017).

[22] Eli Greenbaum, *Three-Dimensional Printing and Open Source Hardware*, 2 N.Y. U. J. INTELL. PROP. & ENT. L. 257, 275 (2013) (concluding without further analysis that digital manufacturing files depicting useful articles "easily qualify for copyright protection" because "[c]opyright law protects 'pictorial, graphic and sculptural works,'" including "technical drawings").

excludes "the *design* of a useful article."[23] I argue that the "design" includes the shape and appearance of the work in any instantiation, whether on the article itself or in a drawing of the article. Specifically, in defining PGS works, the statute includes language referred to as the useful article exclusion:

> [PGS] works shall include works of artistic craftsmanship insofar as their form but not their mechanical or utilitarian aspects are concerned; *the design of a useful article*, as defined in this section, shall be considered a pictorial, graphic, or sculptural work only if, and only to the extent that, such design incorporates pictorial, graphic, or sculptural features that can be identified separately from, and are capable of existing independently of, the utilitarian aspects of the article.[24]

The statutory language contains an ambiguity. On one reading, the exclusion from copyright protection is for "the design" – in the abstract – of a useful article, not merely the design as it appears on or in the useful (tangible) article. Stated differently, one view is that the design of the useful article refers to the article's overall shape and appearance whether depicted (1) by the article itself or (2) in a *mere* drawing of the article.[25] Under an alternate reading, the exclusion applies only to the "design of a useful article" (i.e., its appearance or shape) *when that design/shape is portrayed by the tangible useful article itself* (but not when the design is portrayed in a drawing of the useful article). Both views are reasonable under the text.

The remainder of the sentence in the useful article exclusion does nothing to resolve the ambiguity. Supporting the broader interpretation (which I will call the "design anywhere" interpretation), the sentence applies the exclusion not only to "sculptural" works, which are 2D objects, but also to "pictorial" and "graphic" works, which are 2D images. Thus, the statute can be read to exclude anything that would otherwise be a pictorial or graphic work if that picture constitutes merely *the design of* (i.e., an exact representation of) a useful article without separable features. In support of this view, one can look to different, clearer wording in Congress's definition of an architectural work, which is defined as "*the design of a building* as embodied in any tangible medium of expression, including a building, architectural plans, or drawings."[26] Under the architectural works definition, even though a building is useful, the statute defines the *work* as *the design* of the building.

---

[23] 17 U.S.C. § 101.

[24] *Id.* (emphasis added).

[25] As will be discussed, drawings of useful articles can be protected by copyright if they do more than merely depict the article; that is, if they contain creative expression.

[26] 17 U.S.C. § 101 (emphasis added).

The statute also makes clear that "the design of the building" can be manifested (1) in the building itself or (2) in a drawing of the building. With the useful article exclusion, in contrast, the design of the useful article is only a protected work if it has separable PGS features. Textually, the useful article exclusion is arguably independent of whether the design is manifested (1) in the useful article itself or (2) in a drawing of the article.

On the other hand, those favoring the narrower reading (which I will call the "tangible article only" interpretation) can point to legislative history suggesting that the reference to "pictorial" and "graphic" works is meant to refer to designs applied on the surface of a useful article (i.e., surface ornamentation).[27] This is undoubtedly correct as far as it goes. The Supreme Court recently confirmed this point by noting that "the 'design of a useful article' can include two-dimensional 'pictorial' and 'graphic' features" such as surface ornamentation.[28] But this does not resolve the ambiguity. Reading the statutory mention of pictorial works to refer to surface ornamentation does not require that it refers *only* to surface ornamentation.[29] In other words, nonprotected pictorial works may also include exact representations of the useful article.

Another textual point is reasonably clear, but also not determinative. Specifically, the design of a useful article includes its shape. In *Star Athletica*, the Supreme Court defined design as referring to "'the combination' of 'details' or 'features' that 'go to make up' the useful article."[30] Shape constitutes a detail or feature that makes up the article. The legislative history

---

[27] STAFF OF H.R COMM. ON THE JUDICIARY, 87TH CONG., REP. OF THE REGISTER OF COPYRIGHTS ON THE GENERAL REVISION OF THE U.S. COPYRIGHT LAW 14 (Comm. Print 1961) ("However, when a [PGS] work is used as a design or decoration of a useful article, it would continue to have all the protection now afforded by the copyright law."); *id.* at 15 ("The copyright statute should make it clear that, for purposes of registration, the 'works of art' category includes pictorial, graphic, and sculptural works even though they may portray or be intended for use in useful articles, but that useful articles, as such, are not acceptable for deposit.").

[28] Star Athletica, L.L.C. v. Varsity Brands, Inc., 137 S. Ct. 1002, 1009 (2017) (discussing surface ornamentation applied to a cheerleading uniform, which the Court identified as a useful object).

[29] As Professor Ned Snow has pointed out to me, virtually all court treatment of the useful article doctrine limits the inquiry to the design as it exists in the useful article. I agree, but do not think it is conclusive because those courts were only analyzing the facts and arguments posed by the particular cases. They simply did not address an argument as to the meaning of the design of a useful article. A notable exception is discussed below regarding the case of Enterprises Int'l, Inc. v. Int'l Knife & Saw, Inc., No. C12-5638 BHS, 2014 WL 1365398 (W.D. Wash. Apr. 7, 2014).

[30] *Star Athletica*, 137 S. Ct. at 1009 (quoting OXFORD ENGLISH DICTIONARY 244 (def. 7, first listing) (3d ed. 1933)).

also demonstrates that shape is part of a design: "Unless the *shape* of an ...
industrial product contains some element that, physically or conceptually, can
be identified as separable from the utilitarian aspects of that article, the *design*
would not be copyrighted."[31] But the ambiguity remains: the phrase "shape of
an article" is no less ambiguous than the phrase "the design of an article."

Sticking with the textual analysis, the useful article exclusion also uses the
phrase "utilitarian aspects of the article."[32] An aspect, like a design, can
connote either a tangible or an intangible concept. As discussed in the
previous subsection, copyright law often operates in abstract concepts, protecting intangible, abstract "works,"[33] suggesting that the terms "aspect" and
"design" should similarly have intangible connotations. If so, the shape of
a utilitarian article is part of its intangible "utilitarian aspect" because the
shape results from the article's function. In fact, the *Star Athletica* Court stated
that "our test does not render the shape, cut, and physical dimensions of the
[useful article] eligible for copyright protections."[34] Because the shape is
constitutive of the utilitarian aspects of a useful article, if a drawing only
depicted the shape of a useful article with no additional content or creativity,
the drawing would not have any separable PGS feature. That being said, it is
also possible that the *Star Athletica* Court was referring only to the shape as
embodied in the physical article.

Of course, the *Star Athletica* Court did not have to consider drawings that
are exact representations of purely useful articles. The only additional relevant
language (besides its observation that the shape, cut, and physical dimensions
of useful articles are not eligible for copyright protection), is found in two
ambiguous pieces of dicta that relate to drawings of useful articles. First, the
Court stated:

---

[31]   H.R. Rep. No. 94–1476, at 55 (1976) (emphasis added).
[32]   Professors Buccafusco and Fromer provide an excellent description of the sorting between
       utilitarian and aesthetic aspects/features that should accompany a separability analysis.
       Christopher Buccafusco & Jeanne C. Fromer, *Forgetting Functionality*, 166 U. Pa. L. Rev.
       Online 119 (2017).
[33]   *See supra* notes 8–9 and accompanying text.
[34]   *Star Athletica*, 137 S. Ct. at 1016. In its analysis of the facts at hand, the Court first stated that
       a decisionmaker must determine whether the separately identified PGS feature "has the
       capacity to exist apart from the utilitarian aspects of the article," which tracked the statutory
       language. *Id.* at 1010. But in the next sentence it dropped the word "aspects" and referred only
       to imagining the feature "apart from the useful article." *Id.* The change did not affect that case,
       but it might affect an analysis of the shape of a useful article because a drawing of its shape is
       easy to imagine separately from the tangible object, but it is not easy to imagine it separately
       from the utilitarian *aspects* of it. *Cf.* Buccafusco & Fromer, *supra* note 32, at 122 (criticizing the
       omission of the word "aspects" in the Court's test).

Nor could someone claim a copyright in a useful article merely by creating a replica of that article in some other medium – for example, a cardboard model of a car. Although the replica could itself be copyrightable, it would not give rise to any rights in the useful article that inspired it.[35]

It also stated that "[a] drawing of a shovel could, of course, be copyrighted."[36] In neither case did the Court provide any details of the model or drawing it was contemplating.[37] Does this suggest that *all* drawings of useful articles are copyrightable? It is not clear.

The Court's dicta relate to other portions of the copyright statute, portions in which supporters of the narrower, "tangible article only" interpretation find more support. First, the statute specifically includes "technical drawings," which are generally drawings of useful articles, as a type of PGS work that may receive copyright protection.[38] The statute also includes a separate provision making it clear that even if a technical drawing of a useful article is protected by copyright, one who manufactures the tangible useful article does not create an infringing copy.[39] Section 113(b), though convoluted in wording, essentially states that "the owner of copyright in a work that portrays a useful article as such" does not have rights against any physical object made from that drawing.[40]

These provisions plainly indicate that some drawings – even technical drawings – of useful articles can receive copyright protection. But they do not foreclose a reading of the phrase "the design of a useful article" as referring to the shape of an article as depicted in a drawing. Stated another way, the possibility that *some* drawings of useful articles can receive copyright protection does not mean that *all* do.

How can this be? I argue that if a drawing of a useful article *does no more* than portray a useful article, it is not protectable. The statute, although ambiguous, does not foreclose this possibility. I believe the resolution to the

---

[35] *Star Athletica*, 137 S. Ct. at 1010.

[36] *Id.* at 1013 n.2.

[37] Whether "could" means "always will be" is debatable. The Court offered no qualifier, but the issue of pure versus embellished technical drawings or models was not before the Court.

[38] 17 U.S.C. § 101 (defining PGS works to include "two-dimensional and three-dimensional works of fine, graphic, and applied art, photographs, prints and art reproductions, maps, globes, charts, diagrams, models, and technical drawings, including architectural plans.").

[39] *Id.* at § 113(b) ("This title does not afford, to the owner of copyright in a work that portrays a useful article as such, any greater or lesser rights with respect to the making, distribution, or display of the useful article so portrayed than those afforded to such works under the law, whether title 17 or the common law or statutes of a State, in effect on December 31, 1977, as held applicable and construed by a court in an action brought under this title.").

[40] *Id.*

statutory ambiguity lies in the constitutional requirement of creativity. As I argue in the next subsection, a drawing doing nothing more than depicting a useful article contains no creativity.

As I discuss immediately below, the creativity requirement is mandated by the U.S. Constitution. A constitutional requirement would even control over a statute that unambiguously attempted to protect uncreative works. As I have argued in this section, however, I believe that the useful articles exclusion is ambiguous. The ambiguity should, therefore, be interpreted to avoid violating the Constitution.[41] This is all the more so because the Supreme Court did not specifically endorse creativity as a constitutional requirement until several years after the 1976 Copyright Act.[42] I turn now to the creativity requirement directly.

Creativity Required

In *Feist Publications, Inc. v. Rural Telephone Service Co.*,[43] the Supreme Court announced a constitutional requirement that works must contain a modicum of creativity to be eligible for copyright protection.[44] The *Feist* Court held that the selection and arrangement in a traditional phone book, which listed alphabetically by last name all the residents' names, towns, and phone numbers in a geographic region, did not contain enough creativity to merit copyright protection.[45] In making its holding, the Court rejected the idea that mere effort, or "sweat of the brow," can merit copyright protection and instead described originality (which it defined as requiring creativity) as the "*sine qua non* of copyright."[46]

The *Feist* Court used the creativity requirement to resolve the "tension" between the uncopyrightability of facts and the copyrightability of compilations of facts.[47] In the same manner, the creativity requirement can resolve the tension between what I have argued is the uncopyrightability of the design of

---

[41] *See, e.g.*, Edward J. DeBartolo Corp. v. Florida Gulf Coast Bldg. & Constr. Trades Council, 485 U.S. 568, 575 (1988) ("[W]here an otherwise acceptable construction of a statute would raise serious constitutional problems, the Court will construe the statute to avoid such problems unless such construction is plainly contrary to the intent of Congress.").

[42] *See infra* note 43. It could be argued that the Court articulated the creativity requirement in Trademark Cases, 100 U.S. 82 (1879), but courts inconsistently applied the requirement until *Feist*.

[43] 499 U.S. 340 (1991).

[44] *Id.* at 346.

[45] *Id.* at 362.

[46] *Id.* at 348.

[47] *Id.* at 345–46.

useful articles and the copyrightability of technical drawings. Focusing on creativity, a drawing that is merely an exact representation of a useful article (i.e., something that does no more than reflect the design of a useful article) contains no separable creativity because the design is required by and inseparable from the utilitarian aspects of the article.[48] Another way to think of it is that the utilitarian aspects of an article are akin to the facts in *Feist*.

When can a drawing of a purely useful article qualify for copyright protection? The answer lies in adding creativity. If the pictorial work does not *merely* depict the design (shape) of the useful article, but instead includes additional, creative material, the overall work is copyrightable subject matter. It is for this reason that artists' paintings of useful articles qualify for copyright protection. Even when an artist attempts to paint an exact replica of the shovel, courts insist that the artist imbues the painting with his or her "personal reaction" of the object.[49] The artist chooses the view and angle at which to depict the article, the lighting to include, and other creative choices.

But the situation is different when a draftsperson creates a CAD drawing that does no more than portray the shape of the useful article, whether the draftsperson is copying an already-existing shovel or is designing the purely utilitarian shovel for the first time. In either case, the draftsperson exercises no protectable creativity – the drawing depicts only the exact dimensions (shape) of the useful article, which is entirely dictated by the utilitarian aspects of the object.

How then, are "technical drawings," which the statute specifically mentions as a type of protectable PGS work, ever protectable? Again, the answer lies in creativity added to the drawing. The creativity does not come from the drawing of the object, because that drawing does nothing more than depict the precise design (i.e., the facts) of the useful article. Rather, the creativity, if any, comes from the additional material included in the technical drawing.

Traditional technical drawings (blueprints) contain many elements in addition to the shape of the article, and the decision about whether and how to include those elements may hoist the drawing over the modest creativity threshold. For example, a draftsperson can decide to include various views of the object, such as a top view, side view, perspective view, various "zoomed in" views, and exploded views (though some of these basic choices may be

---

[48] This section's argument need not rely on my previous statutory construction analysis of the design of a useful article. Nevertheless, I relate the two arguments at times because I think they get to the same point; one tied to statutory language, one tied to doctrines about facts and functionality. Some courts and commentators, however, may be more comfortable with a framework of facts and functionality rather than useful articles.

[49] Bleistein v. Donaldson Lithographing Co., 188 U.S. 239, 250 (1903).

governed by industry convention). Further, a draftsperson can decide which parts to label and how to label them, typically with lines leading from a specific part to a balloon that specifies the part name or number.

But surface-mesh and machine-instruction files differ in important ways from traditional blueprints.[50] The depiction of a useful object in those DMFs contains only one view (because it is a rotatable three-dimensional view) and no part labels. Every aspect of the drawing, every line and curve, exists entirely to depict the exact design (shape) of the utilitarian object. There is only one way to depict that particular shovel – if ten other people independently created a CAD drawing of the same shovel, each drawing (if technically accurate) would show an identical shape. Likewise, each surface-mesh and machine-instruction file, if accurate, would be identical.[51]

Copying from the Physical

The lack of creativity in DMFs of purely utilitarian objects is most apparent when someone creates a DMF by copying an existing utilitarian object. A person can do this by scanning the object and allowing software to create an accurate depiction of the object as a surface-mesh file, as described in Chapter 2. A person can also do this by taking exact measurements of the object and recreating the object in CAD software by hand. In either case, the copier has done nothing authorial or original, but has simply captured reality. In other words, the copier has only copied facts.

One may be tempted to argue that the scan is like a realistic painting or a photograph, which can be copyrightable, but the analogy proves too much.[52] Photographs are only copyrightable to the extent that the photographer

---

[50]   I do not include design files only because they may, but need not, include extraneous material that can be creatively arranged. It is common for design files to include labels, notes, and the like, which can nudge them over the creativity threshold. Software removes these materials when converting design files into surface-mesh files, leaving the surface-mesh file depicting only the design.

[51]   As discussed in Chapter 2, there could be differences in resolution (the size of the triangles used) or in how well the software tessellates features. But these are generated by the software, not the draftsperson.

[52]   As far as realistic paintings are concerned, courts insist that, intentionally or not, the painting includes the "personal reaction of an individual upon nature." *Bleistein*, 188 U.S. at 250 ("The copy is the personal reaction of an individual upon nature. Personality always contains something unique. It expresses its singularity even in handwriting, and a very modest grade of art has in it something irreducible, which is one man's alone."). In contrast, drawing lines in a CAD program is a science, not an art. The draftsperson can specify the length and curvature with precision. Further, shapes in CAD programs are rarely drawn from scratch. Rather, the CAD software has numerous prestored shapes that a draftsperson uses.

includes creative choices like angle, perspective, and lighting.[53] But where these elements are lacking, that is, where the photograph is nothing more than a slavish copy of an unprotected work, it contains no protectable creativity.[54] The same is true for maps that do no more than depict reality.[55]

Detailed 3D scans of useful objects represent nothing more than slavish copying of the object's shape. The person taking the scan is not making choices as to lighting, perspective, or angles. Therefore, there is no creativity in the initial scan.[56]

As discussed in Chapter 2, the surface-mesh file generated by the scanning software may require some manual repair to accurately depict the object. For example, a user may need to edit the file to reflect a sharp corner when the imperfect software rounded the corner. Such edits, however, when made to accurately reflect an existing object do not constitute creative choices. The Tenth Circuit held as much in *Meshwerks, Inc. v. Toyota Motor Sales U.S.A., Inc.*, when it refused to grant copyright protection to a 3D scan of a car even after workers edited the scanned image "to resemble each vehicle as closely as possible."[57] The court concluded that "Meshwerks' models depict nothing more than unadorned Toyota vehicles ... [I]ts models reflect none of the decisions that can make depictions of things or facts in the world, whether

---

[53] Schrock v. Learning Curve Int'l, Inc., 586 F.3d 513, 519 (7th Cir. 2009).

[54] *See, e.g., id.* (recognizing that there exists a "narrow category of photographs that can be classified as 'slavish copies,' lacking any independently created expression"); Bridgeman Art Library, Ltd. v. Corel Corp., 25 F. Supp. 2d 421, 427 (S.D.N.Y. 1998) (applying UK law and finding no originality in exact reproductions of public domain works). *Cf.* Daniel J. Gervais, *Feist Goes Global: A Comparative Analysis of the Notion of Originality in Copyright Law*, 49 J. COPYRIGHT SOC'Y U.S.A. 949, 971–72 (2002) ("[A] photographer trying to take a technically perfect picture is not making creative choices."); Justin Hughes, *The Photographer's Copyright – Photograph as Art, Photograph as Database*, 25 HARV. J. L. & TECH. 339, 374–75 (2012).

[55] Darden v. Peters, 488 F.3d 277, 286–87 (4th Cir. 2007) (affirming Copyright Office's refusal to register pre-existing map with additions "color, shading, and labels using standard fonts and shapes"); Kern River Gas Transmission Co. v. Coastal Corp., 899 F.2d 1458, 1463–64 (5th Cir. 1990) ("[T]he idea of the location of the pipeline and its expression embodied in the 1:250,000 maps are inseparable and not subject to protection."); *see also* Dennis S. Karjala, *Copyright in Electronic Maps*, 35 JURIMETRICS J. 395 (1995) (noting that the *Feist* decision leaves many digital maps unprotected by copyright).

[56] *See generally* Michael Weinberg, *3D Scanning: A World Without Copyright*, SHAPEWAYS (2016), www.shapeways.com/wordpress/wp-content/uploads/2016/05/white-paper-3d-scanning -world-without-copyright.pdf.

[57] *See, e.g.,* Meshwerks, Inc. v. Toyota Motor Sales U.S.A., Inc., 528 F.3d 1258, 1260 (10th Cir. 2008). The scanning process was more manually intensive than scanning technology described herein; it involved placing special tape on the car and using an articulated arm tethered to a computer to map coordinates based on the tape. But the principle is the same.

Oscar Wilde or a Toyota Camry, new expressions subject to copyright protection."[58]

Creating a DMF from Scratch

A more contentious issue is whether a DMF of a useful article (e.g., a shovel) contains protectable creativity when a draftsperson creates the DMF from scratch, as opposed to by copying an existing object. This would commonly be the case in the design phase of a new product. In one sense, creating a DMF of a yet-to-be-manufactured object differs from copying an existing object: the lines cannot be copied from an object because it does not yet exist. The draftsperson is no longer copying the existing facts.

But in another sense, the draftsperson is constrained by the to-be-created physical object. The lines are thus analogous to existing facts. With a little flamboyance, one could say that the draftsperson is copying a Platonic form.[59] The drawing does not emerge from the draftsperson's creativity; it emerges from the designer's utilitarian ingenuity. Every line or shape drawn is dictated by the utilitarian shape of the shovel to be manufactured.

Some might argue that when the draftsperson is drawing a never-before manufactured shovel there are choices to be made, such as how long to make the handle or how wide to make the spade. These choices may be made by the draftsperson or by someone dictating the shovel's dimensions to the draftsperson.

But in my view, and the view of at least one court discussed below, choices as to a useful article's dimensions reflect not creativity in the copyright sense, but only choices about the utilitarian design of the article. In other words, mere choice is not enough. Choice must be coupled with creativity. If choice alone contributed creativity, the tangible object itself would be protected. Some argue that tangible useful objects in fact embody creativity but that the useful article doctrine excludes the inherent creativity in the tangible object to channel useful objects away from copyright law. But as already discussed,

---

[58]   *Id.* at 1265. *Cf.* ABS Entertainment, Inc. v. CBS Corp., 900 F.3d 1113, 1126 (9th Cir. 2018) (stating that digitally remastered sound recordings that merely remove clicking or extraneous noise from the original recording do not contain protectable creativity).

[59]   Plato theorized that "forms" were the most accurate reality even though they were nonphysical. For example, the most accurate, real triangle was a form, but no one could see it. Every triangle drawn by humans was an imperfect copy of the form. *See, e.g.,* JOHN M. FRAME, A HISTORY OF WESTERN PHILOSOPHY AND THEOLOGY 64–65 (2015). Similarly, the digital drawing of a yet-to-be-manufactured utilitarian object can be said to be a copy of a form. This admittedly esoteric analogy should be limited to utilitarian objects lest it wipe out all of copyright. The form is thus a conceptualization of the draftsperson's utilitarian constraints.

section 101 does not exclude only a "useful article," but rather *"the design of a useful article."* In this sense, the issue of "what counts as creativity" when creating a drawing from scratch can be linked to the statutory language already analyzed previously.

Stated another way, choices about the dimensions of the useful object cannot contribute to copyrightable creativity because they are dictated entirely by utilitarian concerns. A shovel designer has the choice to make the handle two feet long or three feet long, but that choice will be made not on the basis of creativity, but on the basis of the best functioning shovel from the end user's perspective. Shorter shovels may be good for some applications and longer shovels better for others, but each shovel is made a certain length based on its function.[60]

That technical drawings are not copyrightable when dictated by function was recognized by the court in *Enterprises International, Inc. v. International Knife & Saw, Inc.*[61] That court refused copyright protection to the plaintiffs' technical drawings because the "designs *admittedly* contain[ed] only functional and utilitarian information, the sole purpose of which [was] to manufacture specific types of knives or blades to precisely fit certain machines."[62] The court's language is probably too broad because creatively arranged utilitarian information can be copyrighted, but the court's emphasis on creativity not constrained by utilitarian concerns is correct.

If ex ante choice were enough to impart creativity, mere written recipes could be protected by copyright, but they are not.[63] In creating a recipe, one chooses the basic dish, ingredients, the cooking time, and the manner of cooking, and yet no protection ensues for these facts. Even the listing of simple cooking instructions does not carry the recipe over the copyright threshold, because the instructions are intimately related to the functional system or method of cooking.[64] As one court stated:

---

[60] Product design can incorporate aesthetic concerns, but when those concerns as reflected in the design are inseparable from the article's utility, they are protected if at all by design patent rights.

[61] No. C12-5638 BHS, 2014 WL 1365398 (W.D. Wash. Apr. 7, 2014).

[62] *Id.* at *6 (emphasis in original). The court did not provide a detailed analysis or description of the drawings, so it is difficult to know whether the drawings had labels, parts lists, or other creative additions.

[63] 37 C.F.R. § 202.1(a) (2018) (stating that "mere listing of ingredients or contents" are not copyrightable).

[64] *See* Publ'ns Int'l. v. Meredith, 88 F.3d 473, 480–81 (7th Cir. 1996); Lambing v. Godiva Chocolatier, 1998 U.S. App. LEXIS 1983 (6th Cir. Feb. 6, 1998); Tomaydo-Tomahhdo, LLC v. Vozary, 629 F. App'x 658, 661 (6th Cir. 2015); Lapine v. Seinfeld, No. 97–5697, 2009 WL 2902584 (S.D.N.Y. Sept. 10, 2009).

The recipes involved in this case comprise the lists of required ingredients and the directions for combining them to achieve the final products. The recipes contain no expressive elaboration upon either of these functional components, as opposed to recipes that might spice up functional directives by weaving in creative narrative ... The identification of ingredients necessary for the preparation of each dish is a statement of facts. There is no expressive element in each listing; in other words, the author who wrote down the ingredients for "Curried Turkey and Peanut Salad" was not giving literary expression to his individual creative labors. Instead, he was writing down an idea, namely, the ingredients necessary to the preparation of a particular dish.[65]

It is the same with a DMF, regardless of the format: everything is included in the drawing for functional reasons to describe the shape of a useful article with the end goal of manufacturing it. To borrow from the words of the *Meredith* court, the drawing merely represents the idea of the utilitarian shovel.

In fact, functional constraints are among the most fundamental limitations on copyright protection.[66] Another common example is found in software cases where the software code is designed to accomplish a utilitarian objective. Any element of software that is dictated by utilitarian concerns like efficiency does not constitute protectable expression.[67] Despite this limitation, complex software continues to garner copyright protection because it can be drafted numerous, arguably creative ways to achieve the same utilitarian objective.[68] But the same is not true for digital manufacturing files of useful objects. Once the design of the useful object is determined based on functionality, the entirety of the design is determined.

In sum, when a drawing does no more than depict the design of a useful article, it contains no protectable creativity. It is important to emphasize that many technical drawings of useful objects will enjoy copyright protection because they include creative choices as to views, labels, parts lists, and the like. This is true whether they are drawn with pencil and paper or in a CAD program. But without such choices, I argue there is no protectable expression.

---

[65] Publ'ns Int'l. v. Meredith, 88 F.3d 473, 480–81 (7th Cir. 1996).

[66] At the extreme, see Lexmark Intern., Inc. v. Static Control Components, Inc., 387 F.3d 522, 544 (2004) ("[A] poem in the abstract could be copyrightable. But that does not mean that the poem receives copyright protection when it is used in the context of a lock-out code."). *See also* Christopher Buccafusco & Mark A. Lemley, *Functionality Screens*, 103 VA. L. REV. 1293, 1316–40 (2017).

[67] The leading case on this front is Computer Assocs. Int'l v. Altai, Inc., 982 F.2d 693, 707–10 (2d Cir. 1992). Analogies can be made to fact works, like books covering science topics, which receive thin protection only for the expression, not the facts.

[68] *See, e.g., id.* at 702. Many disagree that copyright is appropriate for software. *See supra* note 18.

One can speculate why Congress felt the need to include technical drawings within copyright's ambit. At the time the statute was drafted, DMFs were not on legislators' minds. Even though I have argued in the chapter that exact drawings of useful objects, even if done on paper, are not copyrightable, the principle carries increased urgency when one considers the different kinds of technical drawings on a spectrum of functionality. Traditional hand-drawn or computer-generated blueprints were limited in their inherent functionality. Humans had to read, interpret, and apply them. The actual value embodied in the blueprint was miniscule compared to the costs of translating that drawing into a finished product.

With 3D printing technology, however, digital drawings implicate much more directly the boundary between copyright and patent law. That is, they become much more closely associated with the end goal of manufacturing and they house vastly more economic value. Design files are the farthest removed from the manufacturing process, because they must first be converted into surface-mesh files. And surface-mesh files must be sliced into machine-instruction files to provide precise instructions to the printer. But all three DMF formats exist on a smooth path to digital manufacturing that does not require much, if any, human intervention.

Because DMFs can be used directly in the manufacturing process, they should be distinguished from traditional blueprints. My analysis thus far demonstrates there is no need to distinguish them, but because the issue of creativity in drawings is debatable, policy considerations are important. Copyright protection for DMFs more directly impedes utilitarian manufacturing than protection for simple blueprints. It is true that copyright in drawings does not prohibit others from manufacturing the object,[69] but in an age of digital manufacturing, an imitator would need to create its own DMFs. It can presumably do this by obtaining the physical object and creating DMFs from it.[70]

But what is the point in forcing the imitator to create its own DMF from scratch like the law currently requires for application programs? Unlike traditional software, where copyright protection was probably granted as a policy matter because patent protection was uncertain and the reverse engineering process provided valuable lead time to the initial creator, useful objects are clearly patentable subject matter and the reverse engineering process is much

[69] 17 U.S.C. § 113(b).
[70] *See* Bleistein v. Donaldson Lithographing Co., 188 U.S. 239, 249 (1903) ("Others are free to copy the original [if it is not protected by copyright]. They are not free to copy the copy."). Justice Holmes was speaking of object found in nature, but the rationale should extend to anything unprotected by copyright.

quicker. Copyright protection for DMFs would do nothing to advance creativity and would instead serve only to slow competition and catch many imitators unaware.[71] Indeed, the whole point of section 113(b) is that copyright should not unnecessarily impede the manufacture of utilitarian objects. But recognizing copyright in DMFs of utilitarian objects would do just that. Furthermore, how much expensive litigation will ensue with parties arguing over whether a second DMF was independently created versus verbatim copied?

DMFs embody the economic value of utilitarian works in a manner that traditional blueprints never have. To allow the copyright to protect DMFs of utilitarian objects would, therefore, be a poor policy fit from a copyright or a patent perspective. It would serve as friction to the desirable imitation that fuels capitalism and extends utilitarian benefits throughout society.[72]

A Note on Models and the Constitution

The creativity requirement explains why unadorned representations of useful objects are not copyrightable but embellished drawings are. One potential difficulty with this analysis is that the statute also lists "models" as PGS works.[73] Unlike technical drawings, models do not typically include anything more than the depiction of the useful object. They certainly do not include multiple views, because they are three-dimensional. And they would not often include part labels or other annotations. Thus, the inclusion of models in the list of PGS works may suggest a congressional intent to protect exact representations of useful articles.

I do not think that conclusion is required. An alternate explanation is that models are traditionally made by hand or through other processes that do not render *exact* representations. They also often need to abstract away details and features to accommodate size and material requirements.[74] In instances where an artist sets out to paint (or, presumably, model) something to look "real," courts have long (stubbornly?) insisted that regardless of intention, the artist imparts a "personal reaction" in the work.[75] Congress may have intended to

---

[71]   *See* Paul Banwatt & Laura Robinson, *Dispatches from the Front Lines of 3D Copyright*, 28 INTELL. PROP. J. 237, 262 (2016).

[72]   Though I argue from a utilitarian perspective, the same result can be arrived at from a *droit d'auteur*, continental emphasis, which tends to institute a high originality bar that DMFs of utilitarian objects would not cross.

[73]   17 U.S.C. § 101.

[74]   I thank Michael Weinberg for this point.

[75]   *Bleistein*, 188 U.S. at 250.

apply this rationale to models (and for that matter, hand-drawn blueprints), which contain minor variations imparted by their creator. With digital design and manufacturing, however, there is no room for personal reaction in the design of utilitarian articles – the design software renders the drawing devoid of deviation.

In the end, the statutory analysis of protection for models must keep in mind that the *Feist* Court's articulation of the creativity requirement came several years after the 1976 Copyright Act. Because the Constitution must control over a statute, the statute should be interpreted as only referring to models containing expressive choices. Any models (or technical drawings) depicting only the design of a useful article lack creativity and cannot enjoy copyright protection.

Merger

The issue as to whether ex ante design choices for useful articles can constitute protectable creativity in drawings can also be viewed from the perspective of the merger doctrine.[76] The merger doctrine starts with the recognition that copyright protection does not extend to "any idea, procedure, process, system, method of operation, concept, principle, or discovery ... "[77] Under the doctrine, what otherwise might count as creative expression can be so closely linked to the underlying idea, process, etc., that the expression merges into the idea and thereby is not protected by copyright. Among other things, the merger doctrine polices the boundary between utilitarian and creative works.

For instance, the merger doctrine has been used to exclude copyright protection for blank forms and instruction manuals even though they embody ex ante decisions about how they are designed. In *Baker v. Selden*, the plaintiff had a copyright in an accounting book as a whole.[78] The defendant substantially copied not the entire book, but only the blank forms for use in the accounting method.[79] In the face of the plaintiff's allegation of copyright infringement, the Supreme Court held that the blank forms were "necessary incidents" to the accounting method and therefore not copyrightable.[80] The

---

[76] For a deep exploration of the merger doctrine, see Pamela Samuelson, *Reconceptualizing Copyright's Merger Doctrine*, 63 J. COPYRIGHT SOC'Y U.S.A. 417 (2016).

[77] 17 U.S.C. § 102(b).

[78] Baker v. Selden, 101 U.S. 99 (1879).

[79] *Id.* at 100.

[80] *Id.* at 103. The Copyright Office has issued a regulation stating that blank forms and similar materials are not copyrightable. 37 C.F.R. § 202.1(c) (2018). This is harmless as long as courts do not read it as limiting *Baker* to its facts. *Baker* wasn't a case about forms. It was a case about the boundary between copyright law and patent law.

Baker court did not use the term "merger," but it is widely seen as a clear forerunner to the doctrine.

Beyond blank forms, courts have applied the merger doctrine to pictorial and literary works. In *Decorative Aides Corp. v. Staple Sewing Aides Corp.*, the plaintiff claimed copyright protection in its instruction sheet that consisted of an illustrated diagram and brief instructions describing how to make the pleated draperies.[81] The defendant's instructions and diagram were very similar to the plaintiff's, but the court held that they were "dictated by functional considerations" and thus could not be the basis of infringement.[82] In short, any small choices in the words and diagram merged with their function.

The defendant in *Decorative Aides* did not dispute the existence of a copyright in the instructions and diagram; it argued only about infringement. But other courts have applied the doctrine to foreclose copyright protection altogether. The leading case (besides *Baker*) is *Morrissey v. Procter & Gamble Co.*, where the court found that copyright law will not protect the short phrasing of rules for a contest.[83] Despite the numerous alterations that could be made to the wording of the rules, the idea of the contest merged with its expression.

In another image-related case, the Fifth Circuit Court of Appeals used the merger doctrine to deny copyright protection to the plaintiff in *Kern River Gas Transmission v. Coastal-Corp.*[84] The plaintiff drew a proposed gas pipeline route on an existing map and claimed copyright infringement when the defendant copied the map, including the pipeline route. The court held that the idea of the pipeline route and any expression merged, thereby precluding copyright protection because the map was the only effective way to show the pipeline route once it was decided.[85]

The merger cases have important implications for DMFs of utilitarian objects. First, they recognize the insignificance of minor choices and variations in the subject matter. Selden exercised choices when designing his particular accounting forms. He could have arranged his columns slightly differently or titled his headings using different words, but these choices did not imbue the forms with protectable expression. In the same way, draftspersons who generate DMFs of yet-to-be-manufactured useful articles can be said to exercise choices regarding length, width, and curvatures, some of which at small scale would not meaningfully affect function. But these minor

---

[81]   Decorative Aides Corp. v. Staple Sewing Aides Corp., 497 F. Supp. 154, 156 (S.D.N.Y. 1980).
[82]   *Id.* at 157.
[83]   Morrissey v. Procter & Gamble Co., 379 F.2d 675 (1st Cir. 1967).
[84]   Kern River Gas Transmission v. Coastal-Corp, 899 F.2d 1458 (5th Cir. 1990).
[85]   *Id.* at 1464.

variations, even if they arguably cross the "modicum of creativity" threshold, should be held to merge with the function of the object.

Second, merger cases also take account of the functional constraints upon a claimed work, both from the view of the original creator and from the view of follow-on users.[86] The *Baker* Court emphasized that where "the methods or diagrams" used in the book are necessary to the utilitarian purpose, "such methods and diagrams are to be considered as necessary incidents" to the utilitarian purpose.[87] Similarly, the *Decorative Aides* court emphasized that the plaintiff's instructions and diagram were "dictated by functional considerations," limiting their protection.[88]

The recognition that functional considerations can merge small variations with utilitarian goals should eliminate the prospect of copyright protection for DMFs of purely utilitarian objects.[89] *Baker* emphasized the importance of considering the "final end" of a purported work.[90] The purpose of creating a DMF, whether it be a design file, surface-mesh file, or machine-instruction file, is to manufacture an object. Every choice about the design of a purely useful object is made for functional reasons, whether to imbue the object with the required strength, to limit its weight, or otherwise to accomplish a utilitarian purpose. To the extent that there are small variations possible within the design, they merge with the utilitarian objective, just like with Selden's forms. To hold otherwise would inhibit free market competition in utilitarian works.[91]

Previously in this chapter I argued that choices made for utilitarian reasons should not constitute creativity in the copyright sense. To the extent that one disagrees with that proposition, the merger doctrine would have the same effect of limiting copyright protection for choices dictated by function. But the merger doctrine is less preferred as a tool to protect the line between patents and copyrights because courts apply it inconsistently. Some courts use it broadly, foreclosing copyright protection in cases that involve a great deal of

---

[86] Samuelson, *supra* note 76, at 442–44.

[87] Baker v. Selden, 101 U.S. 99, 104 (1879).

[88] *Decorative Aides Corp.*, 497 F. Supp. at 157.

[89] Again, this assumes the file contains nothing more than the shape of the object.

[90] *Baker*, 101 U.S. at 104 ("[T]he teachings of science and the rules and methods of useful art have their final end in application and use.").

[91] *Cf.* Kern River Gas Transmission v. Coastal-Corp., 899 F.2d 1458, 1464 (5th Cir. 1990) ("Such map markings are certainly the only effective way to convey the idea of the proposed location of a pipeline across 1,000 miles of terrain. To extend protection to the lines would be to grant Kern River a monopoly of the idea for locating a proposed pipeline in the chosen corridor, a foreclosure of competition that Congress could not have intended to sanction through copyright law.").

creative expression,[92] while others unrealistically limit it to cases where there is only *one way* to express the idea.[93] More problematically, some courts apply it only as an affirmative defense and limit it to non-verbatim copying, which is inconsistent with *Baker v. Selden* and leads to unnecessary litigation costs.[94]

***

Whether parsing the statute, analogizing to unprotectable facts or ideas, or applying the merger doctrine, there is enough uncertainty as to whether to protect DMFs of purely utilitarian objects that courts are likely to be influenced by policy concerns. I think it is self-evident that these DMFs do not implicate the core aesthetic and creative expression that is at the heart of copyright. Rather, they implicate overwhelmingly (if not exclusively) utilitarian concerns. Protecting these DMFs with copyrights, which would last as long as the author lives plus seventy more years, risks intruding upon and upsetting the carefully balanced patent system, which provides a patent term of only twenty years. It may be that copyrights could provide extra incentive to these utilitarian works, but as will be discussed in Chapter 10, it is not at all clear that extra incentive is needed.

C. OUTSIDE THE UNITED STATES: DMFS OF UTILITARIAN OBJECTS

Not all countries interpret originality as requiring creativity.[95] Without a requirement for creativity, as opposed to mere skill or labor, DMFs of utilitarian objects would be protected by copyright, especially where they are created by a draftsperson rather than scanned. Even when an object is scanned, there can be skill and labor in the scanning process and post-scan editing. The advent of 3D printing technology will put pressure on these jurisdictions to create a legal mechanism that prevents copyright protection for DMFs of utilitarian objects.

---

[92] *See* Herbert Rosenthal Jewelry Corp. v. Kalpakian, 446 F. 2d 738 (9th Cir. 1971) (stating that the idea of a jeweled bee pin was "indistinguishable" from its expression, despite the fact that millions of different jeweled bees could be imagined).

[93] *See, e.g.,* Yurman Design, Inc. v. PAJ, Inc., 262 F.3d 101, 111 (2d Cir. 2001) ("[I]f there is just one way to express an idea, the idea and expression are said to merge.").

[94] Osborn, *IP Channeling, supra* note 21, at 1322; *see also* Samuelson, *supra* note 76, at 435–38.

[95] For example, Canada does not require creativity, but only skill and judgment. Tesh W. Dagne & Chelsea Dubeau, *3D Printing and the Law: Are CAD Files Copyright-Protected?*, 28 INTELL. PROP. J. 101, 122–23 (2015). Australia and New Zealand also traditionally did not either, though Australia's most recent pronouncement requires "independent intellectual effort." IceTV Pty Ltd. v. Nine Network Australia Pty Ltd. [2009] HCA 14 (Austl.). It is not clear whether this raised the level of originality or not.

In the European Union, the law as to originality is evolving. Previously diverse standards are being harmonized through directives and forceful (some would say activist) CJEU decisions.[96] These changes, among others, have raised intense discussions about the interface between copyright, patent, and design law.[97]

For example, UK law was traditionally very permissive toward copyright protection in some works. It did not require creativity, but only skill, judgment, and labor.[98] Commentators lament that the meaning of skill, labor, and judgment is unstable,[99] but regardless, it clearly encompassed even simple design drawings, and would encompass DMFs.[100]

EU law, however, has begun to harmonize the standard of originality, forcing out the skill, judgment, and labor standard.[101] The directives aimed at software, databases, and photographs require a work to be "the author's own intellectual creation." But the CJEU has interpreted that standard to apply to all works, not only software, databases, and photographs. CJEU case law further refines the requirement, speaking in terms of the need for an author's "creativity"[102] and "free and creative choices" having a "personal touch."[103] Under this language, mere choice is not enough to provide originality; the choice must be "creative." The CJEU has also stressed that choices dictated by functionality cannot contribute the requisite creativity.[104]

---

[96] *See, e.g.,* Case C-5/08, Infopaq Int'l v. Danske Dagblades Forening, 2009 E.C.R. I-6569; Case C-604/10, Football Dataco Ltd. v. Yahoo! UK Ltd, 2012 2 CMLR 24; Case C-168/09, Flos SpA v. Semeraro Casa e Famiglia SpA, 2011 E.C.R. I-00181.

[97] *See, e.g.,* The Copyright/Design Interface: Past, Present and Future (Estelle Derclaye ed. 2018).

[98] *See, e.g.,* Indep. Television Publ'ns Ltd. v. Time Out Limited Ltd. & Elliot [1984] Ch 64 (Eng.).

[99] Lionel Bently & Brad Sherman, Intellectual Property Law 94 (2008).

[100] *See, e.g.,* Mackie Designs Inc. v. Behringer Specialised Studio Equipment (UK) Ltd. [1999] 20 RPC 717 (UK); British Northrop Ltd v. Texteam Blackburn Ltd [1973] FSR 241.

[101] *See, e.g.,* Lionel Bently, *The Return of Industrial Copyright?*, 34 E.I.P.R. 654 (2012); Estelle Derclaye, *Assessing the Impact and Reception of the Court of Justice of the European Union Case Law on UK Copyright Law: What Does the Future Hold?*, 240 Revue Internationale du Droit D'auteur 5 (2014); Andreas Rahmatian, *Originality in UK Copyright Law: The Old "Skill and Labour" Doctrine Under Pressure*, 44 Int'l Rev. Intell. Prop. & Competition L. 4, 6 (2013). Of course, the United Kingdom's relationship with the European Union is in flux as "Brexit" continues to unfold at the time of this writing.

[102] Case C-5/08, Infopaq Int'l v. Danske Dagblades Forening, 2009 E.C.R. I-6569.

[103] Case C-145/10, Eva-Maria Painer v. Standard Verlags GmbH 2011 E.C.D.R. 297.

[104] Case C-604/10, Football Dataco Ltd. v. Yahoo! UK Ltd, 2012 2 C.M.L.R. 24 (holding that there can be no originality from aspects of a database that are "dictated by technical considerations, rules or constraints which leave no room for creative freedom"); Case C-406/10, SAS Institute Inc. v. World Programming Ltd., 2012 3 C.M.L.R. 4 ("[T]o accept that the functionality of a computer program can be protected by copyright would amount to

Taken together, these cases suggest an analysis of DMFs similar to the U.S. approach discussed previously in the chapter. That is, DMFs that will manufacture purely utilitarian objects do not contain any creativity in the mere representation of the object.[105] European scholars have recognized the beginnings of this argument, though they conservatively limit its application to the most basic design drawings of utilitarian objects.[106] Alternatively, as in the United States, courts could analogize DMFs to uncopyrightable facts or could apply the merger doctrine to DMFs of purely utilitarian objects.[107]

Additional wrinkles exist in countries that offer sui generis protections for creations that may not qualify for copyright protection. For instance, the EU Database Directive protects databases, defined as "a collection of independent works, data or other materials arranged in a systematic or methodical way and individually accessible by electronic or other means."[108] The CJEU interprets this definition broadly,[109] so much so that DMFs might fall within it. Further, many countries offer copyright-like protection to creations using various tort or unfair competition laws that protect against so-called slavish or parasitic copying.[110] Although the details of these laws are beyond the scope of this

---

        making it possible to monopolise ideas, to the detriment of technological progress and industrial development."); Joined Cases C-403 & 429/08, Football Association Premier League v. QC Leisure, 2012 F.S.R. 1. For a similar line of thinking in Australia, see Burge v. Swarbrick [2007] HCA 17 (Austl.) ("The determination [of whether a work is of artistic craftsmanship] turns on assessing the extent to which the particular work's artistic expression, in its form, is unconstrained by functional considerations.").

[105]   That is not to say a blueprint of such an object as a whole might not be original based on its choices of views, shading, labeling, and the like. Even as to copyrighted drawings, each country's law generally provides that any copyright does not prohibit the manufacture of the utilitarian object displayed therein. *See* Copyright, Designs and Patents Act, 1988, c. 48 §51(1) (UK) [hereinafter, UK CDPA] ("It is not an infringement of any copyright in a design document or model recording or embodying a design for anything other than an artistic work or a typeface to make an article to the design or to copy an article made to the design."). *See also* Mackie Designs Inc. v. Behringer Specialised Studio Equipment (UK) Ltd, [1999] RPC 717.

[106]   Bently, *supra* note 101, at 768 (stating that "drawings of nuts, bolts and even exhaust pipes – might well not pass muster" under the new EU standard for originality); Margoni, *supra* note 3, at 239 ("The blueprint can be of a purely technical nature and lack any possible form of copyright protection. This is an unlikely scenario considering how low the required level of originality usually is.").

[107]   *See, e.g.,* Case C-393/09, Bezpečnostní Softwarová Asociace - Svaz Softwarové Ochrany v. Ministerstvo Kultury, 2011 F.S.R. 18.

[108]   European Parliament & Council Directive 96/9 on the Legal Protection of Databases, 1996 O.J. (L 77) 20 (EC) art. 1(2).

[109]   *See, e.g.,* Case C-490/14, Freistaat Bayern v. Verlag Esterbauer GmbH, ECLI:EU:C:2015:735 (providing database protection for topographical maps).

[110]   *See, e.g.,* Eleonora Rosati, Originality in EU Copyright: Full Harmonization Through Case Law 173 (2013).

book, scholars in the relevant jurisdictions should carefully consider whether providing these protections to DMFs of purely utilitarian objects is necessary or beneficial.

The previous two subsections focused on DMFs as drawings, but DMFs also constitute copies of literary works because the file can be displayed in code (textual) form. Copyright law bends over backward to protect computer program code as literary works, searching scrupulously for creativity despite strong arguments that programs should not be copyrightable.[111] Under U.S. law, DMFs constitute "computer programs" under the statute's capacious definition of "a set of statements or instructions to be used directly or indirectly in a computer in order to bring about a certain result."[112] Australia's definition is similar.[113] The EU Software Directive does not define software other than to state that preparatory design material is included in the undefined term,[114] but commentators contend that DMFs can qualify as literary works in the European Union.[115]

But as with drawings, literary works are only protected to the extent they contain creative expression.[116] If every line of code is dictated by efficiency or other external factors, there is no protectable expression.[117] Moreover, with DMFs the literal code is rarely written by humans. While it is technically possible to create a DMF entirely by typing code, the process is tedious and rarely done except for the simplest of shapes. Rather, a draftsperson uses a CAD program to draw the image, and the computer translates the shapes into textual code using algorithms directed to utilitarian goals, not creative

---

[111] For a list of works discussing computer software, see Osborn, *IP Channeling, supra* note 21, at 1311 n.30.

[112] 17 U.S.C. §101.

[113] Australian Copyright Act § 10(1).

[114] European Parliament & Council Directive 2009/24 on the Legal Protection of Computer Programs, 2009 O.J. (L 111) 16 (EC) art. 1(1) [hereinafter, Software Directive].

[115] *See, e.g.,* Dinusha Mendis, *'Clone Wars' Episode II – The Next Generation: The Copyright Implications Relating to 3D Printing and Computer-Aided Design (CAD) Files,* 6 L. INNOVATION TECH. 265, 271 (2014); Bradshaw et al., *supra* note 3, at 24.

[116] *See, e.g.,* H.R. REP. NO. 94-1476, at 54 (1976) (Conf. Rep.), *as reprinted in* 1976 U.S.C.C.A. N. 5659, 5667 (noting that copyright protects computer programs only "to the extent that they incorporate authorship in programmer's expression of original ideas, as distinguished from the ideas themselves").

[117] *See, e.g.,* Computer Assocs. Int'l v. Altai, Inc., 982 F.2d 693, 707 (2d Cir. 1992); Case C-406/10, SAS Institute Inc v. World Programming Ltd., 2012 3 C.M.L.R. 4.

ones. Further, the software that converts the design file into surface-mesh and machine-instruction files generates the code for those files.

Because humans do not write the actual text of the code, but rather only guide its basic structure by drawing shapes in the CAD program, the literal code does not reflect creativity as to its wording.[118] The only creativity attributable to the draftsperson would correspond to the creativity in the CAD drawing itself, which brings us right back to the previous analysis: drawings that exactly depict useful articles lack creativity.[119]

Some have trouble accepting the argument that textual code of images is not always protectable as a literary work, but they should consider a noncopyrightable photograph.[120] If a physical copy of a photograph is not protected by copyright, it must follow that a digital copy of that photograph would not be protected either. Although a JPEG file is a "computer program" (per the U.S. copyright statute's definition) and can be represented in code format, this fact alone cannot transform the text, generated by a digital camera, into a protectable work.

Another analogy can be drawn to digital files that depict typefaces.[121] Typefaces are not protectable in the United States because they are functional.[122] Congress explicitly considered whether the *design* of typefaces (not just the physical blocks that stamp the letters) should be protected, but concluded the design did not constitute a PGS work.[123] The basic design of

---

[118]   Jane Nielsen & John Liddicoat, *The Multiple Dimensions of Intellectual Property Infringement in the 3D Printing Era*, 27 Australian Intell. P. J. 184, 195–97 (2017); Osborn, *IP Channeling, supra* note 21, at 1318–20.

[119]   Humans can edit the code to fix errors, but because these fixes are for utilitarian reasons, they do not contribute to creativity. They are even less creative than the image editing in *Meshwerks, Inc. v. Toyota Motor Sales U.S.A., Inc.*, 528 F.3d 1258, 1260 (10th Cir. 2008).

[120]   *E.g.*, Bridgeman Art Library, Ltd. v. Corel Corp., 36 F. Supp. 2d 191 (S.D.N.Y. 1999).

[121]   A typeface is "'a set of letters, numbers, or other symbolic characters, whose forms are related by repeating design elements consistently applied in a notational system and are intended to be embodied in articles whose intrinsic utilitarian function is for use in composing text or other cognizable combinations of characters.'" Jacqueline D. Lipton, *To © or Not to ©? Copyright and Innovation in the Digital Typeface Industry*, 43 U.C. Davis L. Rev. 143, 148 (2009) (quoting Terrence J. Carroll, *Protection for Typeface Designs: A Copyright Proposal*, 10 Santa Clara Computer & High Tech. L.J. 139, 141 n.2 (1994)).

[122]   Monotype Corp. PLC v. Int'l Typeface Corp., 43 F.3d 443, 446 (9th Cir. 1994) (noting that "typefaces are not afforded copyright protection which has permitted popular typefaces originally developed by one to be easily and closely copied by a competitor without compensation"). Many other countries do protect typeface. *See* Lipton, *supra* note 121, at 147 n.10.

[123]   H.R. Rep. No. 94–1476, 55–56 n.88 (1976) ("The Committee does not regard the design of typeface, as thus defined, to be a copyrightable 'pictorial, graphic, or sculptural work' within the meaning of this bill and the application of the dividing line in section 101."). It should be noted that some typefaces are very creative and should be protected by copyright. *See* Lipton, *supra* note 121, at 155–64 (giving examples of creative fonts).

any typeface is dictated by function, thereby precluding the needed creativity.[124] Because the typeface is not copyrightable, a computer program that does no more than recreate the typeface is also not protectable.[125]

Others argue that because code can be arranged multiple ways, it embodies creativity in the choice of a particular arrangement. It is true that countless minor permutations of DMF code are possible without changing the final object at all (e.g., move the nozzle in a clockwise versus counterclockwise direction). Even putting aside the fact that people drawing in CAD programs are not typing the code directly, it cannot be that the mere reordering of certain functional steps can bring the file within copyright protection. Were it otherwise, simple recipes would be copyrightable because the ingredients could be listed in multiple orders. But recipes, as mere listings of ingredients, are not copyrightable.[126]

Hence, the copyrightability of the basic code necessary to depict a drawing is tied directly to the copyrightability of the image itself.

E. ANCILLARY COMMENTS OR IMAGES EMBEDDED IN DMFS – APPENDING COPYRIGHT PROTECTION?

This chapter has already described how, on a technical drawing, any materials in addition to the basic depiction of a useful object may contribute protectable creativity. Besides the labels and views discussed already, some files include metadata and comments. Metadata is typically found in design files. It

---

[124] This could be seen as another example of why mere depictions of useful articles do not contain creativity. But there is a difference between typeface, which has its utilitarian end in its two-dimensional depiction, and useful articles, which have their utilitarian end in their three-dimensional form. One could quibble that the mere outline of a typeface could be equated to a drawing of an object, but even the outline of the typeface retains its utilitarian function.

[125] Policy Decision on Copyrightability of Digitized Typefaces, 53 Fed. Reg. 38,110 (Sept. 29, 1988) (codified at 37 C.F.R. § 202 (2017)) [hereinafter *1988 Policy Decision*] ("[T]he Copyright Office has decided that digitized representations of typeface designs are not registrable under the Copyright Act because they do not constitute original works of authorship."). *See also* Osborn, *IP Channeling, supra* note 21, at 1319–20. Font designers lobbied furiously to obtain protections for digital typefaces and received a victory for *scalable* digital fonts, but the rationale for this protection would not extend to protecting DMFs. *Id.* at 1320.

[126] 37 C.F.R. § 202.1(a) (stating that "mere listing of ingredients or contents" is not copyrightable). Further, even inclusion of simple instructions for mixing the ingredients does not make the recipe copyrightable because it is merely a functional system or process. *See* Publ'ns Int'l. v. Meredith, 88 F.3d 473, 480–81 (7th Cir. 1996); Lambing v. Godiva Chocolatier, No. 97–5697, 1998 U.S. App. LEXIS 1983 (6th Cir. Feb.6, 1998); Tomaydo-Tomahhdo, LLC v. Vozary, 629 F. App'x 658, 661 (6th Cir. 2015); Lapine v. Seinfeld, No. 08 Civ. 128(LTS) (RLE), 2009 WL 2902584 (S.D.N.Y. Sept. 10, 2009).

includes additional information, such as the name of the draftsperson or notes about design choices, input via the CAD program. Comments are words in the actual lines of program code that are directed to a human reader and are not executable by a computer. Users can embed comments in any kind of file. Chapter 2 provided an example of comments in DMF code.

Design files often include metadata directed to others, such as design parameters or other engineering information. These can certainly contribute to copyright protection if the expression is creative enough. Once the design file is translated into a surface-mesh file, however, usually all metadata and other extraneous information is stripped away. All that is left is the tessellated surface geometry of the object, which I have argued is unprotected by copyright if the object is purely utilitarian. Further, when software converts the surface-mesh file into a machine-instruction file, that file only contains the instructions for the printer.

Users, however, can choose to insert textual comments into the code form of surface-mesh and machine-instruction files. Alternatively, they could add a creative image overlaid onto the digital version of the object such that it prints along with the tangible object.[127] This raises the possibility that even if courts apply my arguments to render mere drawings unprotectable, DMF creators wanting to control their files can circumvent this limitation by inserting extraneous comments or images to put the file as a whole over the creativity threshold.

Although some may put comments or surface images into surface-mesh and machine-instruction files out of pure motives, others will include them solely to exercise control over the file, especially where the object to be printed is not patentable because it is obvious or not novel. In other words, they will want to make up for the lack of patent protection with copyright protection. Because people wanting to copy the file to use it as a DMF would also need to copy the comments, they would arguably commit copyright infringement based on copying protected expression. This would allow a type of backdoor patent using copyright.[128]

Sometimes the motives of users will be obvious, as where they put a poem in the comments that has no instructive value.[129] More savvy users will include

---

[127]   Only some printers have the ability to print in color, but even the least expensive printer could print a monochrome creative shape on the surface of the object.

[128]   Calling the protection a backdoor patent is an overstatement because copyright law permits an imitator to create its own DMF even by copying the utilitarian features of the product.

[129]   *See, e.g., Habeas Haiku Splatters Spam*, INTABULLETIN (July 1, 2003), www.inta.org/INT ABulletin/Pages/HabeasHaikuSplattersSpam.aspx (describing a company's use of a haiku in a hidden email header in an attempt to use copyright to protect the utilitarian email header).

extraneous material that looks as if it was placed there with altruistic motives. In either case, the content acts as a type of lockout code.[130] Virtually no one values DMFs of utilitarian objects for the creative expression in the comments; they only want the functional features. In that case, copyright law is being used not to protect the value of a creative work, but rather the value of a utilitarian work.

Normatively, this is a misapplication of copyright law, whose goal is to incentivize creative works for the betterment of the public, not to prevent access to otherwise unprotected utilitarian objects. Courts disfavoring such uses of copyright law can refuse copyright protection in several ways. If the expression is miniscule, it may fail the creativity threshold, or its expression may merge with its function. The most aggressive application of the merger doctrine would find that any content acting as a lockout code, no matter how creative, merges with its function as a lockout code.[131]

More aggressively, courts could hold that the lockout codes constitute copyright misuse.[132] Copyright misuse is an equitable doctrine that most

---

[130] *Cf.* Julie E. Cohen, *Reverse Engineering and the Rise of Electronic Vigilantism: Intellectual Property Implications of "Lock-Out" Programs*, 68 S. CAL. L. REV. 1091, 1094–97 (1995) (discussing lockout programs that limit access to video games without a key, wherein the key consists of copyrighted material); Andrea Pacelli, *Who Owns the Key to the Vault? Hold-up, Lock-out, and Other Copyright Strategies*, 18 FORDHAM INTELL. PROP. MEDIA & ENT. L.J. 1229, 1242–46 (2008) (discussing the use of copyrighted material as a password for access to a computer program or other proprietary source).

[131] *Cf.* Lexmark Intern., Inc. v. Static Control Components, Inc., 387 F.3d 522, 541 (2004) ("[T]he fact that [the expression] also functions as a lock-out code undermines the conclusion that Lexmark had a probability of success on its infringement claim."); *id.* at 544 ("[A] poem in the abstract could be copyrightable. But that does not mean that the poem receives copyright protection when it is used in the context of a lock-out code."). In this regard, it is worth noting that 3D printing companies use lockout codes to limit the useable feedstock (ink) to 3D printers. *See* Exemption to Prohibition on Circumvention of Copyright Systems for Access Control Technologies, 80 Fed. Reg. 65,958 (Oct. 28, 2015) (codified at 37 C.F.R. § 201).

[132] *See, e.g.*, Lasercomb Am., Inc. v. Reynolds, 911 F.2d 970, 979 (4th Cir. 1990) (extending copyright misuse to a license that required licensees to agree not to create competing software); Practice Mgmt. Info. Corp. v. Am. Med. Ass'n, 121 F.3d 516 (9th Cir. 1997); Alcatel USA, Inc. v. DGI Techs., Inc., 166 F.3d 772 (5th Cir. 1999) (extending copyright misuse to a license that required licensees to agree not to create competing software); Omega S.A. v. Costco Wholesale Corp., No. 04-CV-05443, 2011 WL 8492716 (C.D. Cal. Nov. 9, 2011) (finding copyright misuse where Omega placed a copyrighted design on the back of its watches to control parallel importation of lawfully sold goods); Brett Frischmann & Dan Moylan, *The Evolving Common Law Doctrine of Copyright Misuse: A Unified Theory and its Application to Software*, 15 BERKELEY TECH. L.J. 865, 912 (2000); Karen E. Georgenson, *Reverse Engineering of Copyrighted Software: Fair Use Or Misuse?*, 5 ALB. L.J. SCI. & TECH. 291, 313 (1996) (supporting copyright misuse defense for necessary intermediate copying and any derivative uses).

often arises with behavior that violates antitrust laws, but it has also been used to ensure copyright law is cabined within its constitutional mandate to incentivize creative works for the public. "The question is not whether the copyright is being used in a manner violative of antitrust law . . ., but whether copyright is being used in a manner violative of the public policy embodied in the grant of a copyright."[133] As an equitable doctrine, it would probably be reserved for obvious uses of lockout codes.

It should be recognized that the use of copyrightable material in a DMF differs somewhat from many lockout codes used to prevent interoperability between competing hardware. Traditionally, lockout codes have been used to stop competing video games from working on a proprietary console or remote garage door transponders from communicating with a proprietary garage door opener. Circumventing a lockout code in the hardware context does not permit cost-free, instantaneous copying of the hardware. The competitor must build its own hardware. With a DMF, unlocking the code allows instant, cost-free copying of the file (assuming no other IP right is implicated), which means that the copier might not independently develop anything. Whether this free riding alters the balance of equities will be a matter of debate, but as Chapter 10 spells out, there are a number of mechanisms outside of copyright by which creators can appropriate the returns on their investment in creating the files. If these incentives are sufficient, and I believe they are likely to be as I discuss in Chapter 10, providing copyright protection to the entire DMF via lockout codes will needlessly slow utilitarian progress and competition.

That being said, in most cases it will be difficult, if not impossible, to discern whether users include copyrightable content through improper motives. Courts could ignore the content, enforce copyright law against copying it, or take a middle ground. Ignoring it altogether goes too far, especially where a creative design is overlaid on an object.[134] Such aesthetic expression is at the core of copyright law, and some might value surface decoration. Always enforcing copyright law against copying the content is also too broad, because it sweeps in instances where inconsequential expression hinders the dissemination and use of otherwise unprotected files.

To take a middle ground, courts could analyze the issue under fair use, which is a robust doctrine in the United States.[135] Fair use requires the

---

[133] Lasercomb, 911 F.2d at 978.
[134] This is not to say that any image is worthy of copyright protection. *See Omega S.A.*, 2011 WL 8492716 (finding copyright misuse where Omega placed a copyrighted design on the back of its watches to control parallel importation of lawfully sold goods).
[135] Israel, Liberia, Malaysia, the Philippines, Singapore, South Korea, Sri Lanka, and Taiwan have flexible fair use provisions similar to the United States, and other countries like Australia

balancing of several factors to determine whether a defendant can be excused from infringement.[136] With computer programs, courts have used fair use to preserve "public access to the ideas and functional elements embedded in copyrighted computer software programs."[137] Courts have recognized that fair use can excuse the copying of lockout codes.[138]

In applying fair use, courts should be aware that one who copies a DMF with the goal of printing the utilitarian object is usually forced to copy all content in the file. For things like non-executable comments, courts should pay attention to whether the copier was even aware of or benefited from the comments. If not, and especially if users of DMFs generally ignore the comments, then the use should be presumptively fair. This presumption could be couched in terms of transformative use, because users who ignore or remove extraneous material are using the file for a utilitarian purpose rather than a creative one.

The same presumption should apply to inconsequential creative images, such as those not readily visible to users. For ornate and obvious surface ornamentation, on the other hand, courts should probably only apply fair use if the copier removes the surface ornamentation before printing or further disseminating the file. In all cases, any discernible intent on the copyright claimant's part is certainly relevant. Courts should also distinguish between private, individual uses and commercial distribution of files. The latter should be judged by a harsher standard.

Outside of the United States, many countries utilize more limited fair dealing provisions, though there is continual pressure to broaden

---

are actively considering reforms. Peter K. Yu, *Customizing Fair Use Transplants*, 7 Laws 9 (2018), www.mdpi.com/2075-471X/7/1/9.

[136] 17 U.S.C. § 107 (listing as nonexclusive factors: "(1) the purpose and character of the use, including whether such use is of a commercial nature or is for nonprofit educational purposes; (2) the nature of the copyrighted work; (3) the amount and substantiality of the portion used in relation to the copyrighted work as a whole; and (4) the effect of the use upon the potential market for or value of the copyrighted work").

[137] Sony Comput. Entm't, Inc. v. Connectix Corp., 203 F.3d 596, 603 (9th Cir. 2000).

[138] *See* Lexmark Intern., Inc. v. Static Control Components, Inc., 387 F.3d 522, 544–45 (2004). *Cf.* Sega Enters. Ltd. v. Accolade, Inc., 977 F.2d 1510, 1520–28 (9th Cir. 1992) (finding intermediate copying to understand video game compatibility with game console to be per se fair use); *Connectix*, 203 F.3d at 602–08 (finding that intermediate copying of BIOS that was necessary to access unprotected functional elements of video game console constituted fair use); Chamberlain Grp., Inc. v. Skylink Techs., Inc., 381 F.3d 1178 (2004) (refusing to allow a DMCA claim to eviscerate a fair use defense); Julie E. Cohen, *Reverse Engineering and the Rise of Electronic Vigilantism: Intellectual Property Implications of "Lock-Out" Programs*, 68 S. Cal. L. Rev. 1091, 1104–51 (1995).

them.[139] Other jurisdictions do not include fair dealing provisions but excuse certain forms of copying under other names.[140] These laws are generally similar to each other in having closed lists of possible exceptions, none of which maps on well to DMFs. DMFs with only ancillary creative expression may increase the impetus for broader exceptions in these jurisdictions.

Another route to avoid a clash between copyright and patent law would be to excuse individual copying in cases of DMFs containing ancillary creative expression. Many countries provide limited private copying exceptions, but the exceptions do not apply to computer programs, which is a problem for DMFs.[141] Of course, this solution, like fair use and misuse, would involve difficult line-drawing questions, particularly in determining when creative expression is ancillary. But just because it is difficult to draw lines does not excuse courts from trying. It is better to free at least some utilitarian DMFs from copyright law's shadow than simply to throw in the towel.

It might be argued that the low damages available for ancillary copyrightable material make the issue moot – who would bother to sue for trivial sums? It is true that damages are often limited to the proportion attributable to infringement.[142] In the United States, however, statutory damages are available for registered copyrights.[143] More importantly, although the low recoveries will deter many suits, they will not deter them all. There have been many instances in the United States (where each side presumptively pays its own legal costs) of copyright owners pursuing low-value suits in part for the

[139] Canada's Supreme Court significantly broadened the doctrine. *See* Michael Geist, *Fairness Found: How Canada Quietly Shifted from Fair Dealing to Fair Use*, in THE COPYRIGHT PENTALOGY: HOW THE SUPREME COURT OF CANADA SHOOK THE FOUNDATIONS OF CANADIAN COPYRIGHT LAW (Michael Geist, ed. 2013). In addition to other exceptions, the United Kingdom utilizes more traditional fair dealing provisions. UK CDPA §§ 29–30A.
[140] *See, e.g.*, Copyright Directive art. 5(2) (allowing member countries to include the listed exceptions).
[141] The United Kingdom at one time excused private noncommercial copying but excluded "computer programs" from the excuse. UK CDPA § 28B. Since DMFs are computer programs, this excuse would not apply. In any event, the UK courts have quashed the private copying exception as inconsistent with the Copyright Directive. *See* BASCA v. Sec'y of State for Bus. & Innovation, [2015] EWHC (Admin) 1723. The Copyright Directive provides that member states may excuse private, noncommercial copying, but only "on condition that the rightholders receive fair compensation." Copyright Directive art. 5(2)(b). Providing compensation should be unnecessary for DMFs with only ancillary creativity.
[142] *See, e.g.*, 17 U.S.C. § 504(b); Sheldon v. Metro-Goldwyn Pictures Corp., 309 U.S. 390 (1940) (apportioning damages).
[143] 17 U.S.C. § 504(c).

prospect of quick settlement payouts.[144] In jurisdictions where the loser pays all legal costs, a copyright owner has even more incentive to bring suit if the law protects the ancillary expression. The costs of such suits are high – potentially crushing when individuals are involved – and they are not serving the ends of copyright policy.

F. CONCLUSION

As a tentative conclusion to this chapter, it is argued that DMFs of utilitarian objects should be protected if at all by patent law rather than copyright law. Patent law's exacting requirements of novelty and nonobviousness may leave many such DMFs unprotected, but a rich public domain of utilitarian technology is an important gear in a capitalist, innovation-centric society. Providing copyright protection to DMFs of utilitarian objects would gum up innovation's gears without obvious return benefit in terms of creativity. Some may argue, as they did with traditional software, that copyright protection provides a necessary incentive to the creation of even utilitarian DMFs. But unlike the uncertain legal climate at the time courts granted copyright protection to software, patent law clearly protects utilitarian objects and provides at least some protection for the corresponding DMFs.

But this conclusion must be only tentative at this point. It may be that, however poorly copyright protection fits as a theoretical matter, it provides a needed appropriability mechanism for creators of utilitarian DMFs. A full exploration of this potential is taken up in Chapter 10, where I conclude that copyright protection does not appear to be necessary based on current evidence.

---

[144] *See, e.g.,* Matthew Sag, *Copyright Trolling, an Empirical Study*, 100 Iowa L. Rev. 1105, 1111–13 (2015) (discussing copyright "trolls," which he defines as companies who make a business model out of suing and collecting settlements).

9

Design Rights, Tangibility, and Free Expression

Chapter Outline:

Conceptually, design rights sit roughly somewhere between copyrightable subject matter and patentable subject matter. If a perfect division between the three IP rights existed (it does not), utility patents would protect the purely utilitarian aspects of objects, copyrights would protect purely aesthetic aspects, and design patents would protect nonobvious blends of the two aspects that garner neither patent nor copyright protection.[1] In fact, however, there is overlap among the categories. In many jurisdictions, the same aspects of an object can enjoy both copyright and design rights.[2]

Whether the appearance of a given tangible object can enjoy design protection, as opposed to being purely dictated by function, can be a difficult question.[3] So too can issues of whether a particular design is too similar to prior designs. Design regimes also sometimes struggle to apply so-called must-fit and must-match exceptions.[4] Although 3D printing technology may

---

[1] *Cf.* Mark P. McKenna & Katherine J. Strandburg, *Progress and Competition in Design*, 17 STAN. TECH. L. REV. 1, 4 (2013) ("The integration of form and function is what distinguishes industrial design from both purely artistic expression (for which we have copyright) and technological invention (for which we have utility patent).").

[2] *See* Mazer v. Stein, 347 U.S. 201, 217 (1954) ("Neither the Copyright Statute nor any other says that because a thing is patentable it may not be copyrighted."); *In re* Yardley, 493 F.2d 1389 (C. C.P.A. 1974).

[3] *See, e.g.,* Council Regulation 6/2002 on Community Designs, 2002 O.J. (L 3) 1 (EC), art. 8(1) ("A Community design shall not subsist in features of appearance of a product which are solely dictated by its technical function.") [hereinafter Design Regulation].

[4] The must-fit exception is a corollary to the functionality rule and prohibits protection for features necessary to permit the product "to be mechanically connected to or placed in, around or against another product so that either product may perform its function"). *Id.* art 8(2). Whereas the must-fit exception concerns mechanical compatibility, must-match focuses on the compatibility of appearance. *See* UK CDPA § 213(3)(b)(ii).

implicate these issues, it doesn't make them any more difficult to analyze. Rather, the primary way that 3D printing technology challenges design regimes is via physitization. This chapter focuses on that phenomenon.

A. DESIGN PATENT PROTECTION FOR DMFS UNDER U.S. LAW

Under U.S. law, design rights only extend to a "design for an article of manufacture."[5] An alert reader will recognize that this phrase is remarkably similar to the useful article exclusion in copyright law, which was discussed at length in Chapter 8. The useful article exclusion refuses copyright protection for "the design of a useful article."

Even though it is not the focus of this chapter, I note that, as with the copyright provision, the design patent provision is ambiguous. Do design rights protect a design in the abstract (i.e., regardless of the object on or in which it appears)? Or is protection limited only to the design as applied on the claimed article of manufacture? Professor Sarah Burstein has considered this issue in depth, and I refer the reader to her analysis on this point.[6] For reasons of history, case law, and policy, Professor Burstein concludes that design patent protection is limited only to the design as applied to a specific type of article of manufacture. I agree with her analysis, and I note it here because it interprets the ambiguous phrase in the opposite direction of my copyright analysis. But it doesn't undermine my analysis because copyright law's useful article exclusion and design patent law's basic protection provision have different histories and policies. Indeed, the useful article exclusion in copyright was meant to channel utilitarian works *away* from the copyright system, whereas section 171 of the patent act *grants* an IP protection.

Digital Article of Manufacture?

As with utility patents, a looming issue for design patents is whether digital versions of otherwise protectable tangible objects are eligible for protection. For example, imagine a tangible, ornamental chair protected via design rights.[7] Is a DMF of that chair likewise protectable via design rights as a "design for an article of manufacture?"[8] A tangible chair easily qualifies

---

[5] 35 U.S.C. § 171.
[6] *See generally* Sarah Burstein, *The Patented Design*, 83 TENN. L. REV. 161 (2015).
[7] *See, e.g.,* Design for a Chair, U.S. Patent No. D150,683 (filed Mar. 27, 1947) (covering a chair design by Charles Eames).
[8] Throughout this chapter, it is generally not necessary to distinguish among design files, surface-mesh files, and machine-instruction files because each can display an image of the underlying

as an article of manufacture, but a digital file is likely too ephemeral or intangible to qualify as an "article."[9] What might serve as the article of manufacture?

The USPTO has a decades-long history of granting design patents for graphical user interfaces and digital icons. (I will use the terms "digital image" or "icon" to refer generally to any image projectable on a computer screen.) Despite this history, no court decision has addressed the patentability of such icons. Further, commentators strongly disagree about whether they should be patentable.[10] Given the wide-open legal landscape, this chapter will address DMFs as well as digital icons more generally.

As a matter of history, the USPTO has flip-flopped on the digital icon issue. It granted the first few applications for them in the mid-1980s, but then reversed course in 1989.[11] The refusal was warranted, a USPTO examiner reasoned while rejecting an application, because

> [i]f projecting a picture onto a screen were sufficient, then individual frames of a motion picture or animated cartoon would be protectable by design patent by virtue of the fact that they were projected on a screen . . . The requirement that a design be embodied in an article of manufacture requires more than merely placing a picture temporarily on the surface of an article. It requires that the design be a concrete part of the article. An image projected on a screen is no more embodied on the screen than is a photograph placed temporarily on a coffee table is embodied in the table.[12]

That reasoning would foreclose design protection for DMFs, which would be no more than images on a screen. But the USPTO changed course again just a few years later. The course change began somewhat modestly as dictum in a Board of Patent Appeals & Interferences (Board) decision, *Ex parte*

---

object. As I will explain, design rights protect appearances. Of course, the image must be similar enough to the protected image or object to warrant infringement, but that is a separate issue from what file type produces the image. Some countries' laws explicitly state that making a manufacturing drawing of a protected object triggers design infringement. *See* UK CDPA § 226(1)(b) (providing the exclusive right to reproduce the design "by making a design document recording the design for the purpose of enabling such articles to be made").

[9]   *See, e.g.,* William J. Seymour & Andrew W. Torrance, *(R)evolution in Design Patentable Subject Matter: The Shifting Meaning of "Article of Manufacture,"* 17 Stan. Tech. L. Rev. 183, 206–15 (2013).

[10] *See id.* at 206–15 (arguing against patentability); Jason J. Du Mont & Mark D. Janis, *Virtual Designs,* 17 Stan. Tech. L. Rev. 107, 111–28 (2013) (arguing in favor of patentability).

[11] Seymour & Torrance, *supra* note 9, at 200.

[12] Robert Barr & Susan Hollander, *Design Patents Revisited: Icons as Statutory Subject Matter,* 9 Computer Law. 13, 14–15 (1992) (quoting a USPTO examiner's office action).

Strijland,[13] which held that the icons as claimed (i.e., with no relationship to a computer) could not be patented. The Board went on to say,

> [W]e do not think that merely illustrating a picture displayed on the screen of a computer or other display device, such as a television or movie screen, is sufficient, alone, to convert a picture into a design for an article of manufacture. Mere display of a picture on a screen is not significantly different, in our view, from the display of a picture on a piece of paper. Only the medium of display is different. However, appellants *have expressly stated in the specification and claim*, as amended, that the article of manufacture which embodies or to which the claimed design is applied is a programmed computer system, and they have provided declaration evidence demonstrating *that the icon is an integral part of the operation of a programmed computer*.[14]

The *Strijland* dicta would foreclose protection for DMFs because they are not "an integral part of the operation of a programmed computer" (as opposed to an icon that can be clicked or touched to activate a program). Subsequent cases provided broader suggestions that merely claiming the icons as a part of a computer display should lead to eligibility.[15]

On March 20, 1996, the USPTO broadened protection when it issued final "Guidelines for Examination of Design Patent Applications for Computer-Generated Icons."[16] These guidelines, which are not binding on courts and have only limited persuasive value, specified that designs for computer-generated icons comply with the article of manufacture requirement if they are "shown on a computer screen, monitor, other display panel, or a portion thereof," without any further requirement of the icon being an integral part of the operation of a programmed computer.[17]

As Professor Sarah Burstein observes, this turns the article of manufacture requirement into "something of a farce" because "while the PTO maintains that '[a] picture standing alone is not patentable,' it is perfectly happy to grant patents for such pictures as long as the applicant surrounds it with some broken lines and adds certain magic words in the title."[18] Other commentators

---

[13]　*Ex parte* Strijland, No. 92–0623, 26 U.S.P.Q.2D (BNA) 1259 (B.P.A.I. Apr. 2, 1992).
[14]　*Id.* at 1263 (emphasis added).
[15]　*See* Seymour & Torrance, *supra* note 9, at 202–04.
[16]　Guidelines for Examination of Design Patent Applications For Computer-Generated Icons, 61 Fed. Reg. 11380 (Mar. 20, 1996).
[17]　*Id.* at 11381.
[18]　Burstein, *The Patented Design*, *supra* note 6 at 204–05 (alteration in original) (quoting U.S. Patent & Trademark Office, Manual of Patent Examining Procedure § 1504.01 (9th ed., Rev. Aug. 2015, Nov. 2015) [hereinafter MPEP]).

see nothing problematic about allowing broad design protection for digital works.[19]

Since publishing the guidelines, the USPTO has issued numerous design patents for digital icons as depicted on a computer screen.[20] Interestingly, though, no court decision has squarely addressed the validity of design patent claims to digital icons.[21] In the most famous design patent dispute in U.S. history, *Apple v. Samsung*,[22] the defendant did not challenge the validity of the digital icon design patent.

Objections to Current Doctrine

There are practical as well as theoretical objections to the USPTO's current approach to digital images. On the practical side, since U.S. design patent law does not have a private, noncommercial use exception or a fair use exception, any reproduction on a computer screen, even for news, commentary, or to advertise a physical product, might infringe.[23] The effects on speech, expression, and competition could be dramatic. In addition, manufacturers of tangible products (even objects not protected by design patents) could obtain

[19]   Du Mont & Janis, *supra* note 10, at 127 ("In sum, the USPTO practice has equilibrated around a concept that we regard as relatively conservative: an embedded virtual design constitutes eligible subject matter because it is self-evident that such a design is associated with a computer display and integral with the operation of that display."). What Du Mont and Janis mean by "integral with the operation of that display" is unclear. It could mean there is a functional relationship between the computer and the icon, or simply that the display screen causes the image to be portrayed.

[20]   Du Mont & Janis, *supra* note 10, at 128–61.

[21]   Seymour & Torrance, *supra* note 9, at 205. One decision has, however, upheld a claim to type font, reasoning that the "program which creates the type fonts is the article of manufacture." Adobe Sys., Inc. v. S. Software, Inc., 45 U.S.P.Q.2d (BNA) 1827 (N.D. Cal. 1998). The case the court cited for support, however, did not hold that computer programs could be the article of manufacture. Instead, it reasoned that type fonts are design patentable because of "the long-standing interpretation of type font designs as configuration-type designs or [solid] pieces or blocks of type." *Id.* (quoting *Ex parte* Tayama, 24 U.S.P.Q.2d (BNA) 1614, 1618 (B.P.A.I. Apr. 2, 1992)). The Guidelines are ambiguous as to whether the article of manufacture for type fonts can be a computer screen or computer program. Guidelines for Examination of Design Patent Applications For Computer-Generated Icons, 61 Fed. Reg. at 11380 ("PTO personnel should not reject claims for type fonts under Section 171 for failure to comply with the 'article of manufacture' requirement on the basis that more modern methods of typesetting, including computer-generation, do not require solid printing blocks.").

[22]   Apple, Inc. v. Samsung Elecs. Co., 926 F. Supp. 2d 1100 (N.D. Cal. 2013), *vacated and remanded by* 786 F.3d 983 (Fed. Cir. 2015), *rev'd and remanded by* 137 S. Ct. 429 (2016).

[23]   *Cf.* Dennis Crouch, *Apple Patents an Encircled Musical Note*, PATENTLY-O (Oct. 25, 2012), http://patentlyo.com/patent/2012/10/apple-patents-an-encircled-musical-note.html (showing the drawing from U.S. Patent No. D668,263 and asking, "Is Patently-O infringing the design patent by showing the image on your screen?").

design patents for digital images of their products and assert them against any online retailer who displayed similar images of the products while trying to sell the product.[24] The USPTO's position leads to other bizarre results: a photograph printed on paper (and paper is undoubtedly an article of manufacture) is not eligible for a design patent,[25] but the same image on a screen (even a digital picture frame) would be. This cannot be correct; if a photograph is not eligible (and it should not be), neither should the same image merely portrayed on a screen.[26]

These practical absurdities point to theoretical problems with permissive protection of digital images via design patents. The first issue concerns tangibility, particularly whether the article of manufacture is the computer screen or the computer program. Each of these alternative possibilities has problems.

A couple of district court cases have suggested, with little reasoning, that the software itself can be the article of manufacture.[27] It is difficult to see how software constitutes an article of manufacture in any way meaningful to digital icons. Under current law, an article must be tangible. The Supreme Court has never considered the issue of tangibility in the design patent context, but it has

---

[24]   *See* Daniel H. Brean, *Enough Is Enough: Time to Eliminate Design Patents and Rely on More Appropriate Copyright and Trademark Protection for Product Design*, 16 TEX. INTELL. PROP. L.J. 325, 377–81 (2008), ; Ralph D. Clifford & Richard J. Peltz-Steele, *The Constitutionality of Design Patents*, 14 CHI.-KENT J. INTELL. PROP. 553, 590–613 (2015); Michael Risch, *Functionality and Graphical User Interface Design Patents*, 17 STAN. TECH. L. REV. 53, 68 (2013) ("[T]here is no theoretical bar to protecting every displayed copyrightable work [including photographs and movies] with a design patent."). Unlike copyright, which might protect the photo but would require copying to infringe, design patents are infringed even absent copying. The strategy of patenting photographs of products could be used even for nonnovel utilitarian objects, because photos of objects can be novel based on angles and lighting. Courts could perhaps combat this by deeming basic photos of products obvious or by giving narrow scope to the claim, but the effort seems unnecessary. What incentive is served by such design patents?

[25]   *Cf. In re* Schnell, 46 F.2d 203, 209 (C.C.P.A. 1931) ("We think that Assistant Commissioner Clay was right in saying that the design must be shown not to be the mere invention of a picture, irrespective of its manner of use . . .").

[26]   One might argue that photographs should be design patentable, but that has never been the law in the United States. The Supreme Court seemed to foreclose this long ago. Gorham Co. v. White, 81 U.S. (14 Wall.) 511, 524–25 (1871) ("[Design patents] contemplate not so much utility as appearance, and that, *not an abstract impression, or picture*, but an aspect given to those objects mentioned in the acts." (emphasis added)). The statutory language has changed since *Gorham*, but not in any way that signals the desire to protect mere photographs. In fact, it has moved in the opposite direction. *See infra* note 35 (discussing legislative history and the Constitution). *See also Schnell*, 46 F.2d at 209.

[27]   *See, e.g.*, Microsoft Corp. v. Corel Corp., No. 5:15-CV-05836-EJD, 2018 WL 2183268, at *4 (N. D. Cal. May 11, 2018) (stating in dicta that "[s]oftware is a thing made by hand or machine, and thus can be an 'article of manufacture.'") (quotation omitted); Adobe Sys., Inc. v. S. Software, Inc., 45 U.S.P.Q.2d (BNA) 1827, 1827 (N.D. Cal. 1998).

defined the term "article" in the design statute as "simply a thing made by hand or machine."[28] This definition is not helpful as to tangibility, because a "thing" could arguably include intangible concepts like images and files. Under Federal Circuit law, however, as discussed in Chapter 4, the relevant definitions of "articles" and "manufacture" require "tangible articles or commodit[ies]."[29] Although these cases focused on the utility patent statute,[30] there is no hint in the text or legislative history that related terms should have different meanings in sections 101 and 171. Furthermore, case law supports reading them the same way.[31]

Is software tangible? That depends on which of the multiple concepts of software one has in mind. Software can refer to an abstract set of instructions, which obviously cannot constitute a tangible article. It can also refer to a tangible storage medium like a CD or computer memory. In that case, the storage medium is obviously tangible, but it does not bear any image or design.

Design patent law has always had a visual focus.[32] True, a storage medium has code embedded on it that will generate an image when run on a computer, but calling data a design is a bit like saying a box of crayons with drawing instructions is a design because I can use them to draw a pretty design on a vase.[33] Whatever the relevant article is must visually display the design when someone is looking at the article.

Another problem with calling a computer program an article of manufacture is that it causes the design patent regime to conflict with other areas of IP. Computer programs have been broadly defined as "a set of statements or

---

[28] Samsung Elecs. Co. v. Apple Inc., 137 S. Ct. 429, 435 (2016).

[29] *In re* Nuijten, 500 F.3d 1346, 1356–57 (Fed. Cir. 2007); *see also* Digitech Image Tech., L.L.C. v. Elecs. for Imaging, Inc., 758 F.3d 1344, 1350 (Fed. Cir. 2014) (stating that "[d]ata in its ethereal, non-physical form is simply information that does not fall under any of the categories of eligible subject matter under section 101."). In a related context, the Federal Circuit has also interpreted the term article to require tangibility. ClearCorrect Operating, L.L.C. v. Int'l Trade Comm'n, 810 F.3d 1283, 1286 (Fed. Cir. 2015) (holding that the word "articles" in the Tariff Act of 1930, which provides the International Trade Commission with "authority to remedy only those unfair acts that involve the importation of 'articles,'" includes only material things and does not include transmission of digital data).

[30] *See Nuijten*, 500 F.3d at 1357 n.9.

[31] For a list of cases equating the meaning in both, as well as an exception, see Sarah Burstein, *The "Article of Manufacture" in 1887*, 32 Berkeley Tech. L.J. 1, 33 n.193 (2017).

[32] *See* Gorham Co. v. White, 81 U.S. (14 Wall.) 511, 524 (1871) ("The acts of Congress which authorize the grant of a patent for designs ... contemplate not so much utility as appearance."); *In re* Hruby, 373 F.2d 997, 1001 (C.C.P.A. 1967) (describing "enjoyment by the beholder" as "the ultimate purpose of all ornamental design"); MPEP § 1502 ("The design for an article consists of the visual characteristics embodied in or applied to an article ... [A] design is manifested in appearance ...").

[33] The instructions might lay the groundwork for a claim of inducement (indirect infringement).

instructions to be used directly or indirectly in a computer in order to bring about a certain result."[34] This definition would encompass files for photographs and movies, categories that design patents have never protected. In fact, Congress crafted modern copyright law to provide the relevant incentives for photos and movies. Although the law allows for dual protection in some circumstances, design patents should not protect works of solely aesthetic features.[35] To allow protection for photos and movies as they appear on a digital screen would trample on copyright law's sphere of purely aesthetic works.[36]

If the computer memory or computer program itself is not the relevant article of manufacture, an alternative view regards the relevant article as the

---

[34] 17 U.S.C. § 101.

[35] This assertion, which no one has yet explored in depth, would meet opposition from some commentators, who might, for example, point out that design patents have protected statues and busts. Act of Aug. 29, 1842, ch. 263, § 3, 5 Stat. 543, 544 [hereinafter 1842 Act] (listing statues and busts among items specifically protected). Though fully exploring my assertion is not possible here, I offer a few observations. First, a constitutional argument can be made that Congress, having chosen the "patent" portion of the so-called IP clause, U.S. CONST art. I. § 8, cl. 8, to justify design patents, cannot use design patents to protect purely aesthetic creations. Protection for aesthetic creations can be justified, if at all, by the "copyright" portion of the IP clause. *See generally* Clifford & Peltz-Steele, *supra* note 24. The patent portion of the IP clause is limited to inventors, and there is no meaningful way to call someone who creates a purely aesthetic creation an "inventor" of a "useful art." *Id.* at 569–77; *see* Sarah Burstein, *Visual Invention*, 16 LEWIS & CLARK L. REV. 169, 173–75 (2012). Second, textually, the 1842 Act protected anyone who "invented *or produced*" things, including statues and busts. 1842 Act §3 (emphasis added). Later statutes, including the current one, dropped the "or produced" language and the reference to statues and busts, possibly suggesting that those items should not be protected by design patents. Third, at the time of the 1842 Act, copyright law did not protect statues and busts, but it does now (and began doing so in 1870), and therefore including them in design patents' orbit is unnecessary (though revision of the design patent statute in 1870 retained the listing of statues and busts, see REVISED STATUTES OF THE UNITED STATES 954 (2d ed. 1878) (reproducing Rev. Stat. § 4929, as then in force), and the reference to them was finally removed in the 1902 Act, see Thomas B. Hudson, A Brief History of the Development of Design Patent Protection in the United States, 30 J. PAT. OFF. SOC'Y. 380, 390 (1948)). Though he does not address the constitutional aspect, Hudson's article discusses important history on the appearance and removal of the term "useful" in design patent statutes. *Id.* at 384–93. Fourth, statues and busts qualify under the traditional meaning of *fine* art, as distinguished from *decorative* arts. Burstein, *supra*, at 172–73. Design patents are "plainly intended to give encouragement to the decorative arts." *Gorham*, 81 U.S. at 524. *See also In re* Hruby, 373 F.2d at 1001 ("We think [the statute's] spirit is as stated by the Supreme Court in Gorham Mfg. Co. v. White, to encourage the decorative arts, over and above those classically known as 'the fine arts.'"). Finally, to circle back to the first point, a statute enacted to promote "decorative arts" stands in some tension with a constitutional provision that requires promotion of the "useful arts."

[36] *See* Burstein, *The Patented Design*, *supra* note 6, at 170–71 ("Drawing a beautiful picture or sculpting an attractive shape without any application in mind is an act of art, not an act of design.").

computer screen bearing the visual image. This is the USPTO's approach.[37] According to this view, the image on a screen is analogous to traditional surface decoration on tangible articles like vases. This broad approach would qualify images of DMFs on screens as eligible subject matter.

The USPTO's approach makes any image on a screen eligible for design protection, and thus gives rise to the same copyright boundary problem just discussed. It also creates a second difficulty concerning the issues of permanence and fixation.[38] Digital images do not permanently appear on the screen and therefore might not be sufficiently embodied in the screen. Some argue the lack of permanence dooms design patent eligibility.[39] But I do not think that permanence can serve as a categorical requirement, if for no other reason than because traditional surface ornamentation on articles could, in some cases, be washed away or otherwise removed.[40]

Instead, I argue, provocatively, that the concepts of permanence and fixation for digital works are better addressed under a concept of intended use. Nondigital design law did not often contemplate intended uses because the use was generally plain from the nature of the claim.[41] But pro forma claim and title requirements (e.g., "digital icon for a portion of a screen") coupled with the dramatic flexibility of computers make the issue urgently salient.

A taxonomy of intended uses of digital icons compared to traditional design patents provides insight into how courts might shape eligibility doctrine. Digital images on screens can be divided into two broad categories: those that have a functional relationship with the computer's operation, and those

---

[37] Guidelines for Examination of Design Patent Applications for Computer-Generated Icons, 61 Fed. Reg. at 11380.

[38] Professors Seymour and Torrance have argued there was an historical requirement of fixation, no longer formally in place, that continues to exert influence in design patent jurisprudence. Seymour & Torrance, *supra* note 9, at 190–93. The fixation concept goes to a broader question of whether and when a design patent for one article can be *enforced* against the design appearing on a different article. *See generally* Burstein, *The Patented Design, supra* note 6.

[39] Seymour & Torrance, *supra* note 9, at 206–14.

[40] Permanence was considered in a well-known case involving a design patent for a water fountain that included the sprayed water as part of the claim. *In re* Hruby, 373 F.2d at 999 (stating that "the permanence of any design is a function of the materials in which it is embodied and the effects of the environment thereon"). *See also* Am. Patents Dev. Corp. v. Cabrice Corp. of Am., 38 F.2d 62, 64 (2d Cir. 1930) ("In thinking of an article of manufacture, one naturally thinks of a permanent contrivance, which does not operate upon a subject that is part of itself."), *rev'd on other grounds by* 283 U.S. 27 (1931).

[41] Intended use was (and is) considered in cases refusing protection for objects that would never be seen during normal use. *See, e.g.,* Contessa Food Prods., Inc. v. Conagra, Inc., 282 F.3d 1370, 1379–80 (Fed. Cir. 2002), *abrogated by* Egyption Goddess, Inc. v. Swisa, Inc., 543 F.3d 665 (Fed. Cir. 2008).

that do not.[42] Images with a functional relationship would include menus and icons that can be clicked or touched to perform an operation. These might constitute eligible subject matter because they do something beyond merely portraying their appearance, just as wallpaper, which can be protected by a design patent, covers a wall.[43]

Images without a functional relationship to a computer include digital displays of mere photographs and movies, which, as to their nondigital form, have not been protectable by design patents.[44] These nonfunctional images would not constitute eligible subject matter.[45] Also included would be any images that do no more than portray their appearance. The design patent system cannot be justified as incentivizing the production of these kinds of works[46] – the current copyright system does this. And while cumulative protection is permissible, different protections typically relate to different aspects of the work.[47]

In between the clearly functional and clearly nonfunctional groups would sit difficult cases. For example, a screensaver is an image or series of images, but it also has a functional relationship with the screen to protect pixels from burning out. Therefore, the images might be protectable as claimed and used

---

[42] The Board provided this distinction in *Ex parte Strijland*, but it has never been developed. *Ex parte* Strijland, No. 92–0623, 26 U.S.P.Q.2D (BNA) 1259, 1263 (B.P.A.I. Apr. 2, 1992) (requiring the icon to be "an integral part of the operation of a programmed computer").

[43] Moreover, they are not limited by their functionality because the icon could be designed numerous ways.

[44] An analogy could be drawn to the judicially created printed matter doctrine in utility patent law. That doctrine holds that "if a limitation claims (a) printed matter that (b) is not functionally or structurally related to the physical substrate holding the printed matter, it does not lend any patentable weight to the patentability analysis." *In re* Distefano, 808 F.3d 845, 848 (Fed. Cir. 2015). Further, "a limitation is printed matter only if it claims the content of information." *Id.* Analogously, a design claim to mere photographs or movies on a screen attempts to claim the content of the images that have no functional relationship to the computer. I thank Professor Mark Janis for this observation.

[45] Being generated by a computer alone cannot constitute a meaningful functional relationship because everything on a screen is generated by the computer. The relationship must affect the computer's functionality, such as an icon that opens a program when touched or clicked.

[46] *See supra* note 35 (discussing the constitutional and other concerns with offering design patent protection to purely aesthetic creations). *Cf.* Gorham Co. v. White, 81 U.S. (14 Wall.) 511, 524–25 (1871) ("[Design patents] contemplate not so much utility as appearance, and that, *not an abstract impression, or picture, but an aspect given to those objects* mentioned in the acts." (emphasis added)); *In re* Schnell, 46 F.2d 203, 209 (C.C.P.A. 1931) ("We think that Assistant Commissioner Clay was right in saying that the design must be shown not to be the mere invention of a picture, irrespective of its manner of use . . .").

[47] On the disadvantages of overlapping protection, see Viva R. Moffat, *Mutant Copyrights and Backdoor Patents: The Problem of Overlapping Intellectual Property Protection*, 19 BERKELEY TECH. L.J. 1473, 1518–20 (2004).

as a screensaver. Other images, like images of cigarette lighters for concerts[48] or characters in a video game,[49] would be excluded.

Another difficult case would be images of products used in online advertising that simultaneously serve as hyperlinks to make the purchase or provide more information.[50] Given their role in speech and competition, advertising images should not be protected by design patents, even though they might have a functional relationship to the computer.

A final difficult case is how to treat the images of DMFs projected onto a computer screen. Images will be shown when a DMF is being created or modified (e.g., in a CAD program) and – usually – when the DMF is being offered for download.[51] But that image does not have a functional relationship to the computer's operation.

These difficult cases of hyperlinked images and DMFs demonstrate that a "functional relationship" test is too blunt an instrument. It does not adequately take account of design patent law's theoretical underpinnings. Given the flexibility of computers and the myriad roles digital images can play on computer screens, a similarly flexible subject matter eligibility approach is warranted.

A Teleological Approach to Protection for Digital Images

What is needed to maintain the design patent regime's policy goals in a digital realm is a teleological approach to subject matter eligibility.[52] The eligibility analysis should not begin and end with whether an image is on a screen. Computers are too flexible compared to traditional articles of manufacture and that flexibility allows digital images to serve a variety of functions. Historically, things were simpler: a pretty design applied to wallpaper could be design patent eligible, but because wallpaper has limited functionality, the claim would identify the intended use as wallpaper. In contrast, a claim to a digital icon on a portion of a computer screen could cover a passive photo,

---

[48] Moving Image for the Display Screen of a Wireless Communication Device, U.S. Patent No. D549,715 (filed Jul. 10, 2006).

[49] Portion of an Electronic Display with a Computer Generated Image, U.S. Patent No. D503,407 (filed Sep. 6, 2001) (Sega's Virtua Fighter video game character).

[50] It should be recognized that the cost of obtaining a design patent in the United States would decrease the incidence of these sorts of design patents. But it would not eliminate them.

[51] Nothing requires an image to accompany a file offered for download, but every website of which I am aware includes an image of what the DMF will print, presumably because people want to know that information before downloading the file.

[52] The approach could go further and protect the files directly, though this would require more substantial changes to subject matter eligibility.

a photo used in news or advertising, a GUI, or an interactive icon. Some of these functions do not fit with the design regime's purpose or history.

Because computers are multifunctional machines, design patents for digital images should be required to state a specific use in their claims (or preamble or title), and that specific use should limit the eligibility and scope of the design patent.[53] The use should be specific enough to exclude uses geared toward entertainment (pictures and movies) and information (including advertising). Thus, for example, instead of a claim merely to a design "for a user interface for a portion of a display screen," the claim should specify the function of the design in the user interface.[54] The function would be taken into account to tie protections to screen ornamentation that is sufficiently similar to traditional surface ornamentation to warrant protection.

For images of DMFs, the claim should be able to specify at least the use of the DMF image in connection with making available the DMF for download. When examining such a claim, the intuitive rule is also the best one: examine what object the DMF will print. If that tangible object is protected by a design patent, then an image of it should be protected *if* it is used in an offer to download the file (but not, for example, if it is used in a news story). If instead the DMF will print a purely utilitarian object or any object not actually protected by a design patent, the image should not be protected by design patent rights.[55] There is simply nothing in design patent policy to justify such protection; otherwise, the tangible version of the object would be protectable.[56]

There are doctrinal issues with this approach that need to be worked through, but this chapter is not the place to flesh out a systematic approach to all design patents to digital images. I outline the approach, however, because there is a strong possibility that, as courts begin to look closely at eligible subject matter for digital images, they will make changes to current

---

[53] In contrast, others have proposed bifurcating eligibility functionality from functionality as it relates to enforceable scope and making the former very permissive. Jason J. Du Mont & Mark D. Janis, *Functionality in Design Protection Systems*, 19 J. INTELL. PROP. L. 261, 302 (2012).

[54] Currently, the MPEP does not permit statements of function in the specification. MPEP § 1503.01, ¶ 15.41 (Rev. Aug. 2017). This rule makes sense when the claim to the tangible object (wallpaper, dinner plate, etc.) implicitly specifies a lot of information about function. It does not make sense with a multifunctional computer screen.

[55] Unless the image is used in an otherwise qualifying function, like as an app icon or part of a GUI. In that case, however, infringement would be limited to the image being used in a like function.

[56] This of course assumes design patent law is properly calibrated, a question that is beyond this book's scope.

doctrine. I hope, therefore, that this outline provides a framework that accommodates design patent claims to DMFs as well.

Digital Images of DMFs

Under either current USPTO practice or a teleological approach, design patent law can protect screen images of objects that DMFs will print. As a matter of policy, assuming the design patent regime itself is properly calibrated, this protection prevents a digital gap in protection: unlike with utility patents, surface-mesh and design files of design patentable objects could trigger direct infringement. But the USPTO approach, because it is not limited to the function of the image on the screen or the design patent status of the tangible object portrayed, is overbroad, as already discussed.

A teleological approach to DMF images of design patentable objects avoids most of the overprotection concerns, but some underprotection would persist. The underprotection persists because the article of manufacture is a computer screen, which is not sold or offered for sale. Only the file, not the tangible screen, is offered and sold, and thus liability is not triggered under the text of section 289.[57] It is less clear whether liability is triggered under section 271(a) for selling the file.[58] (The liability issues under sections 271 and 289 exist even under the broad USPTO approach.) The offeror would generally be liable, however, for "making" or "using" the image on the screen because most offers would include an image of the file.[59] Anyone who downloads the DMF and views the image of it on a computer screen would also directly infringe (though detection might be difficult).

In contrast, the teleological approach would eliminate most of the overprotection. First, protection would only be granted to DMFs of objects that are protected by design patents. In addition, the claim would limit the scope of

---

[57]   The second part of section 289 expressly limits liability to one who "sells or exposes for sale any article of manufacture to which such design or colorable imitation has been applied." 35 U.S. C. § 289. When people offer to sell a DMF, they don't offer the computer screen for sale too. The first part of section 289 triggers liability if someone "applies the patented design . . . to any article of manufacture for the purpose of sale." *Id.* This probably means "for purpose of selling the article so made," but no court has considered the issue.

[58]   Section 271(a) triggers liability for anyone who, among other things, "offers to sell, or sells any patented invention." *Id.* § 271(a). Section 171 in turn defines the patented invention not as the article of manufacture (the computer screen), but as a "design *for* an article of manufacture." *Id.* § 171 (emphasis added). Arguably, selling the file is selling a design that is meant for a computer screen.

[59]   It is possible to sell a DMF without an image demonstrating what it will print, but it would be rare. Buyers usually want to see what they are buying.

protection for uses *as a* DMF. Note that there are no overbreadth concerns with restricting images of the object in connection with advertisements because offering to sell an infringing tangible object is already an act of infringement.[60] In short, the teleological approach would allow design patents to offer digital versions of otherwise-protected objects some of the same protections as the tangible versions, but without the overbreadth of the current approach.

Digital Design Patent Infringement

The difficulties and shortcomings of either the USPTO or teleological approaches to design patents and DMFs could be avoided if courts adopted a doctrine of digital patent infringement for design patents similar to that outlined in Chapter 5 for utility patents. Under this doctrine, if a design patent claim protected a tangible object, anyone who sold or offered to sell a DMF of the object would directly infringe the claim to the tangible object. In contrast, merely making the file would not constitute infringement. This theory has essentially the same benefits and drawbacks as discussed in Chapter 5 with utility patents.

Indirect Infringement

Even if U.S. design patent law does not protect digital files directly or completely, it offers design patent holders the opportunity to sue for indirect infringement if the file will manufacture an object protected by a design patent.[61] Like with utility patents, however, indirect infringement claims for design patents have significant limitations. The accused infringer must have knowledge of the patent and an intent to infringe,[62] and the patent owner also must identify underlying acts of direct infringement, which can be difficult

---

[60] *See id.* §§ 271(a), 289. Under the current case law, an offer to sell must be a formal contract law offer. Lucas S. Osborn, *The Leaky Common Law: An "Offer to Sell" as a Policy Tool in Patent Law and Beyond*, 53 SANTA CLARA L. REV. 143, 171–202 (2013). Thus, mere advertisements, most of which do not rise to the level of an offer to sell, would not trigger infringement. For an argument that the Federal Circuit's restrictive rule is a poor policy fit, see *id.* As with utility patents, it is unclear how the infringement provisions, which require sales and offers for sale, will apply to DMFs that are downloadable for free.

[61] Indirect infringement under 35 U.S.C. § 271(b) applies to design patents. *See, e.g.*, Wing Shing Prods. (BVI), Ltd. v. Simatelex Manufactory Co., 479 F. Supp. 2d 388, 407–08 (S.D.N.Y. 2007).

[62] Global-Tech Appliances, Inc. v. SEB S.A., 563 U.S. 754, 765–66 (2011).

with decentralized 3D printing. If the choice is between the current overbroad USPTO approach or indirect liability, the latter is preferable. But a middle approach like the teleological focus more closely aligns with protections for tangible objects.

Print Shop Intermediaries

Print shop intermediaries that print DMFs on behalf of others would be liable for making the protected design, whether the design was a registered image or a tangible product.[63] Just as with utility patents, this liability exposure puts print shops in a difficult spot. The costs of determining whether each print job would infringe a registered design would be enormous without a sophisticated technological solution. The risks of liability might cause print shops to close, which would deprive the public of the benefits of all the noninfringing print jobs. Therefore, the law should provide a safe harbor provision for good faith print shops that accidentally infringe.[64]

B. DESIGN PROTECTION FOR DMFS UNDER THE EU DESIGN DIRECTIVE

This section will focus primarily on design protection provided by the EU Design Regulation, with occasional references to other countries' design laws where they differ in relevant respects.[65] Design protection is generally stronger in Europe than in the United States, and many companies see it as a key aspect of digital image protection. As one attorney stated, with digital icons the client doesn't rely on copyright protection

> because it's not harmonized; [the client doesn't want] trademarks – [because they are] difficult to be obtained, and the scope is limited to the class and goods you have registered; so it's about design rights, basically. And it's not

---

[63] In contrast, if the print shop merely rented time on its printers for customers to use, the individual would be the one making the invention.

[64] *See supra* Chapter 5 (outlining a safe harbor for print shops under utility patent law).

[65] The Design Regulation has the same eligibility requirement for registered and unregistered designs. As discussed in Chapter 3, infringement for unregistered designs requires copying, but not for registered designs. Unless otherwise mentioned, this section focuses on registered design rights under the Regulation. Recall that individual country's unregistered design rights have not been harmonized and can vary greatly from each other and from the Design Regulation. For instance, the United Kingdom's unregistered design rights can last up to fifteen years and exclude surface decoration from protection. UK CDPA § 213(3)(c).

about unregistered design rights, because these are only against copying and have three years' term of protection only.[66]

Although the EU's Design Regulation uses very different wording than the U.S. statute, the primary issue of whether and how a DMF can be protected by design rights raises many of the same basic issues.[67] In contrast to the United States, which has virtually no scholarly commentary specific to 3D printing and design rights, Europe has a wealth of analyses.[68]

The interpretive difficulty starts with article 3 of the Design Regulation, which defines design as "the appearance of the whole or a part of a *product* resulting from the features of, in particular, the lines, contours, colours, shape, texture and/or materials of the product itself and/or its ornamentation."[69] Focusing on this definition only, it could be argued that digital shapes serve as ornamentation to a tangible product, namely a computer screen. Commentators in Europe, however, have not made this argument.

Rather, arguments about protection for digital images have focused on the definition of product under article 3, which is "any industrial or handicraft item, including *inter alia*, parts intended to be assembled into a complex product, packaging, get-up, *graphic symbols* and *typographic typefaces*, but excluding computer programs."[70] The phrase "industrial or handicraft item" sounds distinctly tangible. Yet the industrial or handicraft item, we are told, can be a "graphic symbol" or "typographic typeface." The phrase graphic symbol is not defined, but it seems strange to think of a graphic symbol as an

---

[66] Rainer Filitz, Joachim Henkel, & Jörg Ohnemus, *Digital Design Protection in Europe: Law, Trends, and Emerging Issues*, CENTRE FOR EUROPEAN ECONOMIC RESEARCH DISCUSSION PAPER 1, 12 (2017), http://ftp.zew.de/pub/zew-docs/dp/dp17007.pdf (quoting an interviewed attorney whose client registers many digital designs).

[67] Commentators report that creating a DMF would not constitute primary infringement under Australian design law, which requires a tangible product bearing the design. See, e.g., Jane Nielsen & John Liddicoat, *The Multiple Dimensions of Intellectual Property Infringement in the 3D Printing Era*, 27 AUSTRALIAN INTELL. P. J. 184, 191 (2017); Mitchell Adams, *The "Third Industrial Revolution": 3D Printing Technology and Australian Designs Law*, 24(1) J.L. INFO. & SCI. 56, 70 (2016). Neither of these commentators addresses whether a computer screen depicting a design could constitute the relevant product. Adams states that a "user would likely infringe if they 3D scanned an existing product and offered it for sale." Id.

[68] See, e.g., Viola Elam, *CAD Files and European Design Law*, 7 J. INTELL. PROP., INFO. TECH., & ELEC. COM. L. 146 (2016); Pedro Malaquias, *Consumer 3D Printing: Is the UK Copyright and Design Law Framework Fit for Purpose?*, 6 QUEEN MARY J. INTELL. PROP. 321 (2016); Thomas Margoni, *Not for Designers: On the Inadequacies of EU Design Law and How to Fix It*, 4 J. INTELL. PROP., INFO. TECH., & E-COM. L. 225 (2013); Dinusha Mendis, *"The Clone Wars": Episode 1*, EURO. INTELL. PROP. REV. 155, 162–65 (2013).

[69] Design Regulation art. 3(a) (emphasis added).

[70] Id. art. 3(b) (emphasis added).

"item." Graphic symbols typically appear *on* items. The confusion is all the more abundant because the regulation also states in article 3(a) that design is the "appearance" of a "product" resulting from the features such as the shape and lines of "the product itself and/or *its ornamentation*." Article 3(a) would seem to categorize shapes and lines appearing on a product as "ornamentation," but article 3(b) defines a graphic symbol as a product unto itself.[71] The wording is not ideal.

Regardless, registrations for computer icons and GUIs have grown quickly in recent years.[72] Court decisions have not had the opportunity to clarify the issue. One approach considered in the United States, which interprets the product as the computer program, is expressly foreclosed by article 3(b). Importantly, this exclusion clarifies that DMFs cannot be protected *as such* because they constitute computer programs, broadly defined. I will return to the significance of this after reviewing the other potential interpretations. An interpretation that attempts to salvage the tangible connotation of "product" would construe a graphic symbol as a product only when it is in a tangible form as a stand-alone product, such as a tangible 3D lightning bolt cut from wood. But this definition is unlikely.

The most aggressive interpretive approach would hold that "product" can include any graphic symbol regardless of the article on which it appears, including a computer screen.[73] Under this approach the graphic image is protected almost in the abstract because it is its own "product." The Explanatory Memorandum to the Regulation[74] clarifies that digital icons and menus can receive protection. It states that "product" means "any item to which a design can be applied,"[75] which alone is not illuminating, as "item" might be limited to tangible objects. But the memorandum continues by stating that, while the Design Regulation does not protect computer programs, it "does not exclude the protection of specific graphic designs as *applied*, for example, *to icons or menus* provided the normal requirements for protection

---

[71] This can be explained by noting that an image on its own can constitute a graphic symbol product, but that same image could be applied to the surface of a tangible item and thereby constitute ornamentation of that item's surface. One could imagine a scenario where the image standing alone did not have individual character but the combination of the shape on the surface of another product did.

[72] Filitz et al., *supra* note 66, at 8–9.

[73] *See, e.g., id.* at 6 (stating that the definition of product is "generously broad" and that "[t]here is no requirement that the design must be applied to an article of manufacture.").

[74] EU Commission, Explanatory Memorandum on the Proposal for a European Parliament and Council Regulation on the Community Design, 3 December 1993 [hereinafter Explanatory Memorandum].

[75] *Id.* at 11.

are met."[76] Taking these two sentences together, digital icons or menus constitute "items" to which a design can be applied.

One could, by parsing the memorandum's language carefully (painfully?), detect a distinction between computer icons, which affect the functionality of a computer program, and a mere graphic image on a screen, such as a digital photograph, which has no function other than portraying its appearance. This interpretation would coincide with the "functional relationship" requirement I explored with respect to U.S. design law. But this interpretation demands far too much of the Explanatory Memorandum's sparse language, and the use of the word "icon" does not hint at any limit to icons that have functional relationships to a program.[77]

Scholars have had difficulty determining whether and how DMFs (or the images they portray) might be eligible for design rights. Viola Elam provides a thorough analysis of digital images as qualifying designs, but in the end equivocates, stating that

> it seems rather unrealistic to assume, in the absence of a specific provision, that digital items represented in the form of CAD files could be seen as "products," whose appearance deserves protection in its own right. The definition of "design" would need to be broadened in future legislation in order to cover a wider range of "immaterial" protectable elements.[78]

Thomas Margoni is more confident that digital representations of DMFs are eligible for protection given that computer icons and GUI are.[79] Pedro Malaquias's analysis is similar.[80]

I think the intent of the Design Regulation is discernible, even if it is clumsily set forth: it allows "products" to include any image on a screen.[81] Certainly the EU Intellectual Property Office agrees. Its Guidelines for Examination of Registered Community Designs, although not binding authority, fully endorse protection for all sorts of visual elements, including "[d]esigns of screen displays and icons and other kinds of visible elements of a computer program,"[82]

---

[76]   *Id.* (emphasis added).
[77]   In fact, Elam interprets icon as something that "fulfils its function exclusively once it is displayed on a computer screen." Elam, *supra* note 68, at 150.
[78]   *Id.* at 150–51.
[79]   Margoni, *supra* note 68, at 232.
[80]   Malaquias, *supra* note 68, at 331.
[81]   Further, the list of products in article 3(b) is illustrative, not exhaustive.
[82]   EUIPO Guidelines for Examination of Registered Community Designs (version Jan. 10, 2018) § 4.1.3 [hereinafter EUIPO Design Guidelines].

"fanciful characters,"[83] "a logo or a graphic symbol,"[84] and, in contrast to the United States, a "photograph per se."[85]

But even if the image a DMF portrays on a screen is protected, the DMF *as a computer file* (i.e., program) is not protected because article 3 (b) of the Design Regulation excludes computer programs. The upshot, practically speaking, is that EU law for registered designs is roughly in the same spot as America's design patent law: a DMF will be not be protected directly (i.e., as a file or program); it will only be protected to the extent that the image of the object it will print is projected on a computer screen.[86]

Stated succinctly, it is not the file but the image that a registered design protects. Thus, as in the United States, if the two-dimensional image projected by a DMF is saved as a different file format, such as a "screenshot" (e.g., JPEG) image, that image will infringe. The difference in U.S. versus EU law is that the Design Regulation denotes the image (as displayed on whatever medium) as the "product," whereas U.S. law (as far as it is settled) considers the "product" to be the computer screen. But since in the vast majority of cases a DMF will only have an appearance as projected on a computer screen (as opposed to printed paper), the difference is largely immaterial.

Infringement

If the image and not the file is eligible for design protection, what does this mean for infringement under the EU regime? To avoid questions of whether an accused design produces a different overall impression on the informed user, we will again assume that there is verbatim copying of another's DMF.[87] The Design Regulation specifies that infringement occurs by the "the making, offering, putting on the market, importing, exporting or using of a product in

---

[83] *Id.* at § 4.1.4 (contrasting fanciful characters from "mere words per se and sequences of letters").

[84] *Id.* at § 4.1.2.

[85] *Id.* at § 4.1.6 ("A photograph per se constitutes the appearance of a product and, therefore, complies with the definition of a design, irrespective of what it discloses. The indication of the product can be writing paper …").

[86] EU law would also protect the image as printed on tangible paper, but in practice this will rarely occur for DMFs.

[87] Exact copying would trigger both registered and unregistered design rights. For further discussion of infringement and 3D printing, see Elam, *supra* note 68, at 155–57 and Margoni, *supra* note 68, at 230–31.

which the design is incorporated or to which it is applied, or stocking such a product for those purposes."[88]

In fact, the issue of design eligibility for images of DMFs is less important in the European Union than the United States because EU law is clear that a 2D representation of a protected 3D object constitutes infringement.[89] Thus, whether the design right is directed to a tangible product or a digital image, an unauthorized digital depiction of the same object image will infringe. Infringement would occur (though exceptions may apply) when someone

- recreates the digital object from scratch with a CAD program,
- opens a DMF in any computer program that projects the digital object on the screen, or
- includes an image of the digital object in an offer to sell the DMF.

In the last case (an offer to sell with an accompanying image), it is clear that "making" the image constitutes infringement. Whether the offer to sell *the file* also gives rise to liability is less clear, and it may turn out to be more important than you might think.

It is not always necessary to visually depict the image of the digital object when selling, copying, or transferring a DMF. Just like you can copy an MP3 music file without listening to the song, you can copy a DMF without opening it to view the image.[90] Of course, in practice people will generally want to see an image of what the file will print before buying it, but this will not always be the case. It is easy to imagine situations where sellers try to circumvent direct infringement by offering to sell files with only verbal descriptions, especially for highly sought-after items that buyers will recognize via such descriptions.

In cases where the image is not displayed on a screen, it may be argued that offering, copying, and transferring the file do not constitute infringement. For instance, copying the file does not literally constitute "making" the product, because the product is the visual image, not the file. It would be anomalous to

---

[88] Design Regulation art. 19(1). Unregistered designs are only infringed if the acts result from copying. *Id.* art. 19(2).

[89] *See, e.g.*, Joined Cases C-24/16 and C-25/16, Nintendo v. BigBen (September 27, 2017) (not yet published), ECLI:EU:C:2017:724 (applying the citation exception for infringement when competitor included 2D images of Nintendo's design-protected 3D products in advertisement claiming compatibility with Nintendo's system); Birgit Clark, *ICE, ICE . . .. – the BGH and the Citation of a Design*, The IPKat (Apr. 11, 2011), http://ipkitten.blogspot.com/2011/04/ice-ice-bgh-and-citation-of-design.html (discussing a German court decision finding infringement of a design patent for a train based on image of the train used in advertising).

[90] The same is true for selling or transferring a DMF – there is no technical need to view the image to complete the transaction. This same point was made when analyzing U.S. law, but there the product is the screen, whereas in the European Union the product is the symbol.

say that someone has made or used a graphic symbol when that symbol is not visually in existence.

What about offering to sell (or importing or exporting) a DMF file with only a verbal description – will that constitute an infringing act? This presents a more difficult issue. Literally speaking, if someone offers a DMF for sale, it can be argued the seller is not offering *an image* for sale. It is offering a file qua file. Against this, it can be argued that both parties contemplate that the buyer will open the file and portray the image on a screen, if not also print it. It would not, therefore, be strange to interpret the offering of a DMF as the offering of an image for sale. As an analogy, when someone buys a digital file containing music, it is common to talk of buying "a song" even though software must run the file to produce the music. This issue is unclear, and courts will need to clarify it.

There is much at stake here. Imagine a seller offers to sell a DMF of a design-protected object. If the offer does not include any image, the seller arguably doesn't infringe. What about the buyer? If the buyer prints the file for personal, noncommercial use, the acts will be excused based on the private, noncommercial use exception.[91] This would leave a substantial protection gap for some transactions. A recent European Commission review of design rights expressed particular angst about the private, noncommercial use exception in light of 3D printing technology.[92]

Exceptions to Infringement

The EU Design Directive includes two important exceptions in addition to the private, noncommercial use exception. Recall that U.S. design law's broad protection of images created concerns about free speech. If it were not for the statutory exceptions, EU design law would create similar concerns. The Design Regulation's exceptions insulate the following:

(a) acts done privately and for noncommercial purposes;
(b) acts done for experimental purposes; and

---

[91] Design Regulation art. 20(1)(a). Australia provides a similar exception in some cases. Adams, *supra* note 67, at 70.

[92] European Commission, *Legal Review on Industrial Design Protection in Europe*, 128–34, 132 n.315 (2016), http://ec.europa.eu/growth/content/legal-review-industrial-design-protection-europe-o_en [hereinafter, Commission Design Review] (discussing TRIPS article 26(2), which limits any infringement exceptions to those that "do not unreasonably conflict with the normal exploitation of protected industrial designs and do not unreasonably prejudice the legitimate interests of the owner of the protected design, taking account of the legitimate interests of third parties").

(c) acts of reproduction for the purpose of making citations or of teaching, provided that such acts are compatible with fair trade practice and do not unduly prejudice the normal exploitation of the design, and that mention is made of the source.[93]

Each of the exceptions alleviates some of the uneasiness about restricting expression. The private, noncommercial use exception, introduced above, means that people viewing protected images on their computers or printing protected objects for personal use would not infringe. The contours of this exception are similar to those for utility patents discussed in Chapter 5, and case law from patent law will likely be influential. Thus, "private" probably does not mean "secret," but rather "not for the benefit of the public," and "noncommercial" probably means "lacking economic benefit to the user."

The experimental use exception is important for researchers who view, copy, and study images protected by design rights. This exception has not been tested in the courts very often.

The citation/teaching exception, if interpreted broadly, could prove valuable for news and commentary that include protected images. The CJEU signaled a willingness to interpret the citation exception broadly in *Nintendo v. BigBen*.[94] BigBen made video game controllers in competition with Nintendo's controllers and advertised the compatibility online by including images of Nintendo's design-protected controllers. The court held that

> a third party that lawfully sells goods intended to be used with specific goods corresponding to Community designs and reproduces the latter in order to explain or demonstrate the joint use of the goods it sells and a product corresponding to a protected design carries out an act of reproduction for the purpose of making "citations" within the meaning of Article 20(1)(c) of Regulation No 6/2002.[95]

The court noted that an alternative holding "could discourage innovation."[96] The *BigBen* decision suggests that the CJEU will interpret the citation and teaching exceptions broadly enough to alleviate the strongest concerns for free speech and comparative advertising, assuming all the conditions of article 20(1)(c) are met.[97]

---

[93] Design Regulation art. 20(1).

[94] Joined Cases C-24/16 and C-25/16, Nintendo v. BigBen (September 27, 2017) ECLI:EU: C:2017:724.

[95] *Id.* at [77].

[96] *Id.* at [76].

[97] For discussion of a German case holding the use of an image in advertising constituted infringement, see Clark, *supra* note 89.

Intermediaries

If a DMF-hosting website is organized as a passive conduit for its users to make, offer, or put on the market DMFs and accompanying images, it may not be a direct infringer even if many images are posted. If, however, the website is considered the maker of the images, it would be a direct infringer. Liability will need to be determined on a case-by-case basis depending on the website and computer architecture. Note, however, that if a website takes images and files from a competitor and puts them on its own site, it would be a direct infringer for making and offering any protected images.[98]

3D print shop intermediaries in the European Union face the same concerns as in the United States and thus the law should provide good faith print shops with an appropriate safe harbor.[99] Another route would be to transfer liability exclusively to the person ordering the print. Some countries, such as Australia, make the person who ordered the printed object vicariously liable as an infringer[100] (but presumably also maintain liability for the print shop). Note, however, that if the individual is excused as a private, noncommercial user, the design owner would be left without any remedy.

Indirect Infringement

The Design Regulation does not provide for indirect infringement liability or direct liability for authorizing infringement.[101] Thus, even if a website intermediary knows of infringing activity on its site, it will not be liable for indirect infringement under the regulation.[102] Because intermediaries represent a centralized enforcement option, some have called for an exploration of liability to be extended to them.[103] An indirect infringement provision that

---

[98] *Cf.* Scott J. Grunewald, *When eBay Sellers Try to Defend Their Illegal Sale of 3D Models from Thingiverse, Comedy Ensues*, 3DPRINT.COM (Feb. 20, 2016), https://3dprint.com/120727/ebay-licensing-3d-models/ (describing an individual who bulk downloaded numerous DMFs from Thingiverse.com and offered them for sale on eBay).

[99] *See supra* Chapter 5 (outlining a safe harbor for print shops under utility patent law).

[100] Adams, *supra* note 67, at 68–69 (discussing *Review Australia Pty Ltd v. Innovative Lifestyle Investments Pty Ltd*, 166 FCR 358 (2008) (Austl.), which held that where a principal hires an independent contractor to perform acts that would infringe, the principal is held to be the infringer).

[101] Through a possible drafting error, neither does Australia. *See* Nielsen & Liddicoat, *supra* note 67, at 194.

[102] National laws may differ in this respect. For example, unregistered design rights in the United Kingdom prevent authorization of infringement. UK CDPA § 226(3). *See also* Malaquias, *supra* note 68, at 336.

[103] Commission Design Review, *supra* note 92, at 128–34.

limits liability to cases of actual knowledge of specific infringement would make sense, just as it does in other IP contexts. But anything more stringent risks shutting down good faith actors who fear high legal costs. Much like with utility patents, it will be exceedingly difficult for webhosts to police design infringement (without sophisticated software to match images).

C. RECOMMENDATIONS AND CONCLUSION

Digital images effectively enjoy broad design protection in the United States, European nations, and many other countries. Unlike the European Union, U.S. design law does not currently offer exceptions that would protect things like free speech, news reporting, and comparative advertising. This chapter has provided high-level thoughts about design protection for all images and has offered focused attention on ways to continue protecting DMFs without perpetuating the harms of overprotection.

As with utility patents, the European Union's provision of a private, non-commercial use exception alleviates fairness and political concerns about innocent infringers who unintentionally violate design rights. At the same time, the exception may swallow the rule when it comes to goods that users can print (and file images they can view) in their homes. But because the holder of the design rights would generally be able to pursue a direct infringement claim against distribution of such files via websites, where the file and associated images would be public, the value of the design right will not necessarily be eviscerated.

On the other hand, individuals who upload files to public websites and who did not know they were violating another's design rights may be liable for substantial damages, not to mention legal costs. A middle course would be to make liability for intermediary-related uses turn on the knowledge of the responsible actor(s), who could include the individual uploading the file and the website hosting it. This could be accomplished via a claim for indirect infringement. The EU Design Regulation does not provide for indirect infringement claims and should consider permitting them.

On the opposite side, the American design patent system should consider adopting a private, noncommercial use exception to insulate innocent infringers from potentially devastating legal expenses. To preserve the value of the design right in an era of 3D printing, the exception (in both the European Union and the United States) could be limited to actions taken without knowledge of the design right.

A personal use exception could also be tailored to allow the download of a DMF, even with the knowledge of a design right, as long as the downloader does not print the object or share the file. The downloader would then be able to take advantage of digital tools that enable easy redesigns of digital objects. Tailoring protection in this way could encourage additional creativity because the downloader would be able to digitally alter the object in such a way as to avoid infringement before printing or sharing, thereby adding diversity to the objects on offer.

10

DMFs and Optimizing Innovation Incentives

Chapter Outline:

Having introduced and analyzed the novel ways in which 3D printing impacts IP law, it is now time to turn to a broader policy analysis. Should IP law be changed in view of these new challenges, and if so, how? I have already offered some recommendations regarding specific aspects of IP law in the preceding chapters. This chapter will look more expansively at the potential IP changes needed to secure an optimum level of innovation. By "innovation," I mean to include both the invention and commercialization of a product.

At the outset, one might ask, why focus only on innovation policy, a distinctly utilitarian area, to the exclusion of policies focusing on the creative arts? There are a couple of responses. I believe 3D printing technology's most novel impact is in the area of utilitarian innovation. Copyright law, the primary legal sphere concerned with aesthetic creation, is mostly well prepared for 3D printing technology because of its history of protecting the same work in different embodiments. This does not mean that the current copyright system is necessarily optimal, but only that 3D printing doesn't upset the balance in significant ways. Therefore, debates about, say, fair use or innocent individual infringement will mirror the debates in other contexts, such as blogging or photography.

In contrast, DMFs of purely utilitarian objects present an exceptional case in which a sea change in the economic and business structure of a definable subset of goods (3D printable utilitarian objects) presents unparalleled stresses to IP law. Further, the stresses to IP law and policy are more localized to 3D printable products, making them amenable to individualized assessment.

Because this chapter focuses on DMFs of purely utilitarian objects, the primary mode of IP protection will be utility patents. But as will be seen, other areas of the law influence the optimal level of innovation incentive.

A. PATENT POLICY AND PROTECTION GAPS

The current doctrinal landscape of patent laws across the world results in an effective weakening of patent rights for 3D printable inventions. Chapter 4 established that patent law will likely allow patent claims directed to machine-instruction files but not surface-mesh or design files. At the same time, a 3D printable invention's economic value is tied up to a large extent in the surface-mesh file format, so failure directly to protect that format weakens any patent claims to the physical object or the machine-instruction file.

Because claims to the valuable surface-mesh files are not available, Chapter 5 described how direct infringement under current legal doctrine is not available for the making, selling, etc. of those files. Further, even if an individual 3D prints a patented object, many countries provide exemptions for private, noncommercial uses. Finally, Chapter 6 demonstrated that indirect infringement claims, while helpful to the patentee, are more difficult to prove and require a showing of the infringer's intent or knowledge of the infringement.

Patent holders will consider this weakening of patent rights unfair and undesirable. But the patent system's fundamental goal is not to reward inventors for their societal contributions. Although patents give inventors exclusive rights to the invention, this grant is a means to a greater end. The greater end is a higher, hopefully optimal, level of innovative activity.

Whether the patent system optimally incentivizes innovation has been debated as long as it has been around. And the truth is, no one knows for certain. At the same time, those who study the patent system generally agree that different types of inventions require different incentive levels.[1] For instance, pharmaceuticals' high research and development costs and comparatively low copying costs necessitate incentives. At the other end of the spectrum, many commentators doubt whether software needs a patent incentive.

Theoretically, then, it would be ideal to calibrate patent protection specifically to the needs of 3D printable inventions. Yet the patent system does not

---

[1] *See, e.g.,* DAN L. BURK & MARK A. LEMLEY, THE PATENT CRISIS AND HOW COURTS CAN SOLVE IT 37–48 (2009).

explicitly modulate its protections based on industry. It is facially a one-size-fits -all system.[2] The political and administrative difficulties from tailoring the system based on industry are simply too high, not to mention the TRIPS Agreement forbids significant differentiation.[3]

Therefore, the question for DMFs becomes: Given the changes brought by 3D printing technology, will patent law as currently calibrated adequately incentivize invention and commercialization for 3D printable inventions? Stated differently, where do 3D printable inventions fall on the spectrum of requiring patent incentives? Do patent laws designed in an industrial age of tangible inventions optimally promote this subset of inventions?

It is impossible to answer such questions empirically with precision,[4] but a thought experiment of sorts can help guide patent policy for 3D printable goods. First, start the thought experiment with the assumption that patent law is currently well calibrated for tangible inventions manufactured by traditional means.[5] Second, analyze 3D printing technology's effects on patent policy by comparing how the technology alters the costs of innovation for the subset of tangible inventions that can be profitably manufactured with 3D printing. Inventions in this category would include GE's fuel injection nozzle described in Chapter 1 or a simple object like a smartphone holder that mounts to a car's air conditioning vent,[6] assuming they are novel and non-obvious. Finally, compare the changes in the costs of innovation for this subset of inventions with the changes in strength of patent rights for them.

[2] Although the patent system is facially neutral, it can de facto discriminate against certain technologies. See id. at 55–65. For instance, so-called business method patents are incredibly difficult to obtain. See Daniel Harris Brean, *Business Methods, Technology, and Discrimination*, MICH. ST. L. REV. 307, 321–41 (2018). Courts also arguably require heightened claim specificity or enabling description for certain fields. See, e.g., Janice M. Mueller, *The Evolving Application of the Written Description Requirement to Biotechnological Inventions*, 13 BERKELEY TECH. L.J. 615 (1998); Arti K. Rai, *Intellectual Property Rights in Biotechnology: Addressing New Technology*, 34 WAKE FOREST L. REV. 827 (1999).

[3] TRIPS Agreement art. 27(1) ("[P]atents shall be available and patent rights enjoyable without discrimination as to ... the field of technology ")

[4] Cf. ROBERT P. MERGES, JUSTIFYING INTELLECTUAL PROPERTY 3 (2011) (speaking to the patent system generally and stating that "[t]he sheer practical difficulty of measuring or approximating all the variables involved means that the utilitarian program will always be at best aspirational").

[5] Put very simply, the balancing of the patent system weighs the incentives to innovate and disclose provided by patents on one side against the societal costs of patents, which primarily include higher prices and slowing the pace of follow-on innovation. For more on the patent balance, see Lucas S. Osborn, Joshua M. Pearce & Amberlee Haselhuhn, *A Case for Weakening Patent Rights*, 89 ST. JOHN'S L. REV. 1185, 1185–90 (2015), and sources cited therein.

[6] For one example of a patented smartphone holder, see Holder for Holding Portable Device, U.S. Patent No. 9,586,530 (filed May 6, 2016).

3D Printing Lowers the Costs and Risks of Innovation

Step one in the thought experiment is simply an assumption, so I will proceed to step two, looking at changes in costs of innovation.[7] Innovation begins with a mental act of conceiving of the invention. 3D printing technology does not make "thinking" any easier, of course. The best that can be said on this front is that the technology may help create a culture where more people are putting increased effort into "thinking" about inventions. For example, 3D printing has helped usher in an entrepreneurial "maker" movement in which individuals engage in making things.[8] The maker movement may not lower the costs of mental steps, but by increasing the number of people engaging in inventive enterprises, it increases the odds that a given invention will be invented. Even so, the effects of 3D printing on conception of inventions is arguably small.

After mentally conceiving of an invention, an inventor needs to concretize it, either by creating design drawings or building a prototype (or both). On this front, the abundance of available free and open source CAD programs enables individuals inexpensively to create quality drawings. Moreover, free software allows them to transform the files into DMFs and to 3D print them. This process, which can be completed in a matter of hours for simple inventions, is far quicker and cheaper than traditional processes.[9] Without this technology, individuals might have needed to hire a draftsperson to create technical drawings. They also would have needed to take those drawings to a manufacturing intermediary who would facilitate prototype construction. Depending on the invention, prototyping might have required expensive tooling or handcrafting and might have taken weeks to complete. Instead, 3D printing technology dramatically lowers the costs of prototyping. In one publicly available example, Volvo Construction Equipment (Volvo's heavy equipment arm) reduced a single prototype from twenty weeks and $10,000 to two weeks and $770, savings of time and costs totaling to about 90 percent.[10]

Following development of the initial prototype, the typical next step is an iterative process during which the design is tested and refined from both an engineering and marketing perspective. Products typically undergo dozens of

---

[7]   A more robust explanation of the stages of innovation and how 3D printing lowers costs can be found in Osborn et al., *supra* note 5, at 1200–24.

[8]   *Cf.* CHRIS ANDERSON, MAKERS: THE NEW INDUSTRIAL REVOLUTION (2012).

[9]   *See, e.g.,* Osborn et al., *supra* note 5, at 1209–11. 3D printing technology's clear advantages in prototyping allowed it quickly to penetrate the prototyping market, earning it the early moniker of rapid prototyping.

[10] Rod Mackay, *Volvo Digs Up 3D Printed Prototype Savings of 18 Weeks and 92% of Cost*, THE JAVELIN BLOG (Jan. 4, 2018), www.javelin-tech.com/blog/2015/10/3d-printed-prototype-helping-volvo/.

revisions before being market ready.[11] Traditional manufacturing processes made iterative improvements slow and cumbersome. But just like with the initial prototype, 3D printing technology allows quick digital editing and iterative prototyping. As a result, the costs and time required for this step are reduced tremendously.

Once an innovator has settled on a final product design, manufacturing begins. Without 3D printing, manufacturing is a risky proposition that involves large upfront costs. The innovator must pay for tooling or other expenses to prepare mass-manufacturing and/or must pay for customized labor like welding and assembly.[12] The innovator must also decide how many copies of the product to order. Any unsold products represent a sunk cost, as do the upfront manufacturing expenses. With 3D printing manufacturing, on the other hand, there are virtually no upfront costs because manufacturing can be accomplished on an as-needed basis. This eliminates the risk of irretrievable sunk costs.[13] As can be seen, 3D printing can lower initial manufacturing costs and risks.

The final commercialization step is to get the product into the consumers' hands. Traditionally, mass-produced parts were physically distributed to the point of sale locations. This could be a retail store or, in the case of direct mailing to customers, the seller's warehouse. But 3D printing technology has the potential to eliminate the costs of distribution. To the extent that customers own or have access to 3D printers, product distribution consists of transmitting the printable file to the customer's 3D printer.

In sum, 3D printing technology lowers the costs and risks of innovation along virtually the entire cycle, sometimes by staggering amounts. Because innovators of 3D printable goods face less cost and risk, they need correspondingly less incentive to engage in innovative activities. All things being equal, it would follow that the need for a patent as an appropriability mechanism decreases as well. But all things are not equal. One must also consider the effects of 3D printing technology on the other side of the patent equation.

---

[11]   *See* Stephen J. Kline & Nathan Rosenberg, *An Overview of Innovation, in* THE POSITIVE SUM STRATEGY: HARNESSING TECHNOLOGY FOR ECONOMIC GROWTH 275, 289–91 (Ralph Landau & Nathan Rosenberg eds., 1986).

[12]   The reader may recall the examples from Chapter 1, including those of jewelers, *supra* Ch. 1 notes 27–28, and fuel injection nozzle manufacturing, *supra* Ch. 1 notes 3–4, demonstrating these savings.

[13]   Against these benefits, it should be recognized that if demand is high and 3D printing times are slow, a seller may not be able to keep up with demand for a time. Further, other manufacturing processes might be more cost effective on a per-unit basis at higher volumes.

3D Printing Weakens Patent Rights and Lowers Imitation Costs

Chapters 4 through 6 showed how 3D printing technology effectively weakens patents in two ways. First, because patent law does not directly protect surface-mesh files, which are the most commonly sold format, patent holders must often rely on indirect infringement claims to stop centralized DMF distributors and sellers. Second, acts of direct infringement (printing or making machine-instruction files) are more diffuse and difficult to detect.

In addition to issues previously discussed, 3D printing technology also affects the patent calculus in a third way: it lowers the cost and quickens the pace of imitation. In other words, physitization does not only help the innovator, it also helps the imitator. Digital files can be copied costlessly, quickly, and with perfect fidelity. Therefore, if an imitator can legally (an important caveat that will be explored in depth) access and copy the innovator's DMF, the imitation will be extremely easy and fast.[14] Even if the imitator must create a DMF from scratch, this can be accomplished relatively quickly and cheaply either by drawing it in a CAD program or by digitally scanning the first mover's commercial embodiment. Compared to the innovator's time and costs to iteratively improve the initial prototype into the final commercial embodiment, the time and costs of copying only the final product are lower.[15]

Balancing Within the Patent Realm

At this point, we can say that for 3D printable goods (1) the costs of innovating are lower, (2) patent rights are effectively weaker because surface-mesh files are not directly protected and acts of direct infringement are difficult to detect, and (3) the costs of imitating are lower.

This triptych of observations represents an essential framework for analyzing 3D printing technology's effects on patent policy. Lawmakers and commentators should not emphasize any one over another. Importantly, however,

---

[14] There will of course be a material cost to printing the tangible device, which will be borne by whoever does the final printing, often the end consumer. In addition, sometimes having a DMF will not be sufficient to recreate the physical invention, namely when the precise printing materials are not known, as may be the case with specialized alloys or plastics with particularized properties.

[15] Reverse engineering is almost always cheaper and faster than the initial innovation, historically averaging about half of the costs – but varying greatly across products. *See, e.g.,* Richard C. Levin et al., *Appropriating the Returns from Industrial Research and Development,* Brookings Papers on Econ. Activity 783, 808–09 (1987); Edwin Mansfield et al., *Imitation Costs and Patents: An Empirical Study,* 91 Econ. J. 907, 909 (1981). Whether 3D printing technology changes the ratio of imitation to innovation time and costs compared to traditional manufacturing should be studied.

we cannot quantify the magnitude of these changes with precision (or, in the absence of future empirical analysis, anything approaching precision). It may be that the lowered costs and time of innovation outweigh the weakened patent rights and lowered imitation costs, in which case patents should be weakened further.[16]

For example, imagine a simple model whereby before 3D printing technology, inventing and commercializing invention X cost $500,000 and that imitating it cost $200,000. In that case, the patentee would need to recoup $300,000 ($500,000 minus $200,000). Suppose that because of 3D printing, the innovation costs decrease by four-fifths to $100,000 and imitation costs also decrease by four-fifths to $40,000. In that case, the patentee only needs to recoup $60,000 ($100,000 minus $40,000). Because $60,000 is less than $300,000, a weaker innovation incentive, assumed here to be from patents, is needed.

But the opposite may also be true. Suppose using the previous hypothetical's starting point that 3D printing only lowers the cost of innovation $100,000 (from $500,000 to $400,000) but lowers the cost of imitation by the same amount as the previous hypothetical (from $200,000 to $40,000). In that case, the change in relative costs is different: before 3D printing technology arose, the innovator needed to recoup $300,000, but after it the innovator needed to recoup $360,000 ($400,000 minus $40,000). Based on these numbers, the innovation incentive (here again assumed to be from patents) should be strengthened. This could be done by granting direct protection to surface-mesh files or by recognizing the doctrine of digital patent infringement.

It may even fortuitously be the case that the effects roughly balance out on average. Perhaps future empirical work can shed light on this issue.[17] What can be said is that the more dramatic the innovation cost lowering due to 3D printing, the more likely it is that 3D printing technology lowers the necessary innovation incentive. Without lawmakers knowing more, however, they may be wise to do relatively little to current patent laws in the face of 3D printing technology.

There is evidence to suggest that in many cases the needed innovation incentive has been dramatically lowered. For example, millions of relatively

---

[16]   One way to do so would be to reduce the patent term, which would mirror the more rapid innovation and imitation cycle. For more on this and other ways to weaken patent rights, see Osborn et al., *supra* note 5, at 1239–52.

[17]   A very large upfront innovation cost, manufacturing and distribution, can be completely removed from the innovator to the extent that buyers can buy the file and print remotely. Of course, the same is true for the imitator. But the point here is that empirical study may be best focused on the earlier stages of innovation.

simple files (and a few not so simple) are offered for free.[18] In addition, for more complex files, an entire movement exists that offers many DMFs for free, known as the "free and open source hardware" (FOSH) movement.[19] That makers are willing to offer DMFs for free suggests that – for these products and creators at least – monetary incentives were not needed. That certainly does not prove there is no need for patents (or other appropriability mechanisms to be discussed shortly), because the law seeks to foster an *optimal* level of innovation. But the prevalence of free offerings does provide evidence that the innovation costs are low and the need for legal incentives is not a foregone conclusion.

Before moving on from patent balancing, it bears mentioning that 3D printing should not materially affect the disclosure function of the patent system. The disclosure function of patents refers to the incentive to disclose the invention (through the required teachings of the patent document) as opposed to keeping the invention as a trade secret.[20] Disclosure allows others to begin understanding how the invention works and building improvements to it. There are at least two reasons this function should not be greatly disturbed even though patent strength is effectively weakened for 3D printable goods. First, patents remain available and retain much of their strength. Second, and more importantly, many 3D printable inventions are not amenable to trade secret protection (the alternative to patent protection).

3D printable inventions will be difficult to maintain as trade secrets because they are tangible inventions that can be reverse engineered. Methods, not devices, are the easiest to maintain as trade secrets. Of course, it is possible to maintain a trade secret for some tangible devices. A machine that makes products can be kept in a secure warehouse, and the engine of an airplane can be hidden from passengers' eyes. But by and large, most tangible devices fall into the hands of consumers who can study and reverse engineer them.[21] And most 3D printable inventions, especially the ones we have been focusing

[18] Thingiverse's users have uploaded over a million DMFs, all of which are offered without charge. About, THINGIVERSE, www.thingiverse.com/about/.

[19] *See supra* notes 71–72 (describing open source and FOSH projects); *see also* ALICIA GIBB, BUILDING OPEN SOURCE HARDWARE: DIY MANUFACTURING FOR HACKERS AND MAKERS (2015); Daniel K. Fisher & Peter J. Gould, *Open-Source Hardware Is a Low-Cost Alternative for Scientific Instrumentation and Research*, 1 MOD. INSTRUMENTATION 8, 8–9 (2012); OPEN SOURCE HARDWARE ASS'N, www.oshwa.org.

[20] *See generally* Sean B. Seymore, *The Teaching Function of Patents*, 85 NOTRE DAME L. REV. 621 (2010).

[21] There will be cases where things like product tolerances and the preferred printing material could be kept as a trade secret, but patent law does not necessarily require this information to be disclosed in the patent application.

on as being distributable to end users via DMFs, will be of this kind. Therefore, because trade secret protection will often not be an option, inventors will focus their attention on patents, even "weaker" patents.

The Case of Individual Users

Having just recommended that lawmakers not attempt to rebalance patents without additional empirical evidence, I must circle back to a recommendation made in Chapter 5. In that chapter, I recommended that jurisdictions strongly consider implementing an exemption from infringement for individuals making private, noncommercial use of the invention. I continue to support an exemption, and I believe it is justified on grounds other than the overall incentive balance of the patent system.

A private, noncommercial use exception is justified on fairness and political concerns rather than economic ones.[22] As covered in Chapter 5, the difficulty of knowing whether a DMF will print an infringing object and the high costs of patent litigation provide a recipe for disproportionate and unpredictable effects on individuals. An exception could alleviate these concerns. At the same time, to respect the rights of patent owners and to preserve the value of patents for 3D printable goods, at least one, or perhaps both of the following caveats should apply. First, a cause of action for indirect infringement should be available against anyone who knowingly supplies the DMFs to the individuals. This is already the case in many jurisdictions, but U.S. law should deem the required underlying act of direct infringement met. Second, a limitation to the exception should be explored whereby individuals who have actual knowledge of the patent would not benefit from the exemption.

***

The upshot of this analysis is that, although there are signs of reduced need for patent protection for 3D printable goods, the overall patent incentives calculus is inconclusive. But the analysis cannot stop there, because the innovation ecosystem is not that narrow. In addition, nonmonetary incentives and non-

---

[22] Some scholars advocate for fairness and similar social concerns as overarching goals of IP systems. *See, e.g.,* William W. Fisher III, *Reconstructing the Fair Use Doctrine,* 101 HARV. L. REV. 1659, 1744–94 (1988) (exploring how copyright law might "advance a substantive conception of a just and attractive intellectual culture"); Madhavi Sunder, *IP³,* 59 STAN. L. REV. 257, 324–25 (2006) (advocating an IP system that serves human culture and values like autonomy, democracy, equality, and development).

patent appropriability mechanisms must be considered, which Sections B and C tackle in turn.[23]

B. NONMONETARY INCENTIVES TO INNOVATE

IP rights provide indirect monetary incentives to innovate, but people innovate for many nonpecuniary reasons. A growing body of legal research applying behavioral economics research indicates that people innovate for nonpecuniary reasons including personal recognition, intellectual challenge, the joy of solving problems, and the desire to improve social welfare.[24] The magnitude of these nonpecuniary incentives can be debated, but the point here is that they provide some non-patent incentives to the calculus. Indeed, the millions of DMFs offered without charge and the FOSH movement testify to the power of nonmonetary incentives.

The Proportional Role of Nonmonetary Incentives

Because 3D printing technology lowers the costs and risks of innovation, nonpecuniary motivations for innovating might have proportionally stronger effects. To see why this is so, imagine that before 3D printing technology, we could quantify the socially optimal incentive level needed to produce an innovation as one hundred "incentive-units" (a generic and fanciful unit of measurement). Suppose also that ten of the needed incentive-units came from nonpecuniary mechanisms and ninety from the patent incentive.

Further suppose that 3D printing technology reduces the costs of innovation relative to imitation such that the socially optimal incentive level becomes only forty incentive-units. If we assume that nonpecuniary mechanisms stayed steady at ten incentive-units,[25] the patent system would only need to supply

---

[23] The innovation ecosystem is far broader than what will be covered herein. But what is covered is that which is most relevant to 3D printable goods and patents.

[24] *See, e.g.*, Stephanie Plamondon Bair, *The Psychology of Patent Protection*, 48 CONN. L. REV. 297, 325–26 (2015); William Hubbard, *Inventing Norms*, 44 CONN. L. REV. 369 (2011); Eric E. Johnson, *Intellectual Property and the Incentive Fallacy*, 39 FLA. ST. U. L. REV. 623 (2012); Gregory N. Mandel, *To Promote the Creative Process: Intellectual Property Law and the Psychology of Creativity*, 86 NOTRE DAME L. REV. 1999 (2011); Laura G. Pedraza-Fariña, *Patent Law and the Sociology of Innovation*, WIS. L. REV. 813 (2013); Henry Sauermann & Wesley M. Cohen, *What Makes Them Tick? Employee Motives and Firm Innovation*, 56 MGMT. SCI. 2134, 2134–35 (2010) (citing numerous sources that support the hypothesis that inventors are motivated by nonpecuniary rewards).

[25] For reasons discussed below, it is not clear that nonmonetary incentives would remain the same.

thirty incentive units. In that case, nonpecuniary incentives would account for 25 percent of the total innovation needed compared to 10 percent before. As we gain an empirical understanding of the average changes in the needed innovation incentives with 3D printable inventions, the role of nonmonetary incentives can also be better understood. If 3D printing drives down the costs of innovation compared to imitation, the case for weaker patents becomes even stronger.

How 3D Printing Affects Nonmonetary Incentives

In addition to understanding how nonpecuniary incentives affect innovation generally, it is important to analyze how 3D printing technology might affect the nonmonetary incentives. I will discuss four nonmonetary incentives: personal recognition, intellectual challenge, the joy of solving problems, and the desire to improve social welfare. These are not the only four, but they are representative of how the analysis would proceed.

Personal recognition is widely recognized as a powerful motivator.[26] 3D printing technology can both help and harm personal recognition. On the helping side, because DMFs of simple products are often distributed through websites that provide attribution via usernames and the like, recognition among a wide audience is possible. Innovators can also attempt to preserve recognition through the use of online contracts requiring attribution. By downloading a file, the downloader agrees to attribute the file to the original creator, even if the digital object is modified. This private ordering solution can help preserve the right of attribution. If the downloader breaks the contract (and the creator learns of it), the creator can sue the downloader for breach of contract.[27]

But recognition might decrease if an imitator copies (or recreates) the DMF and separately posts it without attribution. The contract only binds the party who specifically agrees to it. If that person transfers the file to a third person with no restrictions, even though the transferor breaches the contract, the third person can post the file online for everyone to download with no restrictions. The contract also cannot prevent people who independently create a similar DMF (perhaps by studying the physical object) without agreeing to the

[26] *See, e.g.,* Bair, *supra* note 24, at 349–50; Jeanne C. Fromer, *Expressive Incentives in Intellectual Property*, 98 Va. L. Rev. 1745, 1790–92 (2012); Justin Hughes, *The Philosophy of Intellectual Property*, 77 Geo. L.J. 287, 349 (1988). The prevalence of attribution clauses in creative commons-type licenses demonstrates the importance of attribution to many people.
[27] Learning the breacher's identity can be difficult, and the damages of such a lawsuit might be low. But the threat of suit can still act as a deterrent.

contract's terms. If any of these things were to happen pervasively and quickly, which has happened before with the massive copying of DMFs from Thingiverse,[28] an innovator would lose much of the recognition incentive.[29]

In addition, personal recognition can be enhanced through trademark law, which can protect the name (or username) of the source of DMFs. As discussed in Chapter 7, consumers faced with an abundance of DMFs may choose to return to particular trusted sources for quality DMFs. Finally, there is evidence for a strong norm among 3D printing online communities toward attribution.[30] When that norm is broken, public shaming of the violator inures to the benefit of the initial creator.[31]

The second nonpecuniary incentive, intellectual challenge, probably will not be appreciably affected by 3D printing. The third and fourth, the joy of solving problems and the desire to improve social welfare, may provide a more powerful incentive for 3D printable inventions. As seen with the innovation stages of prototyping, improving, and distributing, 3D printing technology empowers innovators to quickly design and distribute innovations. For someone who recognizes a problem or wants to improve society by providing access to a gadget, 3D printing provides a path with more immediacy and certainty to doing so compared to traditional methods. One example of this in practice is the worldwide network of people providing prosthetics and exoskeletons using 3D printing technology, as described in Chapter 1.[32]

C. NON-PATENT APPROPRIABILITY MECHANISMS IN THE LAW

Besides patent rights, other IP rights might protect DMFs of purely utilitarian objects and add additional incentive to innovate. Further, other legal mechanisms beyond IP law can do the same thing. Each of these possibilities is discussed in turn.

---

[28] *See* Scott J. Grunewald, *When eBay Sellers Try to Defend Their Illegal Sale of 3D Models from Thingiverse, Comedy Ensues*, 3DPRINT.COM (Feb. 20, 2016), https://3dprint.com/120727/ebay-licensing-3d-models/ (describing the copying of files from Thingiverse).

[29] I do not, however, believe a new legal right to attribution should be created. Unless it is shown that attribution is being systematically and drastically undercut, the legal and transactional costs associated with enforcing such a right seem to outweigh any benefits. *See, e.g.,* Christopher Jon Sprigman et al., *What's a Name Worth?: Experimental Tests of the Value of Attribution in Intellectual Property*, 93 B.U. L. REV. 1389, 1424–34 (2013).

[30] *See* Grunewald, *supra* note 28 (describing widespread objections to the copying, without attribution, of files from Thingiverse).

[31] *See id.*

[32] *See supra* Ch. 1 notes 45–46 and accompanying text (discussing a worldwide, open source network of people who seek to provide 3D printed prosthetics).

Copyright

Ostensibly, copyrights should have nothing to do with purely utilitarian works because copyrights are geared primarily toward aesthetic creativity. Despite this general rule, copyright has played an important appropriability role for utilitarian software.[33] The justifiability of this protection has been subject to debate from the beginning, but the important point here is that copyright protection can provide incentives for utilitarian works.

Chapter 8 discussed the potential statutory and doctrinal debate as to whether copyright law protects DMFs of purely utilitarian objects. It largely deferred normative analysis of whether that protection is needed. It might be justified, for example, because of weakness in patent protection. This, in fact, was one of the reasons copyright protection was first granted to traditional software in the 1970s – it was believed that patents would not protect it. But as we have seen, patent law provides some important protections for DMFs (assuming they meet the patent requirements of novelty and nonobviousness).

Indeed, this chapter allows a more definitive normative statement: copyright law should not be used to protect DMFs of purely utilitarian objects. Besides the poor theoretical fit between copyright law and DMFs of purely utilitarian objects,[34] the patent analysis provided in this chapter demonstrates that there is no clear need for stronger innovation incentives for these files. (Again, empirical evidence may develop that changes this conclusion, but for now it looks as if 3D printing is more likely to decrease the need for IP incentives, if anything.)

Besides, copyright is a poor fit due to the nature of protection (and corresponding incentive) it would provide if it is applied. It would actually be rather narrow in one sense and too broad in another. It would be too broad because it would apply to *all* DMFs of purely utilitarian objects, not just the subset able to overcome patent law's formidable novelty and nonobviousness requirements. The strict legal requirements for patents mean that many DMFs of utilitarian objects will not be covered by patents at all. And this is as it should

---

[33] See, e.g., Stuart J. H. Graham et al.,*High Technology Entrepreneurs and the Patent System: Results of the 2008 Berkeley Patent Survey*, 24 BERKELEY TECH. L.J. 1255, 1289–90 (2009) (stating that high technology entrepreneurs rated copyright protection as between slightly and moderately important in securing competitive advantage from their technology innovations); Pamela Samuelson, *The Uneasy Case for Software Copyrights Revisited*, 79 GEO. WASH. L. REV. 1746, 1781 n.268 (2011) ("[S]oftware firms have a strong interest in copyright protection insofar as mass-marketed software is infringed by users.").

[34] To the extent that U.S. lawmakers tried to justify granting copyright protection to these files to foster utilitarian innovation, it would probably violate the Constitution. *See supra* Ch. 9 note 35.

be if the patent system is properly balanced. A rich public domain of utilitarian technology is beneficial to society because it allows inexpensive access to goods and provides building blocks for future innovations.[35] Providing copyright protection would shrink the public domain and slow competition and cumulative innovation.

Copyright protection would also catch many imitators unaware – even people familiar with IP laws would not expect copyright to protect files having a purely utilitarian nature.[36] This is all the more problematic because the copyright term is so long (life of the author plus seventy years in the United States and Europe). This lengthy term was not much of a problem for traditional software because of its rapid obsolescence. But DMFs of utilitarian objects may have a longer shelf life, assuming the file format does not become obsolete. A screwdriver will probably be just as useful a hundred years from now as it is today.

At the same time, copyright protection would also be rather narrow. Where the underlying object is not protected by copyright (because it has no separable creativity), independently creating a DMF of the same object from scratch is not infringement.[37] In other words, for these kinds of DMFs,[38] reverse engineering is permissible from a copyright perspective.

It is true that forcing the imitator to re-create the file rather than quickly making a digital copy introduces some delay, which can provide incentive to innovate because it slows copying. In fact, the reverse engineering delay was one of the aspects that made copyright protection most appealing for traditional utilitarian software. But the context in which copyright was officially granted to traditional software (in the late 1970s in the United States) differs in important respects from DMFs. Mass-market software was thought deserving – in the innovation sense – of copyright protection in part because patent protection was thought to be unavailable. This is not true for DMFs.

---

[35] Indeed, our economic system's presumption is for freedom to copy. "In general, unless an intellectual property right such as a patent or copyright protects an item, it will be subject to copying." TraffFix Devices, Inc. v. Mktg. Displays, Inc., 532 U.S. 23, 29 (2001). Therefore, if patents are not available to a DMF of a purely utilitarian object, the burden is on those advocating for additional protection to demonstrate the need. Why protect the mere digitization of known (or obvious) objects with copyrights?

[36] *See* Paul Banwatt & Laura Robinson, *Dispatches from the Front Lines of 3D Copyright*, 28 Intell. Prop. J. 237, 262 (2016). In addition, it would lead to expensive (and seemingly useless) litigation arguing about whether a particular DMF was independently created versus digitally copied.

[37] *See* 17 U.S.C. § 113(b); *supra* note 70 and accompanying text.

[38] Where the tangible object enjoys copyright protection, it would be an act of infringement to re-create the digital file by copying from the tangible object.

In addition, most mass-market software took significant time (typically measured in months or even years) and resources (typically measured in hundreds of thousands or millions of dollars) to develop.[39] It also took significant
time and effort to reverse engineer. This will not often be the case with
DMFs.

To see why the re-creation delay is unlikely to provide a needed benefit for
DMFs, it is helpful to consider two scenarios: a simple DMF and a complex
one. For simple DMFs, defined as those that take only a few hours or days to
create, it probably takes a similarly short amount of time to re-create them.
The delay incentive provided by copyright would thus be small. Moreover,
because these files were easy to create in the first place, they will often need
very little in way of monetary incentives[40] (in contrast to much of the traditional mass-market software sold in the 1980s or 1990s).[41] Indeed, nonpecuniary motivations might provide the optimal amount of incentive – consider
again the open hardware movement and the many files offered for free on
websites.

Complex DMFs will take more time and effort to create and thus may need
more protections to incentivize their creation. Whereas simple DMFs will
often be made and purchased by individuals, complex DMFs will more often
be made and purchased by industry, at least in the near term. This has
important implications for a variety of appropriability mechanisms, notably
contract law, which will likely play a key role for many complex DMFs. These
other mechanisms, to be discussed shortly, will likely obviate the need for any
copyright-based incentive for these files.

Trademarks

Trademarks will play an important, if traditional, role as an appropriability
mechanism for DMFs of utilitarian objects. Because millions upon millions
of DMFs will be on offer, buyers will rely on sellers' trademarks as a quality

---

[39] See DANIEL E. SICHEL, THE COMPUTER REVOLUTION: AN ECONOMIC PERSPECTIVE 53
n.26 (1997) (noting an estimate of $10 per line of code for routine software development in
1992). Windows 3.1 comprised over a million lines of code. How Many Millions of Lines of
Code Does it Take?, VISUAL CAPITALIST, www.visualcapitalist.com/millions-lines-of-code/.
Video games were also costly in the 1980s and 1990s. See, e.g., How Much Does It Cost to
Make a Big Video Game?, KOTAKU, https://kotaku.com/how-much-does-it-cost-to-make-a-bi
g-video-game-1501413649.

[40] This will not always be the case. The costs of research and development might be large even
though the final file is easy to create.

[41] See generally SICHEL, supra note 39.

indicator for files.[42] The same will be true at the website level: buyers will seek websites known for offering quality files.

Trademarks allow sellers who gain a reputation for designing quality digital objects to reap the rewards of that reputation. This will be especially important for files that do not have IP protection, because they can be freely copied. Although the imitator can copy an unprotected file and offer it for sale, many buyers may prefer to buy from a trusted source.

Simultaneously, digital copying can undermine some of a trademark's benefits. Copiers might gain a reputation for selling quality files as well. Furthermore, copiers can even truthfully state that they are offering a digital copy of a file made by another person, as long as they word the statement carefully to avoid confusion.

Design Rights

Assuming my views from Chapter 9 are followed, design rights would not play a large role for DMFs of purely utilitarian objects because the functionality doctrine would preclude design protection for the files and the objects. If, instead, design protection is available even for images of utilitarian DMFs, that protection could be used as an appropriability mechanism as described in Chapter 9 . In addition, the functionality doctrine's modest reach means that design rights might protect objects having a large degree of utilitarian character.[43] For the same reason as with copyrights, design rights do not appear to be a needed incentive for highly utilitarian works.

Trade Secrets

Trade secret law could protect DMFs that are kept under reasonable degrees of secrecy. But this will not be possible for the basic paradigm this book has envisioned in which users sell, stream, or give away DMFs to the general public. Because users could easily reverse engineer the file by studying it or the tangible object, trade secret protection will not play a strong role. On the other hand, trade secret protection can benefit those who do not distribute their files

---

[42]   As detailed in Chapter 7, the source indications relied on by consumers will be those outside of the file, such as the seller's name.

[43]   As to the undesirability of the lax functionality standard in design patents, see Christopher Buccafusco & Mark A. Lemley, *Functionality Screens*, 103 VA. L. REV. 1293, 1374–75 (2017). Unlike a copyright in a drawing of a useful article, which does not prohibit the manufacture of the useful article itself (or, presumably, an independently created drawing), a design patent could prevent all copies of the file, to the detriment of utilitarian progress.

widely, such as businesses who keep their files in-house or who sell to a limited number of others under obligations of secrecy.

Beyond IP: Contracts

The most ubiquitous legal protection used with DMFs will likely be contracts. Contracts are legally enforceable promises between parties who have mutually agreed to terms.[44] Contracts offer many benefits, including the efficiency of private ordering. For simplicity I will focus on U.S. law, but the reader should know that the law varies from country to country. (Indeed, it varies among the fifty states of the United States).

Sellers of DMFs not protected by IP will be concerned that a buyer will copy and disseminate the file to others, thus undercutting potential sales by the seller.[45] The seller can use contract clauses accompanying the original sale to prohibit the buyer from copying or otherwise disseminating the file. Assuming proper notice,[46] this clause should be enforceable against the buyer. If the buyer breaches the contract, the seller can sue and obtain damages. Through this simple mechanism, the seller can better recoup investment costs.

Although contracts act as a practical and legal deterrent, they have important limitations. First, it may be difficult to know who out of many buyers breached the contract if a rogue file appears for sale (although technology can allow for tracking of individual files). Second, damages for breach of contract are generally lower than for patent or copyright infringement,[47] although a seller could include a reasonable "liquidated damages" provision that estimates the damages for a breach.

---

[44] *See, e.g.,* RESTATEMENT (SECOND) OF CONTRACTS § 17 (1981) ("[T]he formation of a contract requires a bargain in which there is a manifestation of mutual assent to the exchange . . .").

[45] I focus here on sellers as opposed to those who offer files for free, because I am considering the extent to which contracts can provide an appropriability mechanism. Even files given away without charge are often accompanied by creative commons "licenses" requiring attribution and noncommercial use. There is much to be said about these licenses, particularly when the file does not embody any IP. A "license" is a grant of permission for something the law prevents (like copying something protected by copyright). But if there are no IP rights, there is no license. And without IP rights, the so-called license has no effect on downstream users who don't agree to the terms. Of course, many creators slap creative commons-type license language on all their files without any appreciation for this fact. Any restrictions in the contract can still be effective as to parties who specifically agree to them, but they are not licenses.

[46] Notice simply relates to the requirement that the seller should reasonably alert the buyer to any terms. *See, e.g.,* Specht v. Netscape Commc'ns Corp., 306 F.3d 17, 29–30 (2d Cir. 2002). Providing notice through a pop-up box is very easy and common in an online sale.

[47] *See, e.g.,* Maureen A. O'Rourke, *Rethinking Remedies at the Intersection of Intellectual Property and Contract: Toward a Unified Body of Law,* 82 IOWA L. REV. 1137, 1142–43 (1997).

Third, contracts do not bind third parties who have no notice of the terms. Thus, if a buyer willingly breaches the contract and provides the file to a third party without notice of the terms, that third party is free to sell/transfer the file (assuming no IP right prevents it). Sellers may try to prevent this by including "pop-up" terms that accompany a file, but these can be disabled.[48] Further, a contract will not prevent a third party from reverse engineering a tangible object to re-create the DMF.

Fourth, courts can invalidate contract terms that violate public policy. Terms that might capture a court's attention include "no resale," "single use only," or "no reverse engineering" clauses because they may violate public policies against servitudes and restraints on alienation.[49] I do not wish to diverge into these complex topics,[50] and instead only mention them to note that the strength of contractual provisions may be modulated to some extent.

In sum, despite the limitations of contractual protection, it provides a simple, inexpensive appropriability mechanism that will deter some copying, thereby decreasing the need for copyright protection for purely utilitarian objects. This mechanism will be helpful even for simple DMFs sold to wide audiences. Even though these kinds of files may be more susceptible to circumvention by difficult-to-determine breach or reverse engineering, these files also are unlikely to need much in the way of legal appropriability mechanisms to generate an optimum level of creation.

Contracts and Complex DMFs

Complex DMFs are likely to need stronger appropriability mechanisms than simple DMFs because they more likely involve significant engineering and

---

[48] *See, e.g.*, Robert P. Merges, *The End of Friction? Property Rights and Contract in the "Newtonian" World of On-Line Commerce*, 12 BERKELEY TECH. L.J. 115, 122 (1997); Guy Rub, *Copyright Survives: Rethinking the Copyright-Contracts Conflict*, 103 VA. L. REV. 1141, 1213 (2017).

[49] JOHN CHIPMAN GRAY, RESTRAINTS ON THE ALIENATION OF PROPERTY 244 (2d ed. 1895), *available at* https://archive.org/details/restraintsonalioograygoog (stating that restraints on alienation "are inconsistent with that ready transfer of property which is essential to the well-being of a civilized community, and especially of a commercial republic"); Molly Shaffer Van Houweling, *The New Servitudes*, 96 GEO. L.J. 885, 930–32 (2008).

[50] I think that contractual provisions like "single print only" and "no reselling files after printing" are, in fact, reasonable in a digital environment where the DMF substitutes for purchasing the physical good. Printing the file once generally leaves the purchaser in the same shoes as one who purchased a tangible object. "No reverse engineering" clauses, especially geared toward individuals, are more complicated because they impede competition and follow-on innovation. For more on this topic see Lucas S. Osborn, *Intellectual Property Channeling for Digital Goods*, 39 CARDOZO L. REV. 1303, 1349–52 (2018) and sources cited therein.

development costs.[51] These files are, by their nature, likely to be created by businesses for sale to other businesses as opposed to individuals.[52] They will, therefore, tend to be specially designed for a relatively small group of users. A smaller universe of users decreases transaction costs and in turn makes private ordering an effective avenue for control and remuneration. Sellers can more easily set prices to recoup investment costs quickly.[53]

Happily, business-to-business transactions are best able to mitigate the weaknesses of contracts. First, because the number of transactions will likely be smaller, sellers can better track buyers and identify breachers. The higher value of the files involved also better justifies the use of tracking software to aid in identifying breachers. Second, although damages are still lower than with copyright or patent protection, businesses can better estimate their damages and can include a liquidated damages clause in their contracts.

Third, the smaller number of potential purchasers decreases the difficulty of specifically contracting with all potential users. Fourth, courts are less likely to invoke public policy to invalidate terms in contracts agreed to by sophisticated businesses as opposed to individuals. For instance, clauses prohibiting reverse engineering are much more likely to be upheld, thereby allowing sellers to maintain trade secrecy even after a sale.[54]

In many ways, the market for complex DMFs resembles customized software development. Studying that field in the 1960s, then-professor Stephen Breyer argued that copyright protection was probably not needed even though initial investment was high and copying costs were low.[55] He described how custom-made programs resulted in individualized contracts for sale and

---

[51] These files are also more likely to qualify for patent protection.

[52] This won't always be the case, but a quick glance at websites like Thingiverse.com shows that most files are relatively simple, whereas a DMF generated by GE described in Chapter 1 would qualify as complex. The nature of current home-based printers probably limits most individual print jobs to relatively simple files in the near future. In addition, some complex files will be used internally by a company, in which case traditional trade secret law will prevent their misappropriation.

[53] *Cf.* Stephen Breyer, *The Uneasy Case for Copyright: A Study of Copyright in Books, Photocopies, and Computer Programs*, 84 HARV. L. REV. 281, 345–46 (1970) (studying the software industry in the 1960s and describing how sellers set prices to recoup investment costs).

[54] Simple objects don't receive trade secret protection because they can be easily reverse engineered. Complex objects, on the other hand, can be protected by trade secret. *See, e.g.*, Rockwell Graphic Sys., Inc. v. DEV Indus., Inc., 925 F.2d 174 (7th Cir. 1991) (involving printing press parts and drawings of them).

[55] *See* Breyer, *supra* note 53, at 344. Even today most software sold is either developed in-house or for custom uses; Samuelson, *supra* note 33, at 1777 ("[S]eventy percent of the total investment in the development of software in the United States in the early twenty-first century is either custom-developed software or software that firms develop for their internal uses.").

products that third parties would not want to copy.[56] The same will be true for custom-made or highly specialized parts.

In addition, when complex parts and relatively few buyers are involved, sellers can protect their DMFs by printing the files in-house and only delivering the final product.[57] The final product can of course be reverse engineered, but the higher level of control provided by keeping the actual files in-house decreases the need for legal protections.

It is apparent, therefore, that contracts provide a meaningful appropriability mechanism for many complex DMFs.

D. BEYOND THE LAW: EXTRALEGAL APPROPRIABILITY MECHANISMS

Besides law-related mechanisms, several extralegal appropriability mechanisms will be important for DMFs. These include technological protection measures (TPMs), lead time advantage, and social norms.

Technological Protection Measures

Perhaps the most important category of extralegal mechanisms are TPMs, which were described in Chapter 2. Encryption and password protection can limit the copyability of files. In addition, various tracking and digital watermarking methods can help sellers discover from which authorized file an illicitly copied file originated. Finally, streaming technology, in which the seller streams the DMF data directly to the buyer's printer, can prevent the file from ever getting in the buyer's hands.

As already stated in Chapter 2, TPMs are not foolproof, nor are they without their own problems. Hackers can remove encryption, erase tracking devices, and capture streamed data. And although TPMs will stop unsophisticated users, once a single person has cracked a TPM, the file can be shared by all. TPMs are also worrisome because they impede beneficial uses of files, such as using one file as a starting point to create something new. At the same time, because not all files will be hacked and hacking takes time and expertise, TPMs offer an important protection against copying.

On the legal side, whether a particular DMF is covered by copyright is important in determining the legality of circumventing a TPM. One section of

---

[56]   Breyer, *supra* note 53, at 345.
[57]   Or, as will be discussed, sellers can protect their files by not transferring the file, but instead only streaming the DMF data to the user's printer.

the DMCA prohibits circumvention of a TPM that protects access to a copyrighted work.[58] If, however, the TPM is protecting a file that does not enjoy copyright protection, the circumvention should not be problematic, though there is some uncertainty in the law.[59] The law is even murkier if a person accesses a work that has copyright protection for the purpose of making fair use of the material, which has important implications for files with ancillary creative material, such as creative, non-executable comments.[60]

The DMCA also prohibits trafficking in a product (including a computer program) that

(A) is primarily designed or produced for the purpose of circumventing a technological measure that effectively controls access to a work protected under this title;

(B) has only limited commercially significant purpose or use other than to circumvent a technological measure that effectively controls access to a work protected under this title; or

(C) is marketed by that person or another acting in concert with that person with that person's knowledge for use in circumventing a technological measure that effectively controls access to a work protected under this title.[61]

The upshot of this section is that if a TPM protects both copyrighted and uncopyrighted works, a developer of a circumvention tool *may* – though courts are not clear – be prohibited from offering it to others even if the intent is only to use it for uncopyrighted works.[62] A court might interpret the statute to mean that if a given TPM protected access to only a *proportionally* low percentage of noncopyrighted files, trafficking in a circumvention program would violate the DMCA. If, on the other hand, the TPM protected a proportionally high

---

[58] 17 U.S.C. § 1201(a)(1)(A) ("No person shall circumvent a technological measure that effectively controls access to a work *protected under this title*.") (emphasis added).

[59] *Compare* Chamberlain Grp., Inc. v. Skylink Techs., Inc., 381 F.3d 1178, 1203 (Fed. Cir. 2004) ("We conclude that 17 U.S.C. § 1201 prohibits only forms of access that bear a reasonable relationship to the protections that the Copyright Act otherwise affords copyright owners."), *with* MDY Indus., LLC v. Blizzard Entm't, Inc., 629 F.3d 928, 950 (9th Cir. 2010) (refusing to read a nexus requirement into the statute).

[60] *Cf.* Universal City Studios, Inc. v. Reimerdes, 111 F. Supp. 2d 294 (S.D.N.Y. 2000), *aff'd sub nom.*, Universal City Studios, Inc. v. Corley, 273 F.3d 429 (2d Cir. 2001) (condemning under § 1201(a)(2) an offer of a circumvention tool that enabled lawful owners of DVDs to watch them on computers running the Linux operating system). The DMCA implements a system that, loosely speaking, exempts circumventions likely to be for fair use, though the details are beyond the scope of this book. *See* 17 U.S.C. § 1201(a)(1).

[61] 17 U.S.C. § 1201(a)(2).

[62] *Cf. Universal City Studios*, 111 F. Supp. 2d at 294.

percentage of noncopyrighted works, the circumvention program would not be "primarily designed" or have "only limited commercial significant purpose or use other than" to circumvent TPMs that protected copyrighted works. This is important to DMFs because there will be many that enjoy copyright protection but there will be many that do not. Rather than focus only on proportionality, courts should look at whether there is a large population of files unprotected by IP to which people should have access.

Lead Time Advantage

Another important extralegal appropriability mechanism is lead time advantage, which is the advantage a first mover enjoys in the marketplace. The first mover can establish a reputation as both a source of the new good and as an innovator.[63] In addition, assuming close substitute goods do not exist, the first mover can charge a higher price until competitors can catch up.[64]

With DMFs, lead time might be very short because digital copying is instantaneous. Because the success of imitation products correlates positively with increasing speed to market,[65] rapid digital copying suggests imitators can appreciably limit the originator's sales.

Although the act of digital copying is instantaneous, imitators must first accurately determine which files are worth copying. Imitators' delays and potential information asymmetries in determining which files are successful increase lead time. For instance, imagine an imitator who studies a well-known DMF marketplace. If sales information is not available on the website, the imitator will have to determine which files are successful through some other means. Even if sales information is available, the imitator will have to wait to know which files are selling well. Only then can it copy and promote the desirable files. At that point, it may have to work around a TPM and find a way to copy the file without breaching a contract with the originator or the host website. By that time, the originator has already made some successful sales and built a reputation. For relatively simple files needing little monetary reward to optimally incentivize their creation, these sales may be sufficient.

[63] Marvin B. Lieberman & David B. Montgomery, *First-Mover Advantages*, 9 STRATEGIC MGMT. J. 41, 46 (1988).
[64] *Id.*
[65] *See* Christina L. Brown & James M. Lattin, *Investigating the Relationship Between Time in Market and Pioneering Advantage*, 40 MGMT. SCI., 1361, 1362 (1994) (finding that pioneering advantage is related to a brand's length of time in the market).

In an alternative scenario, an imitator might attempt to continuously and completely copy the entire contents of another's website.[66] Through this wholesale copying, the imitator would eliminate delays. But this strategy would undoubtedly run into legal problems. First, wholesale copying of another company's web repository would almost certainly violate the website's terms of use, not to mention laws against computer fraud and abuse.[67] Second, it is highly likely that at least some of the files on the website would be protected by copyright or other IP rights. Therefore, this strategy would not likely succeed.[68]

Social Norms

Social norms may play a role in incentivizing DMF creations. The study of norms in the legal context has provided a vast amount of scholarship.[69] Rather than delving into the intricacies of norms, I wish to make a few simple observations.

Two related norms in particular could play a role in DMFs offered for sale on the Internet. First, a norm against blatant copying (sometimes referred to as "stealing" even in the digital context) exists among some people. Like most norms, it will be context dependent. Without delving into the theory of norms, I believe it is not controversial to suggest that a norm against copying may reduce the effects of copying in certain contexts.

The norm against copying gives rise to a second, intimately related norm in favor of buying from the originator. As a result, not only will there be fewer copiers, but also those who disapprove of copying may refuse to buy from

---

[66] *Cf.* Craigslist Inc. v. 3Taps Inc., 942 F. Supp. 2d 962, 966 (N.D. Cal. 2013) (discussing allegations that defendant republished Craigslist's online advertisements by scraping the listings "in real time, directly from the Craigslist website" so as to "essentially replicate[] the entire Craigslist website").

[67] *Cf. id.* at 968 77.

[68] Of course, some copyists hide their identities and use websites hosted in rogue jurisdictions, so there will be avenues for wholesale copying. Whether such sites would significantly divert sales is another question.

[69] *See, e.g.,* ROBERT C. ELLICKSON, ORDER WITHOUT LAW: HOW NEIGHBORS SETTLE DISPUTES (1991) (studying the relationship of law and norms); Lawrence M. Friedman, *The Law and Society Movement*, 38 STAN. L. REV. 763 (1986); Eric A. Posner, *The Regulation of Groups: The Influence of Legal and Nonlegal Sanctions on Collective Action*, 63 U. CHI. L. REV. 133 (1996); Mark F. Schultz, *Copynorms: Copyright Law and Social Norms, in* INTELLECTUAL PROPERTY AND INFORMATION WEALTH, 201–25 (2007) (Peter K. Yu, ed.). For a discussion of norms and the law in relation to 3D printing, see Lucas S. Osborn, *Regulating Three-Dimensional Printing: The Converging Worlds of Bits and Atoms*, 51 SAN DIEGO L. REV. 553, 593–607 (2014).

a copyist. Trademark law and laws against false advertising can help those seeking originators to find them.

In addition, these norms can affect websites and communities. To dent the sales of originals, a copied version will need to be offered on a popular website. But norms against copying, not to mention website user agreements, may prohibit the posting of copied files. Even where copying is not specifically prohibited in user agreements, website moderators might remove files that resulted from mere copying. Further, individual users may shame the copyist, further denting any financial impact the copier might have on the originator.[70]

On the other side of the equation, some people exhibit a competing norm in favor of free copying. The norm in favor of copying (even in the face of infringement) was famously embodied in the "file sharing" phenomenon that rocked the music and movie industries beginning in the 1990s (and continues to this day).[71]

Whether a norm in favor of or against copying dominates can be very context dependent, varying on things like whether the copying is for personal use only and whether the authorized channel is perceived as a fair one.[72] Another factor that will modulate competing norms is whether the copying involves any subsequent transformation versus mere copying without building upon it.[73]

This brief overview of the role of norms as appropriability mechanisms does little more than scratch the surface. In a given case, norms may have only limited significance. But in situations where the upfront costs of creation are also small, even a limited influence from norms may contribute meaningfully to an optimal incentive level.

E. CONCLUSION

With respect to 3D printable goods, we can comfortably say that (1) innovation costs are lower, (2) patent rights are effectively weaker, and (3) imitation costs

---

[70] Shaming, norms against copying, and norms in favor of buying from the originator (not to mention breach of contract and probable IP infringement) were on display when someone copied numerous files from Thingiverse.com, printed them, and sold the printed versions via eBay. *See* Scott J. Grunewald, *MakerBot Responds to Shady eBay Store Selling Thingiverse Users' 3D Models*, 3DPRINT.COM (Feb. 24, 2016), https://3dprint.com/121262/makerbot-responds-to-jpi/.

[71] *See generally,* Schultz, *supra* note 69.

[72] *See, e.g.,* Ben Depoorter & Sven Vanneste, *Norms and Enforcement: The Case Against Copyright Litigation,* 84 OR. L. REV. 1127, 1139–43 (2005).

[73] *See, e.g.,* LAWRENCE LESSIG, FREE CULTURE: HOW BIG MEDIA USES TECHNOLOGY AND THE LAW TO LOCK DOWN CULTURE AND CONTROL CREATIVITY 19 (2004).

are lower. Because we do not know the relative changes in these three metrics, we cannot say for certain whether innovation incentives from patents are optimal for 3D printable goods (even assuming they were optimal before 3D printing).

We can also see that several non-patent incentives are likely to play a significant role in incentivizing innovation in this space. These incentives are likely to be strong enough that copyright incentives are not needed for purely utilitarian DMFs.

Different innovations will require different levels of incentives, with simple DMFs requiring relatively little incentive. Indeed, we have seen that millions of DMFs are offered for free across numerous websites, suggesting that no monetary incentives are needed for those particular files and their creators. More complex DMFs may require stronger incentives. But even here the FOSH movement suggests that some complex DMFs do not require monetary incentives. In addition, for those DMFs that require monetary incentives, contracts and other noncopyright incentives are likely to constitute important appropriability mechanisms. Lawmakers should keep all these in mind when assessing desired levels of IP protections.

Conclusion

3D printing technology unquestionably will grow in importance in the coming years. The technology will disrupt the settled processes for the design, manufacture, and dissemination of myriad physical objects. I have used the term physitization to capture the various facets of this disruptive phenomenon whereby objects can move back and forth between digital and physical embodiments and in which economic value has spread from tangible to virtual embodiments.

The disruption will cut across many fields, but none more markedly than the law, and particularly IP law. The technology will interact with IP law in a variety of ways, some unprecedented and others routine. Based on these interactions, IP law will face many calls for change from a variety of constituencies.

IP law is largely about fostering innovation and creativity. It enjoys worldwide recognition as a tool that can, *if* properly calibrated, enhance productivity and well-being. But many aspects of IP law are not designed for a world where bits (digital information) and atoms (physical goods) are increasingly interchangeable. If lawmakers and scholars do not understand the fundamentals of 3D printing technology and physitization or how these phenomena interact with IP laws, the world's IP regimes may poorly serve their purposes. They may overprotect or underprotect.

In thinking about protection levels, I have focused primarily on the most novel issues raised by 3D printing technology. In patent law we see a weakening of effective protection because patents do not directly protect the DMFs holding the most economic value. In trademark law we see that 3D printing technology disrupts assumptions about consumer perceptions of manufacturing and brands. In copyright law we see difficult questions about whether and how to protect digital versions of functional objects. A similar question presents itself for design rights.

We cannot resolve these complex issues through apodictic application of doctrine. Policy must play a key role. For example, innovation policy must take the lead for DMFs of utilitarian objects, and lawmakers and scholars must understand the technology's various effects on innovation incentives. We do not currently have a clear empirical picture of these effects, and future study will be highly important. For the time being, the evidence does not indicate a suboptimal level of innovation incentives for DMFs of utilitarian objects, even in the face of patent protection gaps. Therefore, as of now lawmakers do not need to mend patent gaps, and they should not co-opt copyright or design patent law to provide additional utilitarian incentives. Nevertheless, nor should they ignore the potential for the technology to one day atrophy aspects of IP protection below optimal levels.

When thinking about protection levels, lawmakers and scholars must also consider how 3D printing technology democratizes the design, manufacture, and dissemination of goods. These changes implicate basic premises on which IP laws are constructed. For trademark law, we should take a fresh look at how consumers understand source, affiliation, and sponsorship in an era of digital goods.

Across the IP spectrum, individual access and empowerment in the areas of design and manufacturing create tensions for laws constructed on assumptions about the legal sophistication and monetary resources of the regulated. These tensions raise not only utilitarian concerns, but also fairness and equality issues. Therefore, I have advocated for particular attention and study in the area of exceptions for private, noncommercial use. Here too the exceptions should be balanced to avoid unduly eviscerating IP incentives. An actor's knowledge of IP protection for a DMF or printed object should be an important factor.

Lawmakers and scholars have much left to explore with 3D printing and IP. My focus on the most novel issues has meant that I passed over analysis of many important existing tensions in IP, which 3D printing implicates or even exacerbates. And though this book looked comparatively at popular IP jurisdictions outside the United States, it did not delve into important international dimensions. For example, some countries, such as those that lack sophisticated manufacturing capacity, will desire to take advantage of 3D printing technology and will resist calls for strong IP protection. As this book has revealed, these countries have much room to modulate IP protection when it comes to 3D printing.

In sum, I have not aimed to pronounce the exact optimal contours of IP protection for 3D printable files and goods. Rather, I have aimed to begin a scholarly conversation and to make recommendations where I believe the evidence and policy warrant them. Continuing the study and conversation will be immensely important to achieving a society in which 3D printing technology, innovation, and creativity can optimally flourish.

Index